WordPerfect® 6.1 for Wind[ows]
SmartStart

SAMANTHA PENROD

Purdue University, Calumet

and

READ GILGEN

University of Wisconsin, Madison

COLLEGE

WordPerfect 6.1 for Windows SmartStart

Library of Congress No.: 94-68906

ISBN: 078970008-5

98 97 96 95   4 3 2 1

Interpretation of the printing code: the rightmost double-digit number is the year of the book's printing; the rightmost single-digit number, the number of the book's printing. For example, a printing code of 95-1 shows that the first printing of the book occurred in 1995.

Screen reproductions in this book were created using Collage Plus from Inner Media, Inc., Hollis, NH.

WordPerfect 6.1 for Windows SmartStart is based on WordPerfect 6.1 for Windows.

Publisher: David P. Ewing

Managing Editor: Sheila B. Cunningham

Marketing Manager: Susan Dollman

About the Authors

Samantha Penrod is an instructor in the Information Systems and Computer Programming department at Purdue University, Calumet, in Hammond, Indiana. In addition to her teaching role at Purdue University, Samantha is President of Compuvise, Inc., a company that provides PC software training and development to several Fortune 500 companies.

Read Gilgen is Director of Learning Support Services at the University of Wisconsin, Madison. He holds a doctorate in Latin American Literature. His professional interests include instructional media, microcomputers, and other technology in support of higher education, especially foreign language education. He has taught and written extensively on DOS and WordPerfect. He is author of Que's *WordPerfect for Windows Hot Tips*, contributing author of Que's *Using WordPerfect for Windows*, Special Edition series, and has published several articles in *WordPerfect for Windows Magazine*.

Publishing Manager
Chris Katsaropoulos

Senior Editor
Jeannine Freudenberger

Production Editor
Fran Blauw

Technical Editor
Read Gilgen

Editorial Coordinator
Elizabeth D. Brown

Editorial Assistant
Jane K. Brownlow

Book Designer
Paula Carroll

Production Team
Maxine Dillingham
Chad Dressler
Dimonique Ford
Karen Gregor
Darcy Meyers
Stephanie Mineart
G. Alan Palmore
Clair Schweinler
Kris Simmons
Scott Tullis

Indexer
Michael Hughes

Composed in *1 Stone Serif* and *MCPdigital* by Que Corporation

Preface

Que College is the educational publishing imprint of Macmillan Computer Publishing, the world's leading computer book publisher. Macmillan Computer Publishing books have taught more than 20 million people how to be productive with their computers.

This expertise in producing high-quality computer tutorial and reference books is evident in every Que College title we publish. The same tried and true authoring and product development process that makes Macmillan Computer Publishing books bestsellers is used to ensure that every Que College textbook has the most accurate and most up-to-date information. Experienced and respected college instructors write and review every manuscript to provide class-tested pedagogy. Quality-assurance editors check every keystroke and command in Que College books to ensure that instructions are clear and precise.

Above all, Macmillan Computer Publishing and, in turn, Que College, have years of experience in meeting the learning demands of computer users in business and at home. This "real-world" experience means that Que College textbooks help students understand how the skills they learn will be applied and why these skills are important.

A Smart Start to Learning Word

WordPerfect 6.1 for Windows SmartStart provides a hands-on approach to one of the most popular word processing programs available. The design of the text is flexible enough to meet a wide variety of needs. This text can introduce a student to word processing, or it can supplement a student's previous learning. The abundant step-by-step, hands-on tutorials allow the student to learn independently or within a large lab setting.

Prior to presenting the step-by-step tutorials, *WordPerfect 6.1 for Windows SmartStart* explains the purpose and practical use of each software feature. Within this context, students quickly learn how to use the software. The explanations and abundance of tutorials enable students to remember how to apply the particular skill and to transfer their knowledge easily to other software applications. This approach ensures that students will use their skills in a practical manner.

Organization

WordPerfect 6.1 for Windows SmartStart uses a logical, simple-to-complex organization. Features that are easy to use and understand are presented first. The student can quickly master basic features and develop a framework for learning more complicated features. In addition, software features that students can use to improve efficiency as they are learning are introduced very early in the text.

Each chapter contains many hands-on tutorials, tables, and screen illustrations to facilitate learning. Learning objectives are listed after the introduction and then repeated at the appropriate points within the chapter. Each chapter ends with a summary to help the student absorb and remember the chapter skills. The end-of-chapter exercises include objective questions and hands-on projects to help students check and apply their skills.

Distinctive Features

WordPerfect 6.1 for Windows SmartStart provides many distinctive features to ensure students success, including the following:

- For convenience and easy reference, key terms are defined in the margin where a new term is first used.

- Each tutorial consists of concise, clear steps. These steps are highlighted in the book design for ease of use and later reference.

- Notes, tips, shortcuts, cautions, and other helpful hints provide additional information to enhance learning.

- Each project is realistic and designed to appeal to a wide variety of business skills and interests.

- The numerous end-of-chapter exercises focus on developing and applying critical thinking skills—not on rote memorization.

- Continuing projects are provided throughout the text. The continuing projects help learners "pull the pieces together."

- A glossary is provided.

To the Student:

Although this SmartStart provides a step-by-step approach, it is much more than a button-pushing book. In response to your requests, we have included a short explanation of the purpose for each software feature. Our focus is on teaching you to use the software effectively rather than on simply listing the software's features. We want to make certain that you remember how to apply your knowledge of WordPerfect 6.1 for Windows long after you have taken this course.

You will not spend a great deal of time simply typing documents. We have provided your instructor with a data disk containing example information for many of the hands-on projects. You then can spend your time completing interesting projects with real-life scenarios.

To the Instructor:

As a result of your feedback, this SmartStart includes several improvements over previous books in the SmartStart series. The number of screen illustrations has been increased to help students move through the steps more quickly. The number of skills-checking exercises has been increased; this SmartStart has twice as many end-of-chapter questions and projects as previous SmartStarts. These new end-of-chapter exercises do not test rote memorization; they do reinforce practical knowledge.

Each chapter has enough end-of-chapter exercises to ensure that all objectives have been fully addressed.

The instructor's manual includes a Curriculum Guide to help you plan class sessions and assignments. Each chapter in the instructor's manual contains teaching tips, answers to "Checking Your Skills" questions, transparency masters, and test questions and answers. The manual also offers advice on what to teach when time is short or when the students have a specific need. Additional project ideas and suggestions also are included.

Look for the following additional SmartStarts:

Access 2 for Windows SmartStart	1-56529-874-8
BASIC SmartStart	1-56529-402-5
dBASE IV SmartStart	1-56529-251-0
Excel 5 for Windows SmartStart	1-56529-794-6
Lotus 1-2-3 SmartStart (covers 2.4 and below)	1-56529-245-6
Lotus for Windows SmartStart	1-56529-404-1
MS-DOS SmartStart	1-56529-249-9
Novell NetWare SmartStart	1-56529-411-4
Paradox for Windows SmartStart	1-56529-405-X
Personal Computing SmartStart	1-56529-455-6
Quattro Pro for Windows 1.0 SmartStart	1-56529-409-2
Windows 3.1 SmartStart	1-56529-203-0
WordPerfect 5.1 SmartStart	1-56529-246-4
WordPerfect 6 SmartStart	1-56529-407-6
WordPerfect for Windows SmartStart	1-56529-403-3
Works for DOS SmartStart	1-56529-396-7
Works for Windows SmartStart	1-56529-394-0

For more information, call:

1-800-428-5331

Contents at a Glance

Table of Contents

4 Proofreading Your Text 77

5 Formatting Paragraphs and Characters   99

7 WordPerfect's Customizing Features   163

Introduction

WordPerfect 6.1 for Windows SmartStart enables you to quickly learn and use WordPerfect in the Windows environment. This book uses a step-by-step approach to learning not only basic features of the program, but the more advanced features as well. *WordPerfect 6.1 for Windows SmartStart* uses many illustrations to guide you through procedures and clarify difficult concepts. This book supplies essential information for new WordPerfect users, and provides helpful suggestions to make you a more efficient user of WordPerfect for Windows.

What Is New in WordPerfect 6.1 for Windows?

WordPerfect 6.1 for Windows is a word processing program that meets the needs of people in a variety of industries and professions. The following list summarizes new WordPerfect 6.1 for Windows features that you can use to save time and increase productivity:

- *Charts and Auto Update Tables.* You can make charts based on data in your tables, and WordPerfect automatically can update the charts as you change data in your table.

- *Drag to Create.* You can size a graphics image box before you retrieve the contents.

- *Drop Cap.* You can create various sizes and styles of drop-cap letters or words.

- *Feature Histories.* WordPerfect for Windows remembers the last 10 files that you opened, the last 10 macros played or recorded, and custom sort definitions.

- *Make It Fit Expert.* This feature effortlessly makes one page and a few lines fit into one page.

- *Open as Copy.* You can use this feature to force files to be opened as read-only, requiring you to save under a different file name if you modify the file.

- *Installation Changes.* Several items have been removed or now are installed only on request during a custom installation: graphics files, WordPerfect printer drivers, upgrade advisors, Macro help, TrueType fonts (Brush, Blackletter, Arrus), and conversion drivers.

- *Table Expert.* You can apply several predefined table formats to your existing table, or you can save your own specialized table formats.

- *Word Forms.* You now can find and replace various forms of a root word ("fly" is replaced with "drive," for example, and "flew" is replaced with "drove").

- *Button Bar/Power Bar.* Both of these features have changed in terms of the features found on them. Also, the Button Bar now is called the *Toolbar.*

- *Cut and Paste.* WordPerfect for Windows automatically "cleans up" extra spaces when text is pasted.

- *Grammatik.* This feature has been improved dramatically, with more automated expert replacements.

- *OLE 2.0.* In-place editing has been made simple. TextArt and WPDraw graphics are OLE objects.

- *PerfectOffice 3.0 Integration.* Shared code now is called PerfectFit Technology and is designed to make WordPerfect, Quattro Pro, Presentations, and GroupWise work well together.

- *QuickCorrect.* This feature automatically corrects common spelling and spacing errors, changes to typographically correct quotation marks, and expands abbreviations.

- *QuickFormat.* Applies format styles to headings. Also, changes in one heading are made in all headings.

- *Tables.* WordPerfect 6.1 has added many enhancements to tables, including row/column indicators, table experts, and size-column-to-fit content.

- *Templates.* These now are easier to work with, and you can more easily create custom templates.

- *Undo and Redo.* This feature provides 10 levels (you can change this to 300 levels) of Undo and Redo.

Who Should Use This Book?

WordPerfect 6.1 for Windows SmartStart is designed as an introductory guide for new WordPerfect users. This book leads you through important procedures and provides useful tutorials in which you can put to use the practical skills you have learned.

What Is in This Book?

The chapters in *WordPerfect 6.1 for Windows SmartStart* are arranged so that you learn the basic skills first, and then proceed to more complex tasks.

Chapter 1, "Getting Started," introduces you to the basics of WordPerfect for Windows by teaching you fundamental skills: how to start the application, how to identify the elements of the WordPerfect for Windows screen, and how to make selections from pull-down menus.

Chapter 2, "Creating a Document," teaches you how to create, save, and print a document. You learn the difference between using Typeover mode and Insert mode when entering text, and you learn how to use different views to examine a document.

Chapter 3, "Editing Documents," shows you how to work with multiple documents. You learn how to select text for copying, cutting, and pasting; you also learn how to use the WordPerfect Help feature.

Chapter 4, "Proofreading Your Text," discusses how to use the Reveal Codes window to view hidden codes, and how to locate and replace text by using the Find and Replace feature. You also learn how to use the Spell Checker, the Thesaurus, and the Grammar Checker tools.

Chapter 5, "Formatting Paragraphs and Characters," tells you how to set the appearance of your text for your documents. You learn how to perform most paragraph and character formatting in the document-editing window by using the Ruler and the Power Bar. You learn how to change margin settings; create tab settings; and use different types of indentation, alignments, and justification. You also learn how to use WordPerfect's WYSIWYG feature to view on-screen how your document will look when it is printed.

Chapter 6, "Formatting Pages," examines formatting at the page level, which deals primarily with the overall layout of the page and any recurring elements in the design. You learn how to choose paper size and type; how to add headers, footers, and page numbers; and how to control page breaks in a document.

Chapter 7, "WordPerfect's Customizing Features," tells you how to customize how the program interacts with you. In addition, you learn how to perform many of the file-maintenance capabilities that Windows usually handles, so that you can perform tasks such as deleting, renaming, and copying files from within the WordPerfect program. You also learn how to automate some of the tasks you perform by using macros.

Chapter 8, "Merging Documents," teaches you how to use the Merge feature to insert variable information into a standard format. You learn to use the Merge feature to create personalized form letters, address envelopes, and create mailing labels.

Chapter 9, "Working with Text Columns and Tables," tells you how to easily set up columns and add them to your documents. You learn how to define newspaper and parallel columns, enter text into them, and adjust them by using the Ruler.

Chapter 10, "Adding Graphics to Documents," shows you how to combine graphics with text, and how to resize and reposition the images. You also learn how to insert borders and lines into a document.

Conventions Used in This Book

WordPerfect 6.1 for Windows SmartStart uses a number of conventions to help you learn the program quickly.

Exact quotations of words that appear on-screen are spelled as they appear on-screen and are printed in a `special typeface`. Information that you are asked to type is printed in **boldface and blue** in numbered steps, and in **boldface** elsewhere.

Menu letters you type to activate a command appear in boldface and blue in numbered steps—**F**ile—and in boldface elsewhere—**F**ile. Keys you press are shown as keyboard icons—⏎Enter—and as blue icons in the numbered steps—⏎Enter. Keys you press together are joined by a plus sign—Alt+F2.

CHAPTER 1

Getting Started

WordPerfect 6.1 for Windows is a powerful word processing program that enables you to create documents such as letters, memos, reports, newsletters, and so on. In this chapter, you learn the basics of WordPerfect for Windows. You learn about some special features of WordPerfect 6.1 for windows, and you learn how to start the application. You identify the elements of the WordPerfect for Windows screen, such as the Title Bar, the Menu Bar, the Status Bar, and the document window. You also learn how to activate pull-down menus and Quick-Menus, and how to choose commands from them. Finally, you learn how to use the Toolbar buttons.

Note: *If you have not used Windows before, you need to read Appendix A, "Working with Windows." It provides basic information about working in Windows.*

Objectives

By the time you finish this chapter, you will have learned how to

1. Understand Some Special Features of WordPerfect for Windows

2. Start WordPerfect for Windows

3. Identify the Parts of the WordPerfect for Windows Screen

4. Understand the WordPerfect for Windows Toolbar Buttons

Objective 1: Understand Some Special Features of WordPerfect for Windows

WordPerfect for Windows enables you to enhance text with underline, bold, and italic options. You also can use some of the more sophisticated desktop publishing features in WordPerfect for Windows to create headers and footers, to build glossaries and indexes, and to combine text with graphics.

The following list provides information about some of the features available in WordPerfect 6.1 for Windows:

- You work in *WYSIWYG* (what-you-see-is-what-you-get) mode. In WYSIWYG mode, text always appears in the font, size, and attribute you assign, and graphics used in documents are shown at all times.

- WordPerfect for Windows is oriented graphically and makes extensive use of icons.

- You can manipulate the screen directly. You can move a window containing a WordPerfect document across the screen by using the mouse to *drag* the window to a new on-screen location, for example.

- You can access as many as nine documents at one time.

- By using the *Object-Action Model* feature, you can perform a series of actions on a single block of text without having to select the block of text for each enhancement.

- You can create footnotes, endnotes, headers, and footers in a few simple steps.

- You can create powerful macros to automate repetitive tasks.

- You can merge text documents. You can merge data from an address list into a form letter, for example.

- You quickly can choose the most commonly used features of the program by clicking a specific button on the Toolbar.

- WordPerfect for Windows offers complete compatibility with earlier WordPerfect versions, as well as easy automatic conversion from other text and word processing formats.

Objective 2: Start WordPerfect for Windows

WordPerfect for Windows icon
A small picture representing the WordPerfect for Windows program on the Program Manager desktop.

To use WordPerfect for Windows, you must have Windows loaded on your computer. If Windows is running on your computer, you will see the Program Manager window and the *WordPerfect for Windows icon* on your screen. If Windows is not running, your instructor can explain how to start Windows.

After Windows is loaded, the Windows Program Manager desktop window appears (if you are unfamiliar with Windows, see Appendix A).

Starting WordPerfect for Windows Using the Mouse

To start WordPerfect for Windows using the mouse, follow these steps:

1 Make sure that Windows is running on your computer and that the Program Manager desktop window is displayed. Your instructor will tell you which program group contains the WordPerfect for Windows program icon.

2 Select the program group containing the WordPerfect for Windows icon by double-clicking that group.

❸ Double-click the WPWin 6.1 program icon within the group to load the program (see figure 1.1). When the program is loaded successfully, you see the WordPerfect for Windows screen.

Figure 1.1
The WordPerfect for Windows program icon in the WordPerfect group window.

WordPerfect for Windows program icon

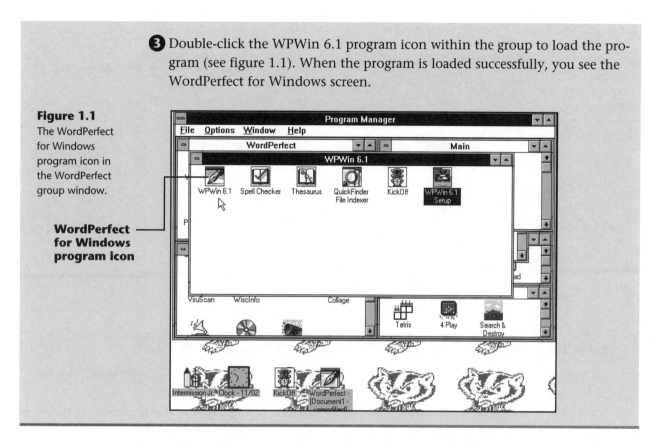

Understanding WordPerfect's Default Settings

When you start WordPerfect, the program puts into effect a number of default settings. These *default settings* affect the way the program interacts with you, the way information is displayed, and the initial formatting used in each new document you create. Typically, the defaults include margin settings, line spacing, justification settings, and tab settings. You can change these default settings by using the **F**ile Pr**e**ferences command, which is discussed in Chapter 7.

Objective 3: Identify the Parts of the WordPerfect for Windows Screen

The WordPerfect program window appears full-size when you start the program. The WordPerfect window contains the following components (see figure 1.2):

- Title Bar

- Menu Bar

- Toolbar

- Power Bar

- Document window with horizontal and vertical scroll bars

- Status Bar

Optionally, you can display the Ruler Bar in the WordPerfect window.

Figure 1.2

The full-size
WordPerfect
program window
you see when you
start the program.

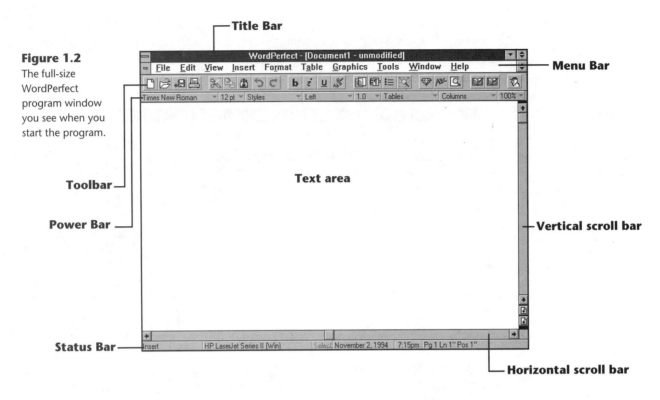

The following sections discuss the various components of the WordPerfect for Windows screen.

Title Bar

The *Title Bar* is the top line of the WordPerfect program window and displays the program name (WordPerfect) along with the name of the currently active document. The currently active document name is displayed in square brackets and is given a default name of [Document1], [Document2], [Document3], and so on until you save the file with a new name. The word unmodified follows the document's name until you add text to a new document or edit an existing document.

Program Control Menu

The *Program Control menu box* is located in the upper left corner of the window, next to the Title Bar. Click this box or press Alt+ to display the Program Control menu. This menu contains commands used to move or resize the WordPerfect program window, to access the Program Manager in Windows, or to close the WordPerfect program window and exit WordPerfect (see figure 1.3).

Document Control Menu Button

The *Document Control menu button* is located below the Program Control menu button to the left of the Menu Bar. The commands on the Document Control menu enable you to restore, move, size, minimize, maximize, close, or edit the next open document.

Minimize Button

The *Minimize button* is a small downward-pointing arrow located at the upper right corner of the screen. When you click the Minimize button, the

WordPerfect program shrinks to an icon at the bottom of the Windows desktop. Even though the program still is running (still loaded in main memory), it no longer uses the full display screen.

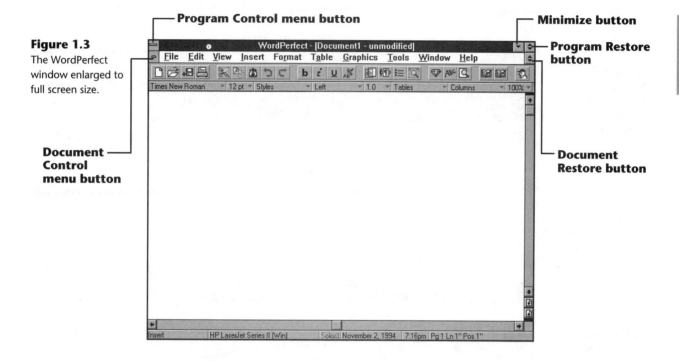

Figure 1.3
The WordPerfect window enlarged to full screen size.

Restore and Maximize Buttons

The *Program Restore button* is located next to the Minimize button in the upper right-hand corner of the screen. The Restore button appears as a vertical double-headed arrow. If you click the Program Restore button, the WordPerfect program window becomes a smaller window on the desktop (see figure 1.4).

The *Document Restore button* is found directly below the Program Restore button. When you click the Document Restore button, the WordPerfect document screen is placed in a medium-sized frame within the larger Windows screen, but does not return to the desktop background. Note that when you click on the Restore button, it changes to a Maximize button that appears as a single arrow. When you click the *Maximize button*, the WordPerfect screen returns to the full-screen size and the desktop is no longer visible, but the Restore button (a double-headed arrow) once again is displayed.

Menu Bar

The second bar on the WordPerfect screen is the Menu Bar. The *Menu Bar* gives you access to various pull-down menus, which contain commands for the topic shown on the Menu Bar. To select a menu from the Menu Bar, click the menu name with the mouse or press (Alt) and the underlined letter in the menu name. For example, (Alt)+(F) opens the **F**ile menu.

Toolbar

Below the Menu Bar is the Toolbar. The *Toolbar* contains buttons that perform frequently performed tasks. To print a copy of a document, for example, position the mouse pointer on the Print button (the fourth button from the left), and click the left mouse button.

Note: *When the mouse is positioned on a Toolbar button, WordPerfect displays a message in the Title Bar telling you what action the button performs.*

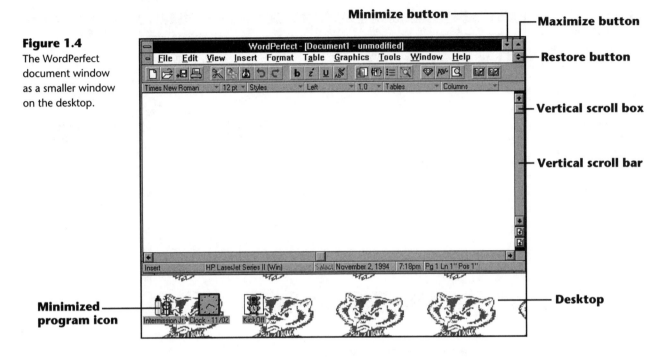

Figure 1.4
The WordPerfect document window as a smaller window on the desktop.

Power Bar

The WordPerfect Power Bar contains buttons that you can use instead of the pull-down menus to select specialized WordPerfect functions. You simply click the mouse on the desired Power Bar button, and WordPerfect executes the function or displays a dialog box for you to enter more information about what you want to do. Some functions of the Power Bar include setting the font, point size, styles, justification, line spacing, tables, columns, and zoom (see figure 1.5).

Text Area

The *text area* is the open area of the screen below the Toolbar. This area is the part of the WordPerfect document window where you enter your information.

Vertical Scroll Bar

The *vertical scroll bar* is the narrow column to the right of the text area; the bar contains an up arrow and a down arrow. You can click the arrows with the mouse to scroll through pages of text in a document. The icons, which resemble pages and are located beneath the down arrow, enable you to use the mouse to view the preceding page and the next page. Another component of the vertical scroll bar is the *scroll box*. You can drag the box with the mouse to scroll through pages of a document.

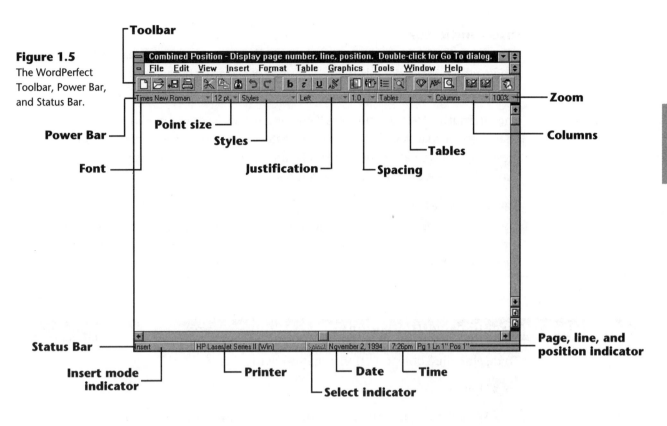

Figure 1.5
The WordPerfect Toolbar, Power Bar, and Status Bar.

Horizontal Scroll Bar

The *horizontal scroll bar* is located below the text area of the document window. This scroll bar contains an arrow pointing to the left and an arrow pointing to the right. You can click these arrows with the mouse to reposition your document horizontally. The horizontal scroll bar has a *scroll box* that can be dragged with the mouse to move the page from right to left or left to right.

Status Bar

The Status Bar is located at the bottom of the WordPerfect program window. This bar displays information about the current document. The right side of the Status Bar contains the *position indicator*, which informs you of the precise position of the insertion point in your document. The position indicator on the Status Bar uses the following abbreviations:

- Pg. Indicates the number of the page on which the insertion point is located.

- Ln. Identifies the vertical position of the insertion point, measured from the top edge of the page. By default, this measurement is shown in inches.

- Pos. Identifies the horizontal position of the insertion point, measured from the left edge of the page, and also shown in inches.

The left side of the Status Bar tells you the printer selected, the date, and the time.

Insert Indicator

When the word Insert appears at the left of the Status Bar, you are in Insert mode, which is the default mode. In *Insert mode,* any characters you type move any existing text over to the right and do not replace the existing text.

The alternative to Insert mode is Typeover mode. *Typeover mode* replaces existing characters or spaces with the new characters you type at the cursor's position. Press (Insert) to activate Typeover mode, and the word Typeover appears in the Status Bar. Press (Insert) again to switch back to Insert mode.

Select Indicator

The *select indicator* near the middle of the Status Bar appears in light gray. This indicator remains dimmed until you select text with the mouse or press (F8) (Select); then Select appears in dark type, indicating that Select mode is on.

Displaying the Toolbar by Using a Pull-Down Menu

To display the Toolbar, perform the following steps:

❶ Open the View menu.

WordPerfect displays a pull-down menu with additional choices (see figure 1.6).

Figure 1.6
The Toolbar option on the View pull-down menu.

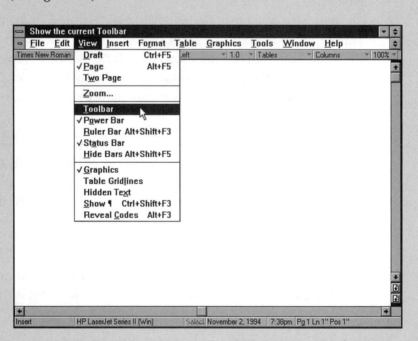

Note: *A check mark next to the Toolbar option indicates that the bar currently is displayed on-screen. When the check mark is absent, you can click the option to display the Toolbar.*

❷ Choose the **T**oolbar option.

The WordPerfect screen now displays the Toolbar.

In WordPerfect for Windows, you easily can move the Toolbar to different locations in the WordPerfect program window. Simply drag the Toolbar to its new position along the borders of the WordPerfect program window or somewhere within the current document window.

Moving the Toolbar

To move the Toolbar to a new location in the WordPerfect program window, perform the following steps:

❶ Position the mouse pointer on one of the gray spaces between the buttons.

The pointer changes to a cupped hand (see figure 1.7).

Figure 1.7
Dragging the Toolbar to a new location.

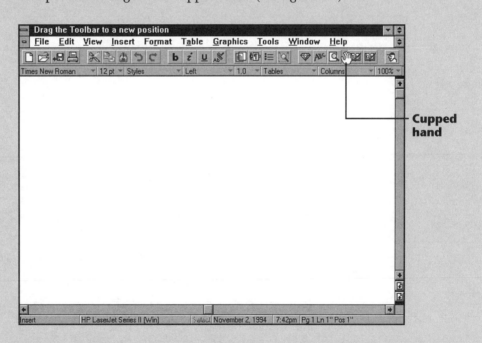

❷ After the pointer has changed, press and hold the left mouse button, drag the outline of the Toolbar to its new position, and then release the mouse button.

To easily change the formatting of a document, use WordPerfect's Ruler Bar. By using the Ruler Bar, you can make changes to the left and right margin settings, as well as the tab settings.

Displaying and Removing the Ruler Bar

To display the Ruler Bar in the document window and then remove it, perform the following steps:

1 Open the **V**iew menu.

2 Choose **R**uler.

WordPerfect displays the Ruler Bar at the top of the document window (see figure 1.8).

Figure 1.8
The Ruler Bar.

Ruler Bar —

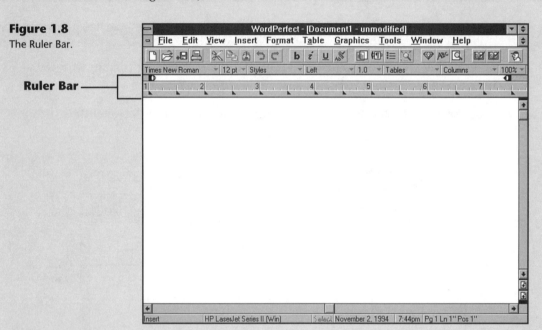

The Ruler Bar operates as a toggle switch. To activate a toggle switch, you issue a command sequence; to deactivate a toggle switch, you issue the same command sequence.

3 Open the **V**iew menu.

Notice that there is a check mark next to the Ruler Bar option, indicating that the ruler currently is activated.

4 Choose **R**uler to remove the Ruler Bar from the document window.

If you display the pull-down menu at this time, you can see that the check mark has disappeared, indicating that the Ruler no longer is activated.

The Reveal Codes Window

The WordPerfect Reveal Codes screen provides one of the easiest ways to edit a document. *Hidden codes* are placed within a document when you use different formatting options (setting tabs, using specialized fonts, and so on) while typing text. These hidden codes inform the printer how the document is to appear. The Reveal Codes window enables you to view and modify these hidden codes. If you want to delete a tab from a document, for example, display the Reveal Codes window while in the document, find the tab code, and press Del to erase the tab code.

When the Reveal Codes window is active, the document window screen splits in half. The upper half shows regular text without codes, and the lower half displays the text with the hidden formatting codes. Figure 1.9 shows the Reveal Codes screen.

Figure 1.9
The WordPerfect screen displaying reveal codes in the lower half of the screen.

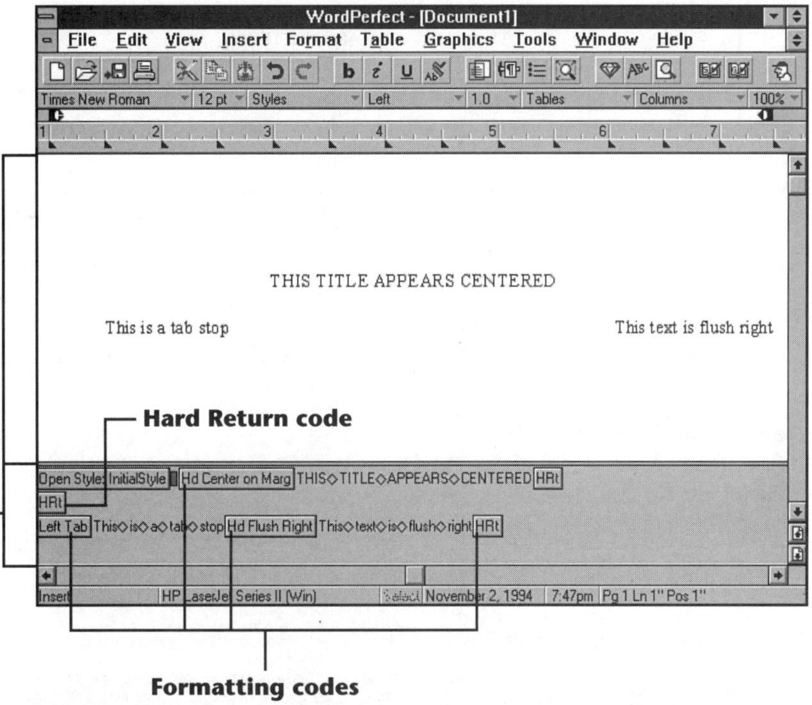

Displaying and Removing the Reveal Codes Window

To display and remove the Reveal Codes window in the WordPerfect document window, perform the following steps:

1. Open the **V**iew menu.

2. Choose **R**eveal Codes.

The document window screen is split into an upper and lower half, with the formatting codes displayed in the lower half (refer to figure 1.9). You can adjust the size of the Reveal Codes window by positioning the mouse on the Reveal Codes window split bar and dragging the bar up or down until you get the desired size. The mouse pointer must be in the form of a two-headed arrow before you can begin dragging it to resize the window (see figure 1.10).

Displaying and Removing the Reveal Codes Window (continued)

Figure 1.10

Drag the Reveal Codes window split bar up or down to change the size of the Reveal Codes window.

❸ Open the View menu.

❹ Choose Reveal Codes.

Because the Reveal Codes option is a toggle switch, repeating the command sequence turns off the option. The screen is no longer split, and the formatting codes do not appear.

> **Tip**
>
> An alternative way to display Reveal Codes is to press Alt+F3.

Using the Mouse

With the mouse, you can efficiently perform a variety of actions. The mouse pointer's shape indicates what you can do with the mouse. The shape changes as the mouse pointer is moved to different areas of the WordPerfect for Windows screen.

Selecting Menu Commands with the Mouse

To select menu commands from the pull-down menu using the mouse, position the mouse pointer on the menu name and click the left mouse button. The menu name is highlighted, and opens to display a list of available commands. You also can open a menu by pressing Alt and the appropriate hot key—the underlined letter in each of the menu names.

If a menu command appears dimmed (a light gray), it currently is not available for selection. If a check mark precedes a command, the command can be toggled on and off. When key combinations follow an option, you can use that keyboard shortcut to select the command without accessing the pull-down menus.

If a menu option is followed by an ellipsis (...), a dialog box with additional options appears as soon as you select the option. If an option is followed by a right-pointing triangle (▶), a cascading menu containing more options appears when you choose that option. After the cascading menu is displayed, you can choose any of the available options.

1

Activating a Pull-Down Menu

To activate a pull-down menu with an associated cascading menu, follow these steps:

1 Move the mouse pointer to the word Format on the Menu Bar.

2 Click the left mouse button.

WordPerfect displays a pull-down menu containing a list of available commands.

3 From the list of commands, choose Line.

A cascading menu appears to the right of the pull-down menu (see figure 1.11).

Figure 1.11
Choosing the Line command from the Format menu opens a cascading menu.

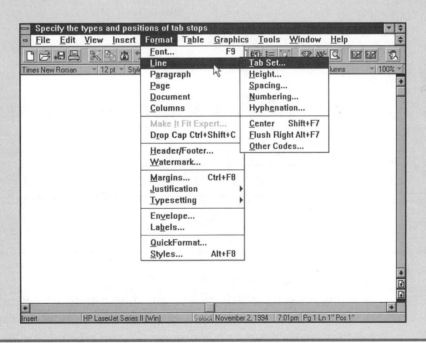

Selecting QuickMenu Commands with the Mouse

When you click the right mouse button on the Power Bar, Toolbar, Status Bar, scroll bars, and so on, a QuickMenu appears. You also can access QuickMenus from margins, the document area, and tables. QuickMenus give you fast and easy access to commonly used features or procedures that you otherwise have to access via the Menu Bar.

Opening a QuickMenu

To open a QuickMenu, perform the following steps:

1 Position the mouse pointer anywhere on the Toolbar.

The Toolbar is located below the Menu Bar and displays small icons representing various functions, such as printing or saving a file.

2 Click the right mouse button to display the QuickMenu (see figure 1.12).

WordPerfect displays a pull-down menu containing the Edit, Preferences, Hide Toolbar, and other options.

Figure 1.12
A WordPerfect
QuickMenu.

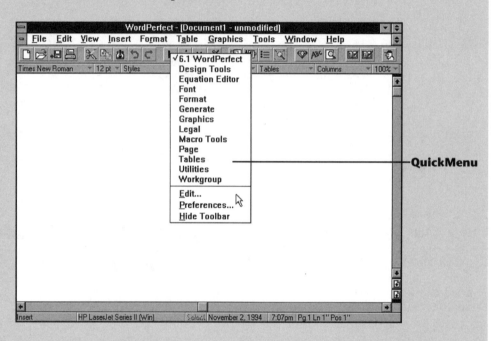

3 To choose an option, point to the option and click the left mouse button.

When you choose the **P**references option, you see a dialog box from which you can choose additional options. If you choose **H**ide Toolbar, you are returned to the WordPerfect screen, and the Toolbar no longer is displayed.

Using the Function Keys

In WordPerfect for Windows, you can choose many commands by using pull-down menus or their function-key equivalents. WordPerfect assigns up to six functions to each function key, depending on whether the key is used alone or in combination with ⚟Shift, Alt, Alt+⚟Shift, Ctrl, or Ctrl+⚟Shift.

Table 1.1 lists the default function key assignments in WordPerfect 6.1. for Windows. This keyboard arrangement is called the *Common User Access* (CUA) keyboard.

Table 1.1   The CUA Function Keys in WordPerfect for Windows

Key	Alone	⬆Shift	Alt	Ctrl	Alt+⬆Shift	Ctrl+⬆Shift
F1	Help	Help: What Is?	Thesaurus	Spell Check	Grammatik	Quick Correct
F2	Find and Replace	Find Next	Find Previous	———	———	———
F3	Save As	Save	Reveal Codes	Redisplay	Ruler Bar	Show Symbols
F4	Open	New	Exit	Close	———	Clear
F5	Print	Full Page View	Page View	Draft View	Hide Bars	———
F6	Next Pane	Prev Pane	Next Window	Next Doc	Prev Window	Prev Doc
F7	Indent	Center Line	Flush Right	Hanging Indent	Decimal Tab	Double Indent
F8	Select	Select Cell	Styles	Margins	———	———
F9	Font	Merge	Sort	Generate	———	———
F10	Menu	Repeat	Macro Play	Macro Record/Stop	Feature Bar/ Menu	———
F11	Image	Text Box Edit	Text Box Create	Horiz Line	———	Vert Line
F12	Table Create	Table Lines/Fill	Table Number	Table Format	Calculate	Table Data

Note: *To use this table, assume that you are pressing one of the keys at the left while pressing the keys listed along the top of the table. The function this key combination performs is shown where the keys would intersect on the table.*

Choosing Pull-Down Menus with the Keyboard

To open a pull-down menu and choose a command by using the keyboard, perform the following steps:

❶ Press Alt.

Notice the dark highlight that appears on the Menu Bar.

❷ Press the underlined letter of the name of the menu you want to display. For this tutorial, press **F** to display the **F**ile menu. (In this book, the underlined letter on-screen is represented by a boldface letter or a blue, boldface letter.)

WordPerfect displays the pull-down menu (see figure 1.13).

(continues)

Choosing Pull-Down Menus with the Keyboard (continued)

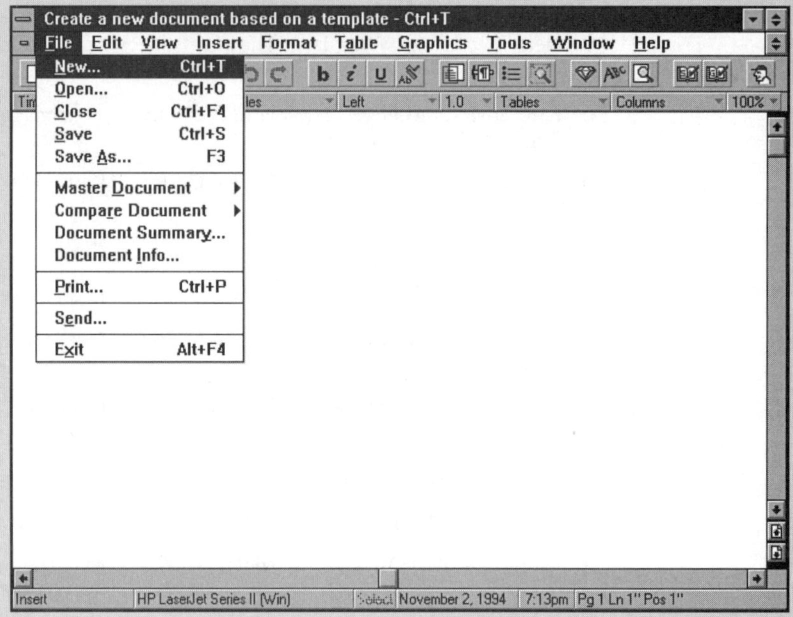

Figure 1.13
The File pull-down menu.

❸ To choose a command from the pull-down menu, press the underlined letter of the command. Or, use the cursor-movement keys to highlight the command you want to execute and then press ↵Enter. For this tutorial, press **C** for **Close**. The File pull-down menu disappears.

Objective 4: Understand the WordPerfect for Windows Toolbar Buttons

WordPerfect for Windows displays a Toolbar across the top of the application window. The *Toolbar* is a group of buttons, or icons, representing commonly used menu commands. To boldface text, for example, click the Bold button on the Toolbar. Table 1.2 lists the buttons on the Toolbar. The buttons are explained in later chapters as you need to use them.

Table 1.2   The Toolbar Buttons

Button	Name	Effect
	New	Creates a new, blank document based on the standard template.
	Open	Opens an existing document (previously saved as a file on disk).
	Save	Saves the active document or template by writing it to a disk.

Button	Name	Effect
	Print	Prints the active document.
	Cut	Cuts the highlighted text to the Clipboard, removing it from your document. The *Clipboard* is where you temporarily keep information to copy to another location.
	Copy	Copies the highlighted text to the Clipboard (leaving it in your document).
	Paste	Inserts the contents of the Clipboard into the current document at the insertion point.
	Undo	Reverses an action (up to the 10 most recent actions).
	Redo	Reverses an undone action.
	Bold	Applies the bold attribute to the current word or highlighted text, or turns on the bold attribute.
	Italic	Applies the italic attribute.
	Underline	Applies the underline attribute.
	QuickFormat	Copies the format of text at the insertion point to other text.
	New Document	Enables you to start a new document based on predefined template documents.
	Paragraph Format	Enables you to change indent, margins, and line spacing of current paragraph.
	Insert Bullet	Inserts a bullet character at the beginning of the current line.
	Make it Fit	Helps you squeeze a document into a specified number of pages.
	Image	Inserts a graphics image into your document.
	TextArt	Creates special effects with text.
	Page/Zoom Full	Enables you to zoom to see a full page, or to move back to the current zoom size.
	Spell Check	Checks the spelling in the active document.
	Grammatik	Checks the grammar in the active document.
	Coaches	Helps you learn specific WordPerfect for Windows features.

Table 1.2	The Toolbar Buttons (continues)	
Button	**Name**	**Effect**
	Chart	Creates special effects with text.
	Draw	Edits or creates graphics images.
	Text Box	Creates a text box that is manipulated as a graphics box.
	Indent	Sets a temporary left margin for the current paragraph.
	Margins	Sets margins for the active document.
	Paper Size	Sets the paper size/orientation for the active document.

Using the Toolbar Buttons

To practice using the Toolbar buttons, first type **Prose is a collection of wurds**. Then follow these steps:

❶ Position the cursor on the word *wurds* and then click the mouse pointer on the B icon on the Toolbar. WordPerfect adds boldfacing to *wurds*.

❷ Click the mouse pointer on the icon that displays an open book with an S and a red check mark. This action starts the Spell Checker, which stops at *wurds* and suggests replacing it with *words*. Click Replace, and then click OK to close the Spell Checker.

❸ Click the icon that displays a printer (the fourth icon from the left). WordPerfect displays the Print dialog box. Choose **P**rint to print the document, or **C**lose to cancel printing.

Chapter Summary

In this chapter, you learned how to start the WordPerfect for Windows program, and how to use the mouse and the keyboard. You also located and learned how to use the various components of a WordPerfect screen.

Checking Your Skills

True/False Questions

For each of the following statements, circle *T* or *F* to indicate whether the statement is true or false.

T F **1.** You can start WordPerfect for Windows from the Windows program icon, the DOS system prompt, or the Windows File Manager.

T F **2.** *Dragging* means to click the mouse button twice in rapid succession.

T F **3.** A check mark next to a pull-down menu command indicates that the command is deactivated.

T F **4.** Dialog boxes give you additional options and may prompt you for more information.

T F **5.** The Toolbar can be moved to a different area on-screen.

T F **6.** One of the easiest ways to edit a document is by using the Reveal Codes window.

T F **7.** The hyphen found next to the Title Bar is called the *Document Control menu button*.

T F **8.** The word wrap feature keeps text within predefined margins.

T F **9.** To activate a QuickMenu, you double-click the left mouse button.

T F **10.** You can use a button on the Power Bar to create an envelope.

Multiple-Choice Questions

In the blank provided, write the letter of the correct answer for each of the following questions.

___**1.** WYSIWYG stands for _____.

   a. where you search is where you go

   b. what you see is what you get

   c. where you seek is where you go

   d. what you style is what you generate

___**2.** The right mouse button is used to _____.

   a. display the Power Bar

   b. display a QuickMenu

   c. move the Menu Bar

   d. execute a Toolbar command

___**3.** The Minimize button is represented by _____.

   a. a small down-facing triangle

   b. a large double-headed arrow

   c. an up-facing triangle

   d. a horizontal arrow

___**4.** The Ruler Bar can be used to _____.

    a. make changes to margins

    b. set tabs

    c. a. and b.

    d. none of these answers

___**5.** The Title Bar contains _____.

    a. menu options

    b. the document name

    c. pull-down menus

    d. icons

___**6.** The alternative to Insert mode is _____.

    a. Select mode

    b. Typeover mode

    c. Num Lock mode

    d. none of these answers

___**7.** The numeric and cursor-movement keys are located on the _____.

    a. left side of the keyboard

    b. center of the keyboard

    c. right side of the keyboard

    d. across the top of the keyboard

___**8.** A menu command that appears dimmed indicates that _____.

    a. it is unavailable at the time

    b. it already is activated

    c. a dialog box follows it

    d. a QuickMenu follows it

___**9.** Key combinations that follow an option are called _____.

    a. menu commands

    b. Control keys

    c. shortcut keys

    d. Escape keys

___**10.** Pressing F8 activates _____.

    a. Insert mode

    b. Select mode

    c. Typeover mode

    d. none of these answers

Fill-in-the-Blank Questions

In the blank provided, write the correct answer to the following questions.

1. A document must contain existing text in order for you to move the _____ _____ _____ through the document.

2. The buttons on the Power Bar are used to perform _____ _____ _____.

3. The three indicators on the right side of the Status Bar include _____ _____, _____ _____, and _____ _____.

4. If you activate the Reveal Codes window, you can see _____ _____.

5. When an option is dimmed on a pull-down menu, that option is _____.

6. To activate the Menu Bar using the keyboard, press the _____ key.

7. You can display the Ruler Bar by choosing _____ from the _____ menu.

8. To move the Toolbar , you first must position the mouse pointer on one of the _____ _____ between the buttons.

9. Both the horizontal and vertical scroll bars have a _____ _____.

10. Pressing ⬆Shift+F7 causes text to _____ on the page.

Applying Your Skills

Review Exercises

Exercise 1: Choosing Menu Options

Using the mouse and keyboard, choose various menu options from the Menu Bar. Activate and deactivate different commands from the pull-down menus. Notice the changes that occur, and write down what you observe.

Exercise 2: Using the Toolbar

Make sure that the Toolbar is displayed. Using the mouse, drag the Toolbar to a new location, and then reposition it back to its original location.

Hide the Toolbar by using the appropriate pull-down menu.

Exercise 3: Using the Function Keys

Using table 1.1, try using several of the function key assignments to carry out commands.

Exercise 4: Listing the Functions of the Toolbar

List the descriptions of the different buttons on the Toolbar. Use the mouse pointer to reveal the descriptions; then write them in list format.

CHAPTER 2

Creating a Document

In this chapter, you learn how to create, save, and print a document. You learn the difference between using Typeover mode and Insert mode when entering text, and you learn how to use different views to examine a document. The procedure for exiting the program also is presented.

Objectives

By the time you finish this chapter, you will have learned to

1. Start a New Document

2. Enter Text

3. View Documents

4. Save a Document

5. Print a Document

6. Exit WordPerfect for Windows

Objective 1: Start a New Document

When you start WordPerfect for Windows, the program displays a blank, full-size document window in which you can enter text for your new document. WordPerfect automatically assigns the temporary name Document1 to the first open document window until you open the File menu and choose the Save or Save As command to name and save the file. This temporary name appears in the Title Bar of the document window (see figure 2.1).

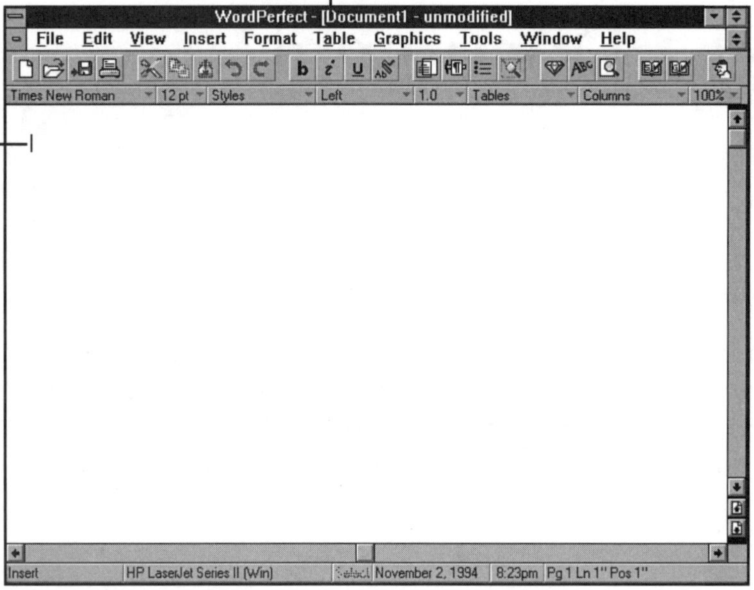

Document name

Figure 2.1
A document window displaying the default document name, Document1.

Insertion point

Cursor (insertion point)
The flashing vertical marker that indicates where the next character will be inserted when you type.

To start a new document in the WordPerfect document screen, simply begin typing text at the insertion point location. The insertion point is indicated by the *cursor*. To move the cursor across existing text, use the cursor-movement keys or position the I-beam pointer in the text and click the left mouse button.

Starting a New Document from a New Window

To open a new document in a separate WordPerfect window, perform the following steps:

1 Open the File menu.

2 Choose New.

3 The New Document dialog box appears. Click Select to use the default standard template.

Notice that the name on the Title Bar is no longer Document1; the name is Document2 because Document2 now is the active document window. If you already have document windows open, such as Document1, WordPerfect assigns the next available numbered name to your new document window—in this case, Document2 (see figure 2.2).

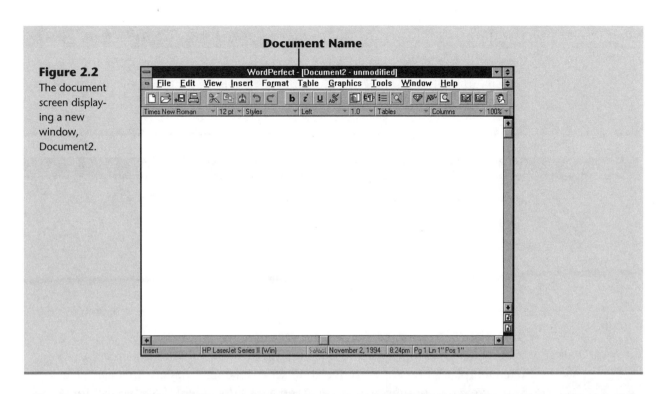

Figure 2.2
The document screen displaying a new window, Document2.

Opening an Existing Document

To retrieve an existing document into the document window, perform the following steps:

① Open the File menu.

② Choose Open.

WordPerfect displays the Open File dialog box (see figure 2.3).

Figure 2.3
The Open File dialog box.

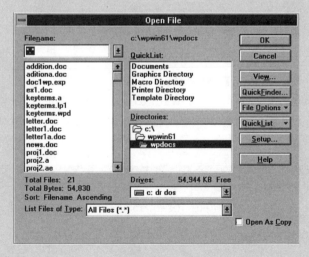

(continues)

Opening an Existing Document (continued)

❸ Highlight a file name from the desired file listing, and double-click the left mouse button; or type the name of the file you want to retrieve in the File**n**ame text box and press ⏎Enter.

Closing a Document Window

To close Document2 and return to Document1, perform the following steps:

❶ Open the **F**ile menu.

❷ Choose **C**lose.

Because Document2 was the active document, it is the one that is closed.

Template
A ready-made document that may contain text, formatting settings, view options (such as hiding or displaying the Toolbar and Power Bar), and graphics.

Selecting a Template for a New Document

WordPerfect for Windows contains more than 40 document *templates*. The supplied templates provide attractive and useful document designs that can save you a great deal of time. When you open a new document, WordPerfect for Windows' default is the standard template. Figure 2.4 shows that the standard template is selected. If you want to use the standard template, click on **S**elect in the New Document dialog box.

Figure 2.4
The New Document dialog box.

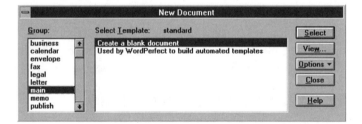

Viewing Different Templates

There may be times when you want to use a template other than the standard template. You can view and select different templates from the Templates dialog box.

Viewing a Template

To view the resume template, for example, perform the following steps:

❶ Open the **F**ile menu.

❷ Choose **N**ew.

The New Document dialog box appears, with the standard options highlighted.

❸ To change the standard template to the resume template, use the mouse to click resume in the **G**roup box. In the Select **T**emplate box, choose Resume-Contemporary.

❹ Click the Vie**w** option button in the dialog box to preview the resume template.

A smaller window appears (called the Viewer) displaying the resume template (see figure 2.5).

Figure 2.5
The Viewer window displaying the resume template.

Document Control Button

❺ Double-click the Document Control button in the upper left corner of the Viewer window to return to the New Document dialog box.

❻ In the New Document dialog box, click **C**lose to return to the WordPerfect screen.

Note: *To choose the **resume** template after you have viewed it, choose **S**elect instead of Close. You can view and select any template listed in the New Document dialog box by following this procedure.*

Understanding WordPerfect's Default Settings

When you start WordPerfect, the program puts into effect a number of *default settings*. These default settings affect the way the program interacts with you, the way information is displayed, and the initial formatting used in each new document you create. Typically, the defaults include margin settings, line spacing, justification settings, and tab settings. You can change these default settings by opening the **E**dit menu and choosing P**r**eferences (see Chapter 7 for more information).

Objective 2: Enter Text

Word wrap
The word processing feature that automatically moves a word to the beginning of the next line if the word will not fit within the current margin settings.

Hard return
The code that WordPerfect inserts when you press ⏎Enter to end a paragraph or line of text.

Soft return
The code that WordPerfect inserts at the end of a line after word wrap occurs.

When you start WordPerfect for Windows, a blank, full-size document window appears in which you can begin entering text at the insertion point location. The *insertion point* is the flashing vertical bar (referred to as a *cursor*) that marks the place in the document where the next character you type will appear. When you open a new document, the insertion point appears in the upper left corner. The insertion point moves to the right as text is inserted and shows you where you are in a document. You can move the insertion point through existing text by using the cursor-movement keys or the mouse. You cannot move the insertion point through a blank text area.

As you type, characters appear at the location of the cursor, and the number represented by the POS indicator in the Status Bar increases. Unlike a typewriter or handwritten methods, word processors enable you to make major revisions within seconds. You can delete, move, format, or copy entire pages of text with one or two keystrokes.

In addition, the cursor indicates where hidden formatting codes will be inserted (codes used to indicate the beginning of a new font style, for example).

WordPerfect's *word wrap* feature keeps track of the insertion point as it moves toward the right margin; when the text has filled a line, word wrap automatically drops text to the next line. With word wrap, you need to press ⏎Enter only when you want to begin a new paragraph or create extra spacing. Each time the word wrap feature drops text down to a new line, an [SRt] (*soft return*) code is inserted into the document. Each time you press ⏎Enter, an [HRt] code (*hard return*) is inserted. You can see these hidden codes when you view the Reveal Codes window (see figure 2.6).

Figure 2.6
The [HRt] and [SRt] codes are displayed in the Reveal Codes window.

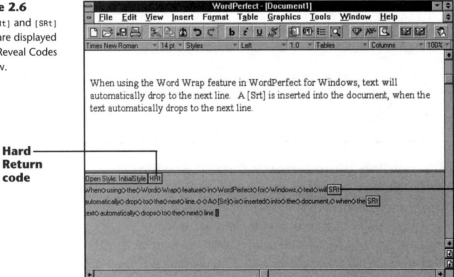

Hard Return code

Soft Return code

Using Word Wrap

To see how the word wrap feature works, type the paragraph shown in figure 2.7 (including spelling errors). Press ⏎Enter twice after the last period of the last sentence.

This paragraph will be used in the following tutorials.

Figure 2.7
Type the text shown in this window.

```
When you key in text using WordPerfect for Windows, remember
to use the word wrap feiture. You don't have to worry about
your sentences going past the right marjin with word wrap; the
program will automatically start new lines for you. The only
times you will need to passs the Enter key are at the end of a
paragraph, at the end of a short line, or when you wish to
insert black lines somewhere in the document.
```

Moving through Text with the Mouse

The quickest way to reposition the cursor in existing text is by using the mouse. Simply position the I-beam pointer so that it is between the characters in the text that need editing, and click the left mouse button.

Moving through Text with the Keyboard

You also can use the keyboard to move through existing text. Table 2.1 shows the key combinations that you can use. Many not only move the cursor in the text, but also scroll the document. Sometimes it is faster to use the keyboard combination methods than it is to use the vertical scroll bar and the mouse.

Table 2.1 Moving the Cursor through Text with the Keyboard	
Key(s)	**Cursor Movement in Text**
↑	Moves up one line
↓	Moves down one line
←	Moves one position to the left
→	Moves one position to the right
Ctrl+→	Moves to the beginning of the next word to the right
Ctrl+←	Moves to the beginning of the word to the left
Ctrl+↑	Moves up one paragraph
Ctrl+↓	Moves down one paragraph
Ctrl+PgUp	Moves to the top of the active document window
Ctrl+PgDn	Moves to the bottom of the active document window
Home	Moves to the beginning of the line
End	Moves to the end of the line
Alt+Home	Moves to the beginning of the page

(continues)

Table 2.1 Moving the Cursor through Text with the Keyboard (continued)	
Key(s)	**Cursor Movement in Text**
Alt + End	Moves to the end of the page
Ctrl + Home	Moves to the beginning of the document
Ctrl + End	Moves to the end of the document

Using Key Combinations to Move through a Document

To practice using key combinations, perform the following steps:

❶ Begin with the insertion point at the beginning of the first line of the paragraph you typed earlier (see figure 2.7).

❷ Press Ctrl + End to move to the end of the document.

❸ Press Alt + Home to move to the beginning of the page.

❹ Press End to move to the end of the line.

❺ Press Ctrl + ← to move to the beginning of the next word to the left.

Understanding Insert Mode

Insert mode
WordPerfect's default editing mode. New text is inserted at the cursor's position, and existing text moves to the right.

As you type text in a new document, WordPerfect uses the default setting of *Insert mode*. You toggle Insert mode on and off by pressing Insert. When you are using Insert mode, the word Insert appears in the Status Bar.

Understanding Typeover Mode

When you want to replace existing text with new text, you can use *Typeover mode*. Typeover mode is the alternative to Insert mode, and is activated by pressing Insert.

Using ←Backspace and Del

Typeover mode
The mode in which existing characters or spaces are replaced with the new characters you type at the cursor's position.

You can use ←Backspace and Del to correct errors as you type a document. Pressing ←Backspace deletes the character to the left of the cursor, and pressing Del deletes the character to the right of the cursor. To edit previously typed text, use the arrow keys to navigate through the document and make corrections with ←Backspace and Del.

Using Insert Mode

To understand how Insert mode works, perform the following steps:

❶ Position the cursor on the first line, in the space between the words *WordPerfect* and *for*.

❷ Type **6.1**.

Notice that the existing text is pushed to the right to make room for the text you enter.

Replacing Text Using Typeover Mode

To replace existing text using Typeover mode, perform the following steps:

1 Position the cursor before the letter *a* in the word *passs* in the third sentence.

2 Press [Insert].

Notice that the Status Bar displays the word Typeover, indicating that you are in Typeover mode. The cursor should be positioned directly before the letter you want to replace. In this tutorial, you replace the letters *as* with *re*.

3 Type **re**.

4 Move to the next line of the paragraph and change the word *black* to *blank* by positioning the cursor on the *c* and typing **n**.

5 Press [Insert] to deactivate Typeover mode.

The word Typeover in the Status Bar is replaced by the word Insert, indicating that the default mode is active again.

Caution

Both [Backspace] and [Del] are repeating keys, which means that if you press and hold down either of these keys, WordPerfect continues to delete characters until you release the key.

Correcting Errors Using [Backspace] and [Del]

To use [Del] to correct an error in a document, perform the following steps:

1 Using the appropriate arrow keys, move to the word *feiture* at the end of the first sentence. Place the cursor before the *i* and press [Del].

The *i* is deleted, and the remaining text moves to the left.

2 Type the letter **a**.

WordPerfect inserts the correction and moves the remaining text to the right.

Follow these steps to use [Backspace] to correct a mistake:

1 Use the arrow keys to position the cursor after the *j* in the word *marjin* in the second sentence.

2 Press [Backspace] to remove the letter *j*.

3 Type the letter **g**.

4 Use either of the methods you have just learned to delete the version number, *6.1,* that you inserted after the word *WordPerfect*.

(continues)

Correcting Errors Using (←Backspace) **and** (Del) **(continued)**

Your document now should look similar to figure 2.8.

Figure 2.8
The edited
document.

> When you key in text using WordPerfect for Windows, remember to use the word wrap feature. You don't have to worry about your sentences going past the right margin with word wrap; the program will automatically start new lines for you. The only times you will need to press the Enter key are at the end of a paragraph, at the end of a short line, or when you wish to insert blank lines somewhere in the document.

Using the Go To Option

The Go To option enables you to quickly reposition the insertion point on a page, or to move to a specific page number.

Using the Go To Option

To reposition the insertion point in the document using the Go To option, perform the following steps:

1 Move the cursor to the top of the document.

2 Open the **E**dit menu from the Menu Bar.

3 Choose the **G**o To option from the pull-down menu.

WordPerfect displays the Go To dialog box. The four round buttons displayed in the dialog box are *option buttons* (also called *radio buttons*). Figure 2.9 shows the Go To dialog box.

Figure 2.9
The Go To
dialog box.

**Option
buttons**

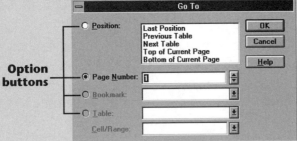

4 Click the **P**osition option button.

A dot appears in the middle of the button. To the right of the option button is a list box containing five options.

5 Click the Bottom of Current Page option to highlight it.

6 Click the OK command button.

You are returned to the document, and the cursor is positioned at the bottom of the page.

Objective 3: View a Document

As you type text, it is displayed in *Page mode*, which is the default setting for WordPerfect. Page mode displays headers and footers as well as WYSIWYG features that enable you to view the font you are using.

An alternative option, *Draft mode*, offers you the same WYSIWYG features but enables the screen display to react more quickly as you type and scroll through text. Headers and footers are not shown in Draft mode. You may find Draft mode more suitable when you are entering text into the document, and then later you can return to Page mode to see how the document actually appears.

2

Changing from Page Mode to Draft Mode

To change from Page mode to Draft mode, perform the following steps:

❶ Open the **V**iew menu.

❷ Choose the **D**raft option.

When the document screen reappears, the repositioned cursor is displayed, and the space for the header and footer have been removed.

Viewing Formatting Symbols

If you want to see where the tabs, spaces, and end of paragraphs occur in the document, you can view these formatting symbols by choosing the **S**how option from the **V**iew menu. This is a toggle switch.

Displaying and Hiding Formatting Symbols

To view the formatting symbols in the current document, perform the following steps:

❶ Open the **V**iew menu.

❷ Choose the **S**how option.

Figure 2.10
The document
screen with the
Show Option
feature
activated.

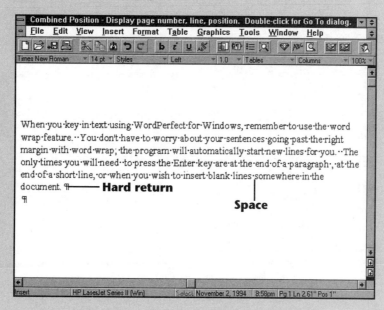

(continues)

Displaying and Hiding Formatting Symbols (continued)

Your document screen displays the formatting symbols (see figure 2.10).

To hide the display of formatting symbols in the document window, perform the following steps:

1 Open the **V**iew menu.

2 Choose the **S**how option again to remove the check mark and deactivate the symbol display.

The paragraph appears without the formatting symbols visible.

Zooming In or Out

You can enlarge or reduce the view of text or graphics on-screen. You may want to reduce the view to see more information at one time. By magnifying the view, you can examine images and text in detail.

Enlarging or Reducing Your View

To use the **Z**oom option, perform the following steps:

1 Open the **V**iew menu.

2 Choose **Z**oom.

WordPerfect displays the Zoom dialog box, showing various percentage option buttons used to magnify or reduce the screen display (see figure 2.11).

Figure 2.11
The Zoom
dialog box.

Note: *If you choose the Two Page option from the* **V***iew menu, the* **Z***oom option is disabled.*

3 Choose the **5**0% option button.

4 Click OK.

Your screen display is reduced.

To enlarge the current display, perform the following steps:

1 Open the **V**iew menu.

2 Choose **Z**oom. The Zoom dialog box appears.

3 Choose the **2**00% option button.

4 Click OK.

Your screen display is enlarged to 200% (see figure 2.12).

Figure 2.12
The screen
displaying a
Zoom option of
200%.

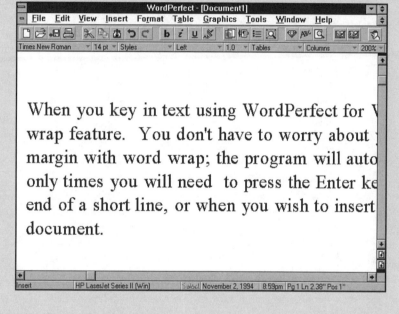

5 Reset the display to 100%.

Objective 4: Save a Document

After you create a document, you can save it for later retrieval. Because the displayed document is temporary until you save the document to disk, the contents of the document will be lost when you turn off the machine. The following section explains how to save a document the first time and then resave existing documents.

File name
A descriptive name
you give your
document when
you save it.

A *file name* is a name you assign to a document. File names can contain up to eight characters and can include an optional extension of up to three characters. Spaces are not allowed in a file name.

Saving a New Document

To save a document the first time, follow these steps:

❶ Open the File menu.

❷ Choose Save or Save As.

The Save As dialog box appears with an insertion point flashing in the Filename box.

❸ Type **WORDWRAP.DOC** in the Filename box (see figure 2.13).

Figure 2.13
The Save As
dialog box.

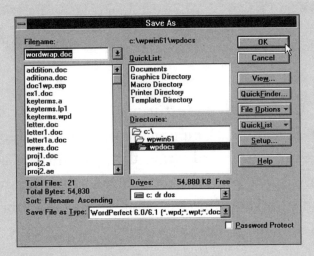

❹ Click OK.

Your document now displays the name of the saved file in the Title Bar (see figure 2.14).

Figure 2.14
The
WORDWRAP.DOC
file displayed in
the Title Bar.

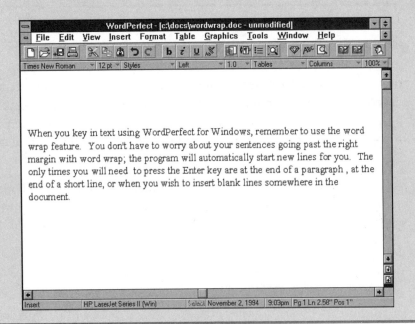

The following options are available in the Save **A**s dialog box:

- *File**n**ame list box*. The area below the File**n**ame box contains a listing of files that exist in the drive and directory in which you are working. You can scroll through this list to choose a file to be retrieved.

- ***D**irectories box*. Informs you of the directory to which the file is being saved and enables you to change the destination of the file.

- *Vie**w** button*. Enables you to examine a file through the Viewer window before retrieving it.

- *Quick**F**inder button*. Enables you to search for a file that meets criteria that you set, such as file pattern, words or phrases, summary fields, or full text.

- *File **O**ptions button*. Enables you to perform various tasks in a file, such as copying, moving, renaming, deleting, and other file-management activities.

- *Quick**L**ist button*. Enables you to display customized file listings quickly. You may want to display certain report files that are stored in a specific directory, for example. Instead of having to type the subdirectory specifications each time you want to view the report files, add them to the QuickList.

- ***S**etup button*. Enables you to change many settings that affect the way file names appear within the Save As dialog box.

Saving an Existing Document

After saving a document the first time, you can save it again by choosing the **S**ave option from the **F**ile menu. WordPerfect saves the document for you without your having to issue additional commands because the program defaults to the file name used the first time you saved the document.

Saving the Document under a New Name

After you have saved your document with a file name, you can save a copy of it under a new name by opening the **F**ile menu and choosing the Save **A**s option. This procedure opens the Save As dialog box, in which you can edit the file name and change the directory and/or drive.

Objective 5: Print a Document

Printing a Document

To print a hard copy of the document using WordPerfect's default print settings, perform the following steps:

❶ Open the **F**ile menu.

❷ Choose **P**rint.

The Print dialog box appears (see figure 2.15).

(continues)

Printing a Document (continued)

Figure 2.15
The Print dialog box.

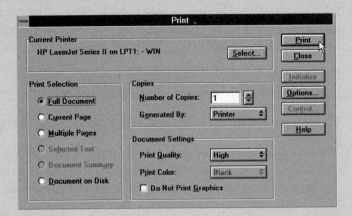

❸ Choose the **P**rint option button.

The message `Preparing Document for Printing` appears, informing you that the file is being readied for printing.

The default print settings that are used follow:

• Printing the full document

• Using the selected printer

• Printing one copy

Clicking the **P**rint button thus prints one copy of the entire document, using your default printer selection. Techniques for changing the default settings are discussed in Chapter 7, "WordPerfect's Customizing Features."

Objective 6: Exit WordPerfect for Windows

When you finish using your documents and want to stop working in WordPerfect, you should be sure to exit the program properly.

Exiting WordPerfect for Windows

When you are ready to close all documents in WordPerfect and return to the Windows operating environment, perform these steps:

❶ Open the **F**ile menu and choose E**x**it.

Alternatively, press Alt+F4.

WordPerfect displays a message box prompting you to save any document that has not been saved, or that contains editing changes you haven't saved (see figure 2.16).

Figure 2.16
The WordPerfect
Save Changes
message box.

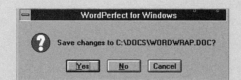

❷ Click **Y**es to save and exit, **N**o to clear the screen, or Cancel to return to the document.

Chapter Summary

In this chapter, you created and entered text into a new document and then edited that document. You learned how to use the different viewing options, how to save a document, and how to print a hard copy of a document. You also learned how to save a document and exit the WordPerfect program.

Checking Your Skills

True/False Questions

For each of the following statements, circle *T* or *F* to indicate whether the statement is true or false.

T F **1.** A *template* is a ready-made document that may contain formatting settings and other special features.

T F **2.** To access the Viewer window, you first must choose the **V**iew menu option.

T F **3.** The insertion point can be positioned anywhere within the WordPerfect document screen.

T F **4.** Each time the word wrap feature automatically drops to a new line, WordPerfect inserts a soft return into the document.

T F **5.** When you start WordPerfect for Windows, Insert mode is activated automatically.

T F **6.** The first time a document is saved, the Save dialog box is displayed.

T F **7.** WordPerfect enables you to have up to nine documents open at one time.

T F **8.** You can include up to two spaces in each file name.

T F **9.** When the **S**how option is activated, you can view hidden codes.

T F **10.** The Vie**w** button in the Save As dialog box enables you to view different templates.

Multiple-Choice Questions

In the blank provided, write the letter of the correct answer for each of the following questions.

___**1.** _____ is not a valid file name.

    a. REPORT.DOC

    b. MEMO

    c. LETTER221.TXT

    d. EXAM10.ANS

___**2.** You press _____ to activate Typeover mode.

    a. ◆Backspace

    b. Del

    c. Insert

    d. ↓

___**3.** You can enlarge or reduce the view of a document by choosing the _____.

    a. **Z**oom command from the **V**iew menu

    b. **Z**oom command from the **F**ile menu

    c. **Z**oom command from the **P**rint menu

    d. **Z**oom command from the **S**ave menu

___**4.** You can save an existing file under a new name by choosing the _____ command.

    a. **S**ave

    b. **E**xit

    c. Save **A**s

    d. **C**lose

___**5.** The Go To option enables you to quickly move to the _____.

    a. end of a sentence

    b. beginning of a word

    c. bottom of the current page

    d. All these answers

___**6.** After saving a file and giving it a name, the Title Bar displays _____.

    a. `WordPerfect [`*Document#* `Unmodified]`

    b. `WordPerfect [`*Document#* `Modified]`

   c. `WordPerfect` [*Document#*]

   d. none of these answers

___**7.** `⏎Enter` is used to do all of the following except _____.

   a. create a new paragraph

   b. create blank lines

   c. end a short line

   d. create a soft return

___**8.** You can turn on and off Insert mode by pressing _____.

   a. `⇧Shift`

   b. `Insert`

   c. `Ctrl`

   d. `Home`

___**9.** The Last Position option in the Go To dialog box moves the cursor to the _____.

   a. last page of a document

   b. last word in a line

   c. preceding position in the document

   d. last paragraph on the page

___**10.** To change the way a file name appears in the Save As dialog box, you click the _____.

   a. File **O**ptions button

   b. Vie**w** button

   c. **S**etup button

   d. none of these answers

Fill-in-the-Blank Questions

In the blanks provided, write the correct answer for each of the following questions.

1. In Page mode, the _____ and _____ are visible.

2. To print a document, choose the **P**rint command from _____ the menu.

3. The **S**how option enables you to view _____ in the document window.

4. Settings that are used automatically when the program is started are called _____.

5. To push characters to the right of the insertion point when entering text, you must be in_____ mode.

6. WordPerfect prompts you with a _____ if you did not save changes before attempting to exit the program.

7. The Zoom option is disabled when the _____ option is selected.

8. WordPerfect automatically uses the _____ template unless otherwise specified.

9. The screen display reacts more quickly in_____ mode.

10. To go to the end of a line, press the _____ key.

Applying Your Skills

Review Exercises

Exercise 1: Creating and Saving a New Document

On a clear screen in a new WordPerfect document, type the following information exactly as shown (including any spelling errors):

Mrs. Mary Mark

116 Ash St.

Indianapolis, IN. 46291

Dear Mrs. Mark:

Thank you for your letter inquireing about the need for protecting critical informtion in your organization. Data protection should be a major concern for all places of bussiness, large or small. One recent warning was the bank fire in Chicago where over 30 years of recorded transactions were destroyed. The problem is that organizations just don't think dissasters will ever happen to them.

Save the document as **LETTER.DOC**.

Exercise 2: Moving through Your Document and Changing the View

Use the various techniques discussed in this chapter to complete the following tasks. On a sheet of paper, make a list of the options, commands, and keys you use to complete these tasks:

1. Move through a document.

2. Use the Go To feature.

3. Use the Show option.

4. Use the Zoom option.

Exercise 3: Saving and Closing a Document, and Exiting WordPerfect

1. Save the LETTER.DOC file under a new name called **LETTER1.DOC**.

2. Print the document.

3. Close the document window.

4. Exit the program.

Exercise 4: Making Changes to an Existing File Using Draft Mode

A common word processing task is to open an existing file, make changes to it, save it, and print it. In this exercise, you do so using WordPerfect's Draft mode:

1. Open the LETTER1.DOC file.

2. With LETTER1.DOC displayed on-screen, open a new file.

3. Activate Draft mode.

4. Type the following document, including all errors. Press ⏎Enter at the end of the short lines or to begin a new paragraph. Use Tab⇥ to indent the beginning of each paragraph.

> **Dear Ms. Ziegley:**
>
> **During the past five years I I have enjoyed working with companies such as Browns Sporting Goods, Telenex Communi-cations, Kay-Mart Office Supples and Stay in Style Clothing Stores. Advertising, being the competative market that it is, demands an individual whose skills include an innovative and creative approach in developing successful campaigns for new product lines. I feel confident that I could trigger new sales for your company and that you would indeed be pleased with the results of my efforts.**
>
> **Acording to an add in the Fort Wayne Gazette on February 12, 1995 an opening exists for a commerial advertising agent. Please cosider me a candidate for the position.**

5. Save the document as **JOB.DOC**.

6. Print the JOB.DOC file.

7. Close both document files.

Exercise 5: Making Changes to an Existing File using Page Layout Mode

Again, you will open, edit, save, and print an existing document, but this time you will use WordPerfect's Page Layout mode.

Follow these steps:

1. Open the JOB.DOC file and activate Page Layout mode. Using the keyboard to move through the document, make the following corrections:

   Insert the letter **c** in the word *Acording,* between the letters *A* and *c* in the second paragraph.

   Correct the spelling of the word *commerial* in the second paragraph to *commercial*.

   Add the letter **n** to the word *cosider* in the second sentence of the second paragraph to make it *consider*.

   Change the word *trigger* in the first paragraph to *launch*.

   Delete the word *indeed* from the first paragraph.

2. Save the file with the new name of **JOB1.DOC**.

3. Print the file.

4. Close the file and exit the program.

5. Review the steps you used to perform this exercise.

Continuing Projects

Project 1: Typing, Saving, and Printing a Document

In this project, you type the basic information for a news release:

1. Type the following document. Press Tab⇥ to indent the first line of each paragraph, and press ⏎Enter twice after each paragraph.

   > **Compuvise has recently hired two new employees to assist in development and sales of computer products at its Chicago and Los Angeles branches. Because of increased business at both of these major branches, the need for additional staff is overwhelming.**
   >
   > **Mr. James Kevin became the new Director of Sales in our Chicago branch on January 25. Mr. Kevin is a native of Peoria, Illinois, and has an extensive background in sales, as well as commercial advertising. For the past five years, Mr. Kevin has developed marketing strategies for major Fortune 500 companies across the country.**

2. Save the document as **NEWS.DOC**.

3. Print the document.

Project 2: Typing, Saving, and Printing a Document

In this exercise, you type a list of key WordPerfect for Windows terms. You get the added benefit of a review while creating this document:

1. Type the following document:

Key Terms in This Chapter

Defaults

Standard WordPerfect settings that are in effect each time you start the program.

Status bar

The bottom line on the WordPerfect for Windows document window is the Status Bar. The Status Bar indicates what the position of the cursor is on-screen.

Insertion point (cursor)

A vertical flashing bar indicating where the next character will be inserted when you type. To move the cursor, use the cursor movement keys or position the I-beam pointer in the text and click the left mouse button.

Word wrap

A WordPerfect feature that eliminates the need to press Enter (Return) each time you reach the right margin. With word wrap you need to press Enter only when you come to the end of a paragraph, short line, or wish to execute a command.

Soft return

The code inserted at the end of each line when the text reaches the right margin and is automatically wrapped to the next line.

Hard return

The code for a carriage return, inserted when you press Enter at the end of a line.

File name

A descriptive title that you assign to a file before storing it in the system memory.

2. Save the document as **KEYTERMS.DOC**.

3. Print the document.

Project 3: Creating a File, Entering Text, Saving a File, and Printing a File

Here, you create a document with several errors. You will use this document later to practice correcting those errors:

1. Type the following text, including the errors:

   Thanks so much for attending our open house celebratian last week. Compuvise is is constantly trying to satisfy the needs of our clients by offering a variety of training options that include word processing, spreadsheet, graphics, database and operating system packages.

   Enclosed is a schedule of classes that will be offered during the month of July 1995. Please feel free to call and ask for any additional information you may need regarding class content as well as specail group discount rates.

2. Save the new file as **TRAINING.DOC**.

3. Print a copy of TRAINING.DOC.

Project 4: Correcting Errors in an Existing Document

Now you can use the TRAINING.DOC document to practice making corrections using the Del, +Backspace, and cursor keys; and using the mouse to move through the text.

Use the methods for making corrections discussed in this chapter and the mouse, to do the following:

1. Insert the word **software** before the word *classes* in the first sentence of the second paragraph.

2. Delete the second occurrence of the word **is** in the second sentence of the first paragraph.

3. Change the *a* to an **o** in the word **celebratian** in the first sentence of the first paragraph.

4. Change the order of the *ai* in the word *specail* in the last sentence of the last paragraph.

5. Save the document as TRAIN1.DOC.

6. Print the document.

7. Close TRAIN1.DOC.

8. Review the steps you used to do the tasks in this exercise.

CHAPTER 3

Editing Documents

In this chapter, you learn how to work with multiple documents. You learn how to select text for copying, cutting, and pasting; you also learn how to use the WordPerfect Help feature.

Objectives

By the time you finish this chapter, you will have learned to

1. Open Existing Documents for Editing

2. Work with Multiple Documents

3. Select Text

4. Use the Copy, Cut, and Paste Commands

5. Use WordPerfect Help

Objective 1: Open Existing Documents for Editing

Before you can edit the contents of a WordPerfect document you have saved to disk, you must open the document into a document window.

Opening an Existing Document

To open WORDWRAP.DOC (which you created in Chapter 2), perform the following steps:

1 Start WordPerfect for Windows using one of the methods described in Chapter 1.

2 Open the File menu; then choose Open.

WordPerfect displays the Open File dialog box, which lists all the files in the current directory.

(continues)

Opening an Existing Document (continued)

❸ Choose the name of the document you want to open (for this tutorial, choose WORDWRAP.DOC) and press ⏎Enter.

❹ Close WORDWRAP.DOC.

Tip

You also can double-click the name of the file to open it. If you get a message saying that the file is not found, check to make sure that the drive and directory are correct.

The Open File dialog box includes the following options not yet discussed:

- *QuickFinder*. Searches for specific files according to their file pattern, words or phrases, summary fields, date ranges, or the QuickFinder Index.

- *List Files of Type box*. Click the arrow next to this box to activate a drop-down list containing options that enable you to choose the type of files you want to display in the list box of file names.

- *View*. Enables you to see a file before opening it into the document window.

Opening a Document from a Different Drive or Directory

You may need to access a file from a drive or directory other than the default drive and directory. If you are using a hard drive (usually drive C), WordPerfect considers this drive to be the default. During the installation of the program, WordPerfect sets up one directory to store its program files (\WPWIN60) and a separate directory to store your work files (WPDOCS). When attempting to access information from a drive other than drive C, you need to specify where you want WordPerfect to look for the information.

Opening a File from a Specific Drive

To open a file from drive A, for example, follow these steps:

❶ Open the File menu and choose Open.

The Open File dialog box appears.

❷ Click the arrow next to the Drives box to activate the drop-down list containing the drives available to your computer.

❸ Choose drive A. Press the up-arrow key until you highlight drive A and then press ⏎Enter. Or, click once on drive A with the mouse.

The file list and directory box show information on files and directories located on drive A (see figure 3.1).

Figure 3.1
The Open File
dialog box
shows a file list
for drive A.

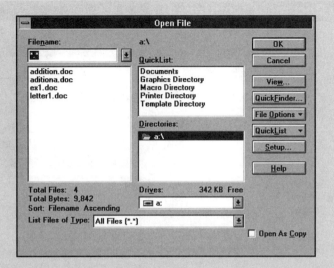

Note: *You must insert a floppy disk into drive A before you choose it. If drive A is empty, an error message appears saying that the drive is not ready.*

Viewing the Contents of a Document

As the list of documents you create in WordPerfect grows, you may not be able to tell what information each file contains just by looking at the file name. You can use WordPerfect's File Viewer to quickly view a document's contents. After you click the Vie**w** button in the Open File dialog box, WordPerfect opens a separate View window that enables you to look at the text of a chosen file. You can move through the text by using the scroll bars.

Viewing a Document

To view the contents of an existing file, perform the following steps:

❶ Open the **F**ile menu; then choose **O**pen.

The Open File dialog box appears.

❷ Click the file name LETTER1.DOC to highlight it. (You created the document in Chapter 2.)

❸ Click the Vie**w** option in the dialog box.

The Viewer window appears, displaying the contents of the LETTER1.DOC file (see figure 3.2). You can maximize or scroll through this window.

(continues)

Viewing a Document (continued)

Figure 3.2
The LETTER1.DOC in the Viewer window.

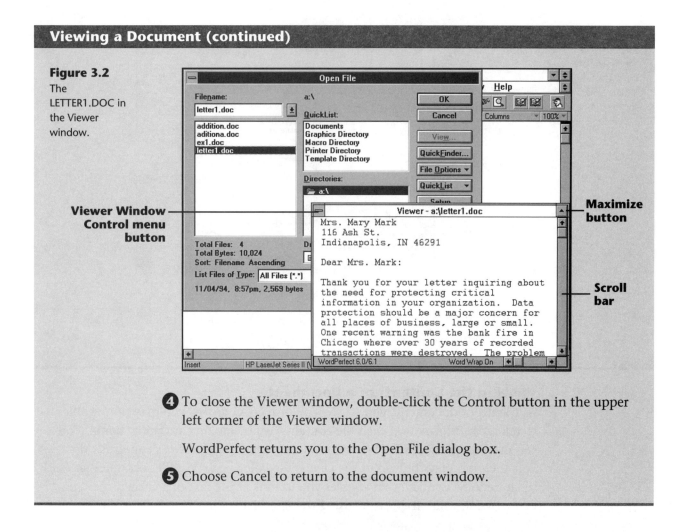

To close the Viewer window, double-click the Control button in the upper left corner of the Viewer window.

WordPerfect returns you to the Open File dialog box.

Choose Cancel to return to the document window.

Objective 2: Work with Multiple Documents

If your computer has sufficient memory, you can open as many as nine documents at one time in WordPerfect. It is important to understand that although nine documents can be open at one time, only one document can be active at a time. In the following tutorials, you open, rearrange, and view multiple documents. You also can easily retrieve one document into another. Finally, you will learn how to close a document when finished with it.

Opening Multiple Documents

To open multiple documents in the WordPerfect document screen, perform the following steps:

Open the File menu; then choose Open.

The Open File dialog box appears.

❷ Hold down Ctrl and click each file you want to open. (For this tutorial, click the LETTER1.DOC and WORDWRAP.DOC file names in the Filename list box.)

❸ Click OK.

The document screen appears and briefly displays the contents of each file that you chose. Only the last open document window is visible in the WordPerfect window.

3

Tip

When you want to open a group of files that are adjacent to one another, you can drag the mouse across them to highlight them all at once and then click OK.

Viewing More than One Document Window

Each WordPerfect document you open appears in its own full-size document window. Each document window can be controlled with its own Maximize and Minimize buttons, drop-down menu, and scroll bars.

To view more than one open document, you can resize and rearrange document windows using the **C**ascade or **T**ile option.

Rearranging Multiple Documents Using the Cascade and Tile Options

To arrange the open documents by using the **C**ascade option, perform the following steps:

❶ Open the **W**indow menu.

❷ Choose **C**ascade.

The windows of the opened files overlap one another. The active file window is displayed in front of all other windows with its Title Bar highlighted (see figure 3.3).

(continues)

Rearranging Multiple Documents Using the Cascade and Tile Options (continued)

Figure 3.3
The cascaded windows displaying WORDWRAP.DOC as the active file.

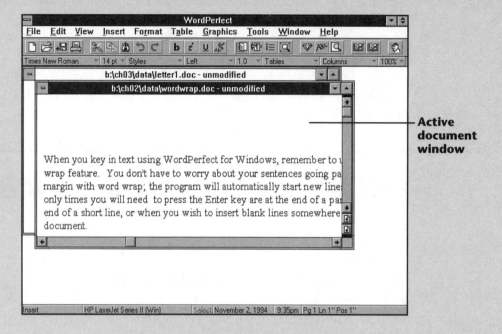

Active document window

To arrange documents by using the **T**ile option, do the following:

❶ Open the **W**indow menu.

❷ Choose **T**ile Horizontal.

The open files are displayed one above the other (see figure 3.4). The Title Bar of the active document is highlighted.

Figure 3.4
The open documents in a tiled display.

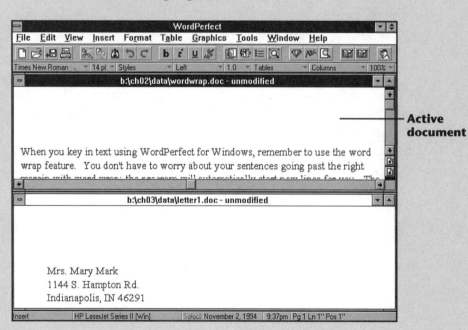

Active document

The following tutorial explains how to activate a document in a cascaded or tiled window.

Activating Cascaded or Tiled Document Windows

1 To make a cascaded WordPerfect document window active, click the Title Bar of the document window you want to make active.

The document window moves to the front of the stack with its Title Bar highlighted and the scroll bars displayed.

2 To make a tiled WordPerfect document window active, click anywhere in the window to make it active.

The active document window's Title Bar is highlighted and the scroll bars are displayed.

Closing Existing Document Windows

After you have finished with a document, you can close its window to free computer memory and reduce clutter on your screen. Before you can close a document window, you must make the document active.

Closing the Document Windows

To close the open documents currently on your screen, perform the following steps:

1 Click the Title Bar for WORDWRAP.DOC to make it the active window.

2 Open the File menu; then choose Close.

3 Close all the remaining windows.

If you have made changes to the document in the window you are closing, WordPerfect prompts you to confirm your changes. To save changes before closing the window, click the Yes button. To clear the active document window of text without closing the active window, press the Clear key combination: Ctrl + Shift + F4.

Retrieving One File into Another File

You may want to incorporate the text of one document into the document in which you're working. WordPerfect makes this an easy task to perform.

Incorporating a File into Another File

To incorporate the text of one document into another document, perform the following steps:

1 On a clear screen, type the following text. Press Enter twice after the last word of the last sentence:

(continues)

Incorporating a File into Another File (continued)

In addition to the word wrap feature, word processors offer many other beneficial features. Some of these include saving a file for later retrieval, deleting files that are no longer needed, and making revisions quickly and easily.

2 Save the document as ADDITION.DOC.

3 Open the Insert menu; then choose File.

The Insert File dialog box is displayed.

4 From the Insert File list, choose WORDWRAP.DOC.

5 Click the Insert button.

WordPerfect displays a message asking you to confirm the insertion of WORDWRAP.DOC into the current document.

6 Click Yes.

The screen displays the addition of WORDWRAP.DOC to ADDITION.DOC (see figure 3.5).

Figure 3.5
The ADDITION.DOC file after WORDWRAP.DOC is inserted.

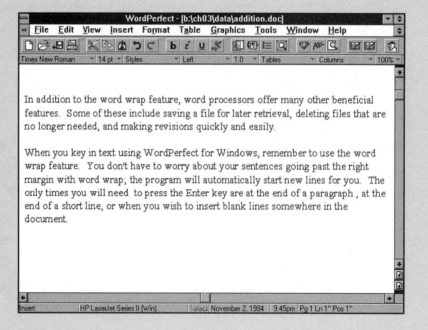

Objective 3: Select Text

WordPerfect's *object-action model* enables you to perform a series of actions on a selected block of text without repeating the selection process. The following sections explain the procedure for selecting text using the keyboard and mouse, and for making changes to selected text.

Using the Mouse to Select Text

Select
To highlight text using the mouse or keyboard so that WordPerfect can identify the text on which you want to perform the next operation.

In a WordPerfect document, you must *select* the text you want to modify before you can choose an editing command. WordPerfect displays the text you select by highlighting it (showing the text in inverse video).

When you move the mouse pointer over text, the pointer changes from an arrowhead to an I-beam.

Note: *Be careful not to press a keyboard character once selected text is highlighted; selected text will be deleted and will be replaced by the keyboard character that was pressed. To get back the accidental deletion, you must immediately choose the* **U***ndo command from the* **E***dit menu or press* Ctrl+Z.

Selecting Several Words on a Single Line

You can use any one of several methods to select portions of text. In the next tutorial, you practice using the mouse to select text in the ADDITION.DOC file.

3

Selecting Several Words on a Single Line

To select several words on a single line of text by using the mouse, perform the following steps:

1 Position the I-beam immediately preceding the first character you want to select. For this example, place the cursor in front of the first word of the first paragraph.

2 Drag the mouse to the right until all the words up to and including the word *other* are highlighted.

3 Release the mouse button. The sentence is highlighted.

4 To cancel the selection of the text, position the pointer in the right margin and click.

Selecting Several Lines of Text

To select several lines of text, perform the following steps:

1 Position the I-beam immediately preceding the first character you want to include. For this example, position the I-beam in front of the first word in the first paragraph.

2 Drag down through the lines you want to select. In this example, drag down to include the third line of the first paragraph.

3 Release the mouse button.

4 To cancel the selection of the text, position the pointer in the right margin and click.

Selecting a Paragraph of Text

To select a paragraph of text, perform the following steps:

1 Position the I-beam immediately preceding the first character you want to select. For this example, place the I-beam in front of the word *When*, which begins the second paragraph.

2 Drag the mouse from the upper left corner of the paragraph to the lower right corner.

3 Release the mouse button.

4 To cancel the selection of the text, position the pointer in the right margin and click.

Using Shortcuts for Selecting Text

When selecting text with a mouse, you can use shortcuts that don't involve dragging. These shortcuts follow:

- To select a single word, double-click anywhere in the word.

- To select a sentence, *triple-click* (three rapid clicks in a row) anywhere in the sentence.

  You also can select a sentence by clicking in the left margin.

- To select a paragraph, *quadruple-click* (four rapid clicks in a row) anywhere in the paragraph.

Using the Keyboard to Select Text

Text also can be selected by using a keyboard function key method. Perform the following steps to select text using the keyboard:

1 Place the insertion point where you want selection to begin.

2 Press F8 to begin selection.

3 Using the cursor-movement keys on the keyboard (the arrow keys) press until the desired amount of text is highlighted.

4 Press F8 again to stop selection.

Note: *When F8 is pressed, the word* Select *in the Status Bar changes from gray to black, indicating that the selection method is activated. The F8 key operates as a toggle switch. When pressed again, the word* Select *in the Status Bar becomes dimmed.*

Using QuickMenus to Select Text

You also can use the mouse to select a sentence, paragraph, or all text in a document without having to click or drag through the text. Instead, you use the QuickMenu attached to the left margin of the document.

Selecting Text with QuickMenus

To open the QuickMenu and select text from the ADDITION.DOC document, perform the following steps:

1 Position the mouse pointer in the left margin of the first line of the first paragraph.

2 Click the **right** mouse button.

A QuickMenu appears (see figure 3.6).

Figure 3.6
One of
WordPerfect's
QuickMenus.

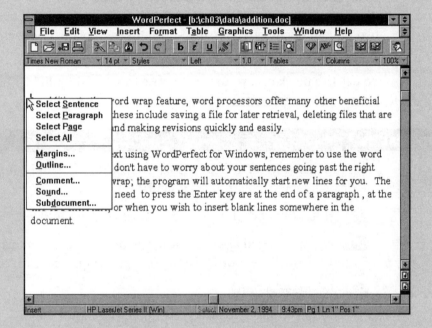

3 Choose Select Sentence to select the sentence on the current line. The sentence is highlighted.

You can choose Select Paragraph to select the current paragraph, or Select All to select all the text in the document.

4 To cancel the selection, position the pointer in the right margin and click.

Replacing Selected Text

You can replace a section of text by selecting the text you want to replace and then typing the replacement text. As soon as you type your first replacement character, WordPerfect deletes all the selected text.

Replacing Selected Text

To replace the first sentence in the second paragraph with a new sentence, perform the following steps:

1 Drag the mouse over the first sentence in the second paragraph to select it.

(continues)

Replacing Selected Text (continued)

❷ Type the following replacement sentence:

When typing text using the WordPerfect program, remember to let word wrap drop to the next line for you.

The old sentence is removed, and the new sentence is inserted.

Inserting Blank Lines and Deleting Text

Press `⏎Enter` to indicate the end of a paragraph and to insert blank lines in the text of your document. Pressing `⏎Enter` inserts a blank line regardless of whether you are in Insert or Typeover mode.

To delete a block of text, use the mouse to select (highlight) the text you want to erase. Then press `⬅Backspace` or `Del`.

Deleting Text

With the ADDITION.DOC file displayed, perform the following steps to delete the first paragraph from the document:

❶ Position the I-beam pointer over the first word in the first paragraph.

❷ Drag the mouse diagonally from the upper left corner of the first paragraph to the lower right corner of the first paragraph in order to highlight it.

❸ Press `⬅Backspace` or `Del`.

The first paragraph is removed from the document.

Using the Undo Command

You can use the **U**ndo command to restore deleted text and to recover from other editing mistakes, such as choosing the wrong WordPerfect command. WordPerfect holds in memory the last action you made in the document and can restore the document to its state before your last action. Remember that in order to reverse the last command you invoked, you must choose the **U**ndo command before choosing another WordPerfect command.

Using Undo to Restore Deleted Text

In the preceding tutorial, you deleted the first paragraph in the ADDITION.DOC file by selecting it and pressing `Del` or `⬅Backspace`. In this tutorial, you will restore that text. Remember that although you can undo your 10 most recent actions, restoring deleted text using **U**ndo works best if you do not perform another action before using **U**ndo.

Restoring Deleted Text Using Undo

To reverse your deletion action using the **U**ndo command, perform the following steps:

❶ Open the **E**dit menu.

❷ Choose **U**ndo.

The first paragraph for ADDITION.DOC reappears on-screen.

Using the Undelete Command

Unlike the **U**ndo command, which restores only the last deletion to a document, the U**n**delete command can restore any of the last three deletions.

Restoring Selected Text Using the Undelete Command

To activate the Undelete command, follow these steps:

❶ Open the **E**dit menu.

❷ Choose U**n**delete.

WordPerfect displays the Undelete dialog box (see figure 3.7).

Figure 3.7
The Undelete
dialog box.

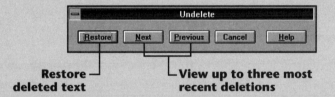

Restore ——
deleted text

└── View up to three most
recent deletions

❸ Click the **R**estore button to restore the highlighted text, or click the **P**revious button to restore the next-to-last deletion you made. You can continue to choose the **N**ext or **P**revious button to cycle forward or backward through the last three deletions you made. When the text you want to restore is displayed, click the **R**estore button again to have the restorations take effect.

Tip

A major difference between **U**ndo and U**n**delete is that U**n**delete enables you to decide where the restored text will be placed, whereas **U**ndo restores text back to its original position only.

Objective 4: Use the Copy, Cut, and Paste Commands

Paste
Places the contents of the Clipboard into a document. After you have copied or cut selected text from a document, you can paste that text into another location.

WordPerfect's *Copy*, *Cut*, and *Paste* commands (located on the Edit menu) enable you to easily move or copy blocks of text to new places in the same document or to other open documents. WordPerfect performs the cut, copy, and paste operations through the *Clipboard*.

Relocating Text by Using Cut and Paste

To reposition text from one area to another in a document, use the Cut and Paste commands. For this tutorial, make sure that ADDITION.DOC is on-screen.

Repositioning Text

To reposition the second paragraph so that it is the first paragraph in the document, perform the following steps:

1 Select the second paragraph by using one of the selection methods previously discussed.

2 Open the Edit menu; then choose Cut.

3 Position the cursor before the first word of the first paragraph in the document.

4 Open the Edit menu; then choose Paste.

The second paragraph is repositioned at the top, and the first paragraph is moved down the page.

5 Position the cursor at the space after the period following the word *document* in the inserted paragraph, and press ⏎Enter. Your document now should look similar to figure 3.8.

Figure 3.8
The ADDITION.DOC file displaying the repositioned paragraphs.

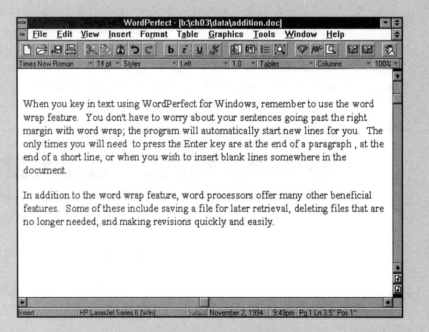

Using the Copy Command

Unlike the Cut command, which removes the selected text, the Copy command duplicates the selected text, which then can be placed in the same document or in another open document.

Copying Information to the Same Document

To place an additional copy of the first paragraph of the ADDITION.DOC file at the bottom of the same document, perform the following steps:

1 Select the first paragraph of ADDITION.DOC.

2 Open the **E**dit menu; then choose **C**opy.

3 Position the cursor on the line below the last paragraph.

4 Open the **E**dit menu; then choose **P**aste.

The document now contains two copies of the first paragraph (see figure 3.9).

Figure 3.9
The ADDITION.DOC file contains two copies of paragraph one.

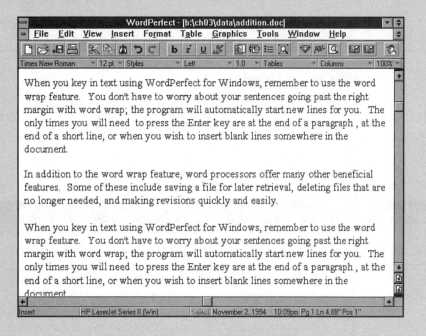

Copying Text from One Document to Another

Clipboard
An area of computer memory that holds the text or graphics you cut or copy. You can paste from the Clipboard into different documents in WordPerfect or into different applications.

Just as you can copy or move text within the same document, you can copy and move text between different documents.

Copying Text from One File to Another

To copy the first paragraph in the ADDITION.DOC file to the WORDWRAP.DOC file, perform the following steps:

1 Open WORDWRAP.DOC so that both ADDITION.DOC and WORDWRAP.DOC appear in the document screen.

2 Click the Title Bar of ADDITION.DOC to activate it.

3 Select the first paragraph of the ADDITION.DOC file.

4 Open the Edit menu; then choose Copy.

5 Click the Title Bar of WORDWRAP.DOC to activate it.

6 Position the cursor one space after the period that follows the last word in the first paragraph (the word *document*).

7 Open the Edit menu; then choose Paste.

The selected text from ADDITION.DOC is copied into WORDWRAP.DOC.

8 Close both documents and save the changes.

Using Paste Simple

To have text that is being pasted take on the same formatting appearance as the existing text at the insertion point, use the Paste Simple command. Paste Simple causes the pasted text to take on the same font size and style, text color, and any attributes (bold, italics, underlining, and so on) that the text at the insertion includes.

Pasting Text Using Paste Simple

To use Paste Simple, follow these steps:

1 Select the text you want to cut or copy.

2 Choose Cut or Copy from the Edit menu.

3 Position the insertion point where the text is to be pasted.

4 Press ⬆Shift+Ctrl+V.

The pasted text appears in the same format as the text at the insertion point. If pasted text is inserted on a blank line, it takes on the default styles, sizes, and attributes.

Note: *Paste Simple is available only to those using WordPerfect 6.0a and 6.1 for Windows.*

Objective 5: Use WordPerfect Help

Copy
Duplicates selected text or graphics. When you combine copying with pasting, you can copy text from one location to another.

WordPerfect for Windows offers extensive on-line help in a special Help window, which you can access at any time while using the program. You can display the Help window along with your document by resizing and rearranging both windows.

Most Help topics contain cross-references indicated by an underlined keyword or phrase in the Help text. On a color monitor, the keyword or phrase is displayed in green as well as being underlined. Each cross-reference leads to related Help topics that give you additional information.

Using Cross-Referencing Help

To select a cross-reference and display a related Help topic using the mouse, perform the following steps:

1 Open the **H**elp menu and choose **C**ontents.

Topics that appear in green on a color monitor include additional subtopic information.

2 Position the mouse pointer on How Do I. Notice that the pointer changes to a hand with a pointing finger (see figure 3.10).

Figure 3.10
Choosing a topic from the Contents menu of the Help command.

Help command buttons

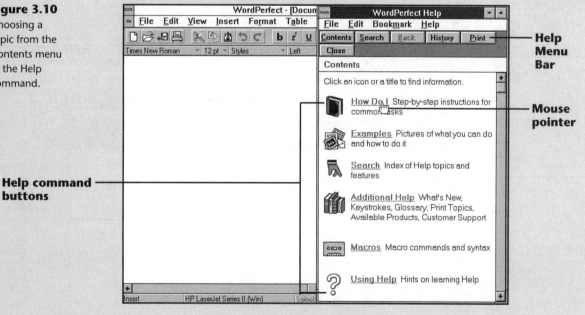

3 Click the topic Use Time Saving Features.

A new Help window appears with subtopics of information for the different time-saving features.

4 Click the topic Use Buttons to see a list of Button topics. Click Use the Toolbar to see specific information for the Toolbar.

Using the Help Command Buttons

The Help window contains five command buttons, which you can use to navigate through Help topics:

Cut

Removes selected text or graphics from a document. When performing cut-and-paste operations, you can move text from one location to another.

- *Contents*. Activates the WordPerfect Help Contents command.

- *Search*. Enables you to search for specific Help topics that contain keywords.

- *Back*. Displays the most recent Help topic you selected and moves you back through topics you have selected.

- *History*. Displays the History dialog box, which lists previously viewed topics.

- *Print*. Prints the current Help topic.

Getting Context-Sensitive Help

WordPerfect supplies context-sensitive help, or help that is directly related to the action you are performing. You can access context-sensitive help while in a dialog box, a menu, or a window.

Using Context-Sensitive Help

To get context-sensitive help about a particular button on the WordPerfect Toolbar, perform the following steps:

1 Position the cursor on the Toolbar for TextArt.

2 Press ⬆Shift+F1.

A question mark inside a bubble appears next to the mouse pointer (see figure 3.11).

Figure 3.11
A question mark in a bubble appears next to the mouse pointer.

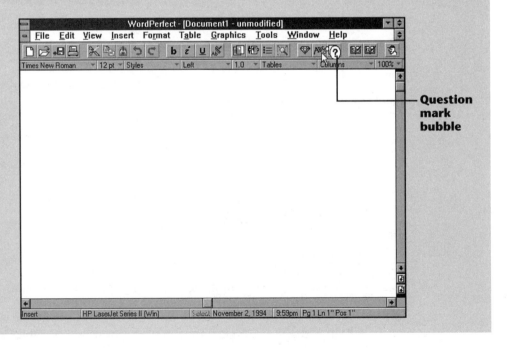

Question mark bubble

3 With the pointer and the bubble positioned on the TextArt button, click once.

WordPerfect displays the Help window for the TextArt button.

4 Choose Close to return to the document.

Using the Help Menus

The WordPerfect Help window has its own Menu Bar that contains the File, Edit, Bookmark, and Help menus. You can choose any Help menu, just as you choose a WordPerfect menu on the Menu Bar in the WordPerfect window. These menus follow:

- *File.* Enables you to open other Help files. You also can print Help topics from this menu.

- *Edit.* Contains the Copy and Annotate options. You use Copy to copy to the Clipboard the text of the selected Help topic. You then can paste this Help information into a document. Annotate enables you to add your own comments and notes to a Help topic.

- *Bookmark.* Contains a Define command, which you use to mark your place in the Help topics to which you frequently refer. By marking these topics, you can return to them quickly.

- *Help.* Contains the options How to Use Help, Always on Top, and About Help. Choose the How to Use Help option to obtain general information about using the various Help screens. Choose the Always on Top option to ensure that the Help window is always on top of any other open windows. Choose the About Help command to display a dialog box that shows the version and copyright notice for WordPerfect Help.

Using the Coaches

The Coach command in WordPerfect for Windows gives you step-by-step instructions for performing common tasks.

Using the Coaches

To use the Coaches feature, perform the following steps:

1 Open the Help menu.

2 Choose Coach.

The Coaches dialog box appears (see figure 3.12).

(continues)

Using the Coaches (continued)

Figure 3.12
The Coaches
dialog box.

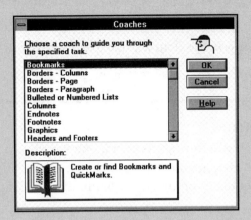

❸ Select the desired task from the list box; then click OK.

Instructions from WordPerfect Coach appear on-screen.

❹ Click the Continue button to walk through the steps.

When the Coach instructs you to do something, you can perform the action or choose the Show Me button, which shows you the action to be performed. Use the Hint button to get more information about a step.

Chapter Summary

In this chapter, you learned how to open and close existing documents; various methods for selecting text; and how to cut, copy, and paste selected text. You also learned how to use the WordPerfect Help windows.

Checking Your Skills

True/False Questions

For each of the following statements, circle *T* or *F* to indicate whether the statement is true or false.

T F **1.** WordPerfect for Windows can open no more than seven documents at one time.

T F **2.** Cascaded windows overlap one another on-screen.

T F **3.** To cause a cascaded display, click anywhere in the document window.

T F **4.** To access a QuickMenu so that you can select text, you must place the mouse pointer in the right margin.

T F **5.** You can double-click to select a sentence.

T F **6.** To make a tiled window active, you must click in the Title Bar.

T F   **7.** You can close all open windows at once by choosing **C**lose from the **F**ile menu.

T F   **8.** You can print a Help topic by choosing **F**ile and then **P**rint Topic from the Help Menu Bar.

T F   **9.** The **B**ack command button in the **H**elp menu takes you back to the first Help screen used.

T F **10.** To cancel a selection of text, position the pointer in the left margin and click the right mouse button.

Multiple-Choice Questions

In the blank provided, write the letter of the correct answer for each of the following questions.

___**1.** To reposition text at another location in the document, you _____.

    a. choose the **C**opy and **P**aste commands

    b. choose the Cu**t** and **P**aste commands

    c. retype the command at the new location

    d. choose the **I**nsert and **P**aste commands

___**2.** You can insert a blank line in a document by _____.

    a. pressing ⏎Enter two times

    b. selecting the line you don't want and deleting it

    c. pressing Spacebar for as long as necessary

    d. using the **I**nsert command

___**3.** To restore the most recent change made to the document, use the _____.

    a. U**n**delete command

    b. **U**ndo command

    c. **E**dit command

    d. Viewer window

___**4.** The object-action model feature is used to _____.

    a. open more than one document at a time

    b. select text for modification

    c. save files

    d. activate the Help windows

___**5.** The **C**oach command is found under the _____ menu option.

    a. **E**dit

    b. **H**elp

3

      c. File

      d. View

___**6.** To issue a command on existing text, you _____.

      a. choose the command and then select the text

      b. select the text and then choose the command

      c. position the cursor before the text and then choose the command

      d. any of these answers

___**7.** You can add one file to another by _____.

      a. using the **C**opy, **Cut**, and **P**aste commands

      b. choosing **I**nsert and then **F**ile

      c. choosing **F**ile, **O**pen, and then **C**opy

      d. a and b only

      e. none of these answers

___**8.** To have text pasted in the same format as the text at the insertion point, you use the _____ command.

      a. Link

      b. Paste Special (⬆Shift+Ctrl+V)

      c. Paste (⬆Shift+Insert)

      d. QuickFormat

      e. none of these answers

___**9.** To cross-reference a Help topic, choose the _____ commands.

      a. **H**elp, **S**earch

      b. **H**elp, **C**ontents

      c. **H**elp, His**t**ory

      d. **H**elp, Book**m**ark

___**10.** To select text using the keyboard, use the _____ key(s).

      a. F10

      b. Alt+F8

      c. F8

      d. none of these answers

Fill-in-the-Blank Questions

In the blank provided, write the correct answer for each of the following questions.

1. Information being cut or copied is placed in the _____.

2. A _____-click is a shortcut method used to select an entire paragraph by using the mouse.

3. Using the _____ command, you can restore the last three changes to a document.

4. To display the contents of multiple windows at the same time, use the _____ option.

5. If you have a color monitor, cross-referenced items in a Help window appear in the color _____.

6. The **S**earch command button in the **H**elp menu enables you to search for specific Help topics that contain _____ _____.

7. The _____ option in the Help Menu Bar contains a **D**efine command that can be used to mark your place in the Help topics to which you frequently refer.

8. Before you can edit the contents of a WordPerfect document, you must _____ the document into a document window.

9. The directory used to store your work files is called _____.

10. When moving the pointer over text, the pointer changes from an _____ to an I-beam.

Applying Your Skills

Review Exercises

Exercise 1: Finding and Working with an Existing Document

Before you can edit an existing document, you must find it. The Viewer can help you see whether the document you are about to open is the correct one. Follow these steps:

1. Start WordPerfect 6.1 for Windows, and view the document LETTER1.DOC. Note the steps you performed to start the program and view the document.

2. After viewing the LETTER1.DOC, open it and make the following changes:

- Change *116 Ash St.* to **1144 S. Hampton Rd**.

- Select and delete the last sentence of the paragraph.

- Restore both of the deletions you just made.

3. Print the document.

4. Close the document without saving changes.

Exercise 2: Using the Help Option

In this exercise, you search for and find a particular Help topic and then print a copy for yourself. Note, however, that Help is so easily accessible that printing Help topics usually is not necessary. Follow these steps:

1. Access help on Create/Edit Text using the mouse.

2. Print a copy of the information.

Exercise 3: Creating a New Document and Inserting It into an Existing Document

Sometimes it is useful to create text that can be incorporated into other documents. In this exercise, you create information related to enclosures, and then incorporate that into your job application letter. Follow these steps:

1. Type the following paragraphs. Press ⌨Tab⌨ to indent each new paragraph:

> **I would appreciate the opportunity to meet with you to discuss my qualifications. Enclosed you will find a resume for your review. A sample portfolio is also included illustrating some of my previous endeavors in commercial advertising.**

> **Please feel free to call or write me at the telephone or address listed above. Thank you for your consideration.**

2. Save the document as **ENCLOSE.DOC**, but do not close the file.

3. Open the JOB1.DOC file.

4. With ENCLOSE.DOC and JOB1.DOC both open, arrange them so the contents of both are visible.

5. Make JOB1.DOC the active document.

6. Switch the location of paragraph 1 with paragraph 2 in JOB1.DOC and then switch them back to their original locations using the cut, copy, and paste techniques.

7. Place the insertion point after the period of the last sentence in the JOB1.DOC file. Retrieve the ENCLOSE.DOC file into the JOB1.DOC file. Press ⌨Enter⌨.

8. Close the ENCLOSE.DOC file and maximize the JOB1.DOC file so that it is a full-screen window.

9. Using the method discussed in "Replacing Selected Text," earlier in this chapter, replace the first sentence of the third paragraph with the following sentence:

> **A resume has been enclosed for your review and I would wel-**

come the opportunity to present myself to you in person to clarify my qualifications.

10. Save the file as **JOB1.DOC.**

11. Print the JOB1.DOC file.

12. Close the file.

13. Review the steps used to perform the steps in this exercise.

Exercise 4: Using the Coach
Use the Coach to take you through information about the QuickStart feature. Write a two-page summary of the covered topics.

Continuing Projects

Project 1: Moving and Copying Text
Follow these steps using cut and paste techniques to arrange a list of key terms alphabetically:

1. Open the document KEYTERMS, which you created in Chapter 2.

2. Add the following text to the document:

Insert Mode

The alternative to Typeover mode. When you enter text in Insert mode, existing characters are moved to the right of the inserted text.

Typeover Mode

The alternative to Insert mode. When you enter text in Typeover mode, existing text is replaced by what you type.

3. Using the copy, cut, and paste techniques you learned in this chapter, rearrange the list of key terms in alphabetical order.

4. Print the document.

5. Save the changes.

Project 2: Working with Multiple Documents and Using the Undelete Feature
Perform each of the following tasks, and write down the steps you used to accomplish each.

1. Open the following documents: NEWS.DOC, ADDITION.DOC, and WORDWRAP.DOC.

2. Make ADDITION.DOC the active document.

3. Delete the first and third sentences in the first paragraph of

ADDITION.DOC, and then delete the last sentence in the second paragraph. Print the document.

4. Undelete the last three deletions. Print the document. Save the changes.

Project 3: Editing an Existing Document

1. Open TRAIN1.DOC.

2. Add the following paragraph to the end of TRAIN1.DOC beginning on a new line. Do not indent before the paragraph.

   Compuvise offers 1, 2, and 3 day seminars on the various software packages. All training is conducted by a staff of highly qualified instructors who specialize in computer training and development. Class size is limited to no more than 10 people per session in order to give individual attention to students when needed. Class time includes a mixture of lecture about the particular software, as well as instructor-led courseware to guide the student through hands-on exercises using the software.

3. Save the file as **TRAIN1.DOC**.

4. Print the file.

5. Make the following changes:

   a. Delete the last sentence of the last paragraph.

   b. Change the first sentence of the last paragraph to read as:

   Seminars are offered as 1, 2, or 3 day sessions covering a variety of software packages.

   c. Switch the locations of the second and third sentences of the last paragraph with each other.

6. Save the file as **TRAIN2.DOC**.

7. Print the file.

8. Save the file as **TRAIN3.DOC**.

9. Print the file.

10. Close the file.

CHAPTER 4

Proofreading Your Text

In this chapter, you learn how to use the Reveal Codes window to view hidden codes, and how to locate and replace text by using the Find and Replace feature. You also learn how to use the Speller, the Thesaurus, and the Grammatik tools.

Objectives

By the time you finish this chapter, you will have learned to

1. Work with Hidden Codes

2. Use the Find and Replace Feature

3. Use the Spell Checker

4. Use the Thesaurus

5. Use the Grammar Checker (Grammatik)

Objective 1: Work with Hidden Codes

As you learned in Chapter 1, WordPerfect for Windows inserts hidden codes into the text of your document when you use various commands. These codes control how your document is formatted when printed. When you open the Reveal Codes window, you can edit the text and the codes in a document.

Deleting Hidden Codes

Deleting codes in the Reveal Codes window is usually more efficient than deleting codes from the editing screen, because in the Reveal Codes window you can more easily identify the location of the codes within the document. Note that as you delete codes in the Reveal Codes window, the editing window reflects your changes.

Deleting Hidden Codes

To delete a hidden code in the Reveal Codes window, follow these steps:

1 Open the document you want to edit.

2 Open the **V**iew menu; then choose **R**eveal Codes.

3 Position the cursor before the hidden code you want to delete.

In figure 4.1, the cursor is positioned before the [Left Tab] code in the Reveal Codes window.

Figure 4.1
This document illustrates where the cursor is placed in the Reveal Codes window when deleting the Left Tab code. Notice that it should be placed directly in front of the Left Tab code before pressing the Delete key.

Cursor—

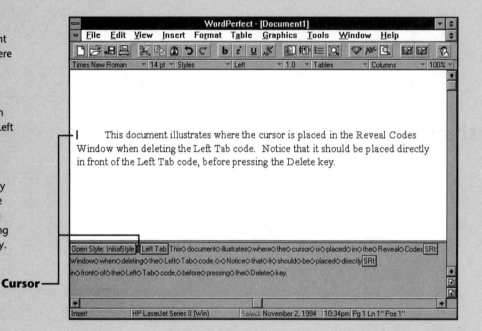

4 Press Del.

Note that the text in the editing window reflects any changes made in the Reveal Codes window. In this example, the deletion of the [Left Tab] code forces the text to align with the left margin.

5 Open the **V**iew menu and choose **R**eveal Codes again to turn off the Reveal Codes feature.

Tip

You can use Alt + F3 as a toggle switch to turn on and off the Reveal Codes screen.

Objective 2: Use the Find and Replace Feature

String
A collection of characters, including codes and spaces, that WordPerfect uses when executing search and replace operations.

The Find feature enables you to search for a character, a word, a phrase, or a hidden code before or after the cursor's position. The set of characters (or characters and codes) that you want to locate in the document is called a *string*. The Find feature enables you to quickly locate sections of a document that require editing.

You can direct WordPerfect to search the entire document from the beginning or from the insertion point location to the end of the document. By choosing the **W**rap at Beg/End of Document option, you can instruct WordPerfect to continue the search until it reaches the insertion point again. In order to find all occurrences of a string without regard to capitalization, you must type the string in all lowercase letters.

Type the text shown in figure 4.2 to use for the following tutorials.

Figure 4.2
Type the text shown in this document.

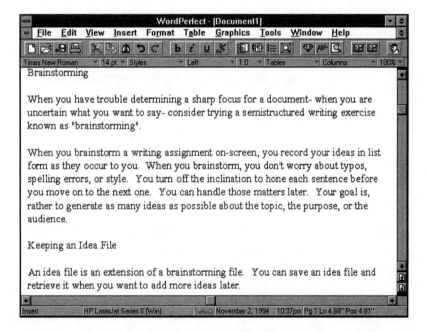

Locating Text with the Find Feature

To locate all occurrences of the word *brainstorm* in the document you just created, perform the following steps:

❶ Move the cursor to the top of the document to begin the search.

❷ Open the **E**dit menu and choose **F**ind and Replace.

WordPerfect displays the Find and Replace Text dialog box.

❸ Choose **O**ptions, and then choose **B**egin Find at Top of Document.

❹ Type **brainstorm** in the Find text box and press ↵Enter.

(continues)

Locating Text with the Find Feature (continued)

> **Tip**
>
> Type a space before or after the word *brainstorm* to distinguish it from words that also contain *brainstorm*, such as *brainstorming*.

WordPerfect highlights the first occurrence of the word (see figure 4.3).

Figure 4.3
WordPerfect finds the first occurrence of the word *brainstorm*.

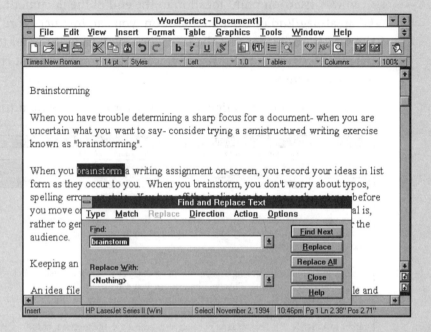

❺ To search the remainder of the document for additional occurrences of *brainstorm*, click the Find Next button.

❻ Continue to click Find Nextuntil WordPerfect prompts you with a box displaying the message "brainstorm" Not Found. This message box, shown in figure 4.4, appears above the Find and Replace Text dialog box, and indicates that no additional occurrences have been located.

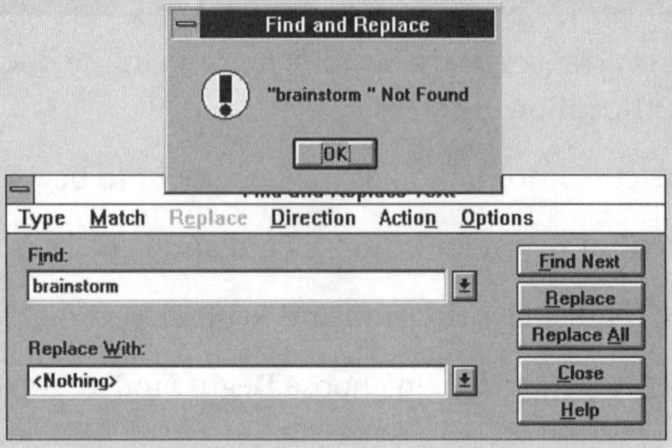

Figure 4.4
The Not Found message.

7 Click OK.

8 To search back through the text, choose **B**ackward from the **D**irection menu and then click the Find **P**revious button in the Find and Replace Text dialog box.

Using Options with the Find and Replace Command

The following search options are available in the Find and Replace Text dialog box.

Choose the Find and Replace Text **T**ype menu to select the following options:

- *Word Forms.* Enables you to replace all forms of one word with some forms of another word. If you replace *fly* with *drive*, for example, WordPerfect also replaces *flew* with *drove*.

- *Specific Codes.* Searches for a specific hidden code of a certain value; for example, `[Left Mar:2"]` indicates a left margin set at two inches. The dialog box for this option supplies a list from which you can choose the codes you want to locate.

With the insertion point in the F**i**nd text box, you open the **M**atch menu to use the following options:

- *Whole Word.* Enables you to avoid finding words that contain the search string. When searching for the word *farm*, for example, WordPerfect finds all words in the document containing the word *farm*, such as *farmer*, *farming*, and *farmed*. The **W**hole Word option is an alternative to typing a space before or after the word for which you are searching.

- *Case.* Locates words or phrases that exactly match the case of the search string; for example, you might want to search for *dBASE* but not *dBase*.

- *Font.* Locates text typed in a specific font and font size.

- *Codes.* Locates formatting codes such as `[SRt]` or `[Right Tab]`.

When you place the insertion point in the Replace **W**ith text box, you then can access the R**e**place menu, which contains the same options that you found in the **M**atch menu (**W**hole Word, **C**ase, **F**ont, and **C**odes).

Choose Actio**n** to select from the following options:

- *Select Match.* WordPerfect selects the search string upon finding it in the text. This option is the default.

- *Position **B**efore.* WordPerfect selects the search string and places the cursor before the located text.

- *Position **A**fter.* WordPerfect selects the search string and places the cursor after the located text.

- ***E**xtend Selection.* Extends a text selection from the location of the insertion point to a specific word, phrase, or code.

Choose the **O**ptions menu to select from the following options:

- ***B**egin Find at Top of Document.* Searches the entire document from the top.

- ***W**rap at Beg/End of Document.* Searches from the cursor forward and then from the top of the document to the insertion point.

- *Limit Find Within Selection.* Enables you to select text before opening the Find text dialog box in order to limit the search to the selected text.

- ***I**nclude Headers, Footers, Etc.* Includes the searching of such elements as headers, footers, footnotes, and endnotes.

- *Limit **N**umber of Changes.* Limits the number of matches that will be found when you use Replace.

Using Wild-Card Characters to Search for Text

WordPerfect includes two *wild-card characters* that you can use in a search string when you are uncertain of the spelling of a particular word or phrase in the document. The ? (question mark) replaces one character, and the * (asterisk) replaces several characters.

Note: *You cannot insert wild-card characters from the keyboard. You must use the Codes option from the Find or Find and Replace Text dialog box.*

Searching for Unknown Characters

To use a wild-card character to search a document for unknown characters, perform the following steps:

1 To begin your search, position the cursor at the top of the document that you created earlier in this chapter.

2 Access the **E**dit menu; then choose **F**ind and Replace Text.

3 In the Find and Replace text box, type **brain** (the letters of which you are sure).

4 Access the **M**atch menu.

5 Choose C**o**des to open the Codes dialog box.

6 Scroll through the Find Codes list box until *(Many Char) is highlighted, and double-click it or choose **I**nsert from the Codes dialog box. *(Many Char) is the first option at the top of the list, as shown in figure 4.5.

Figure 4.5
The *(Many Char) option is selected from the Codes dialog box.

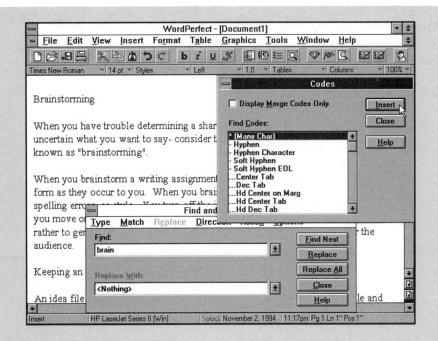

⑦ Click **C**lose.

The [*(Many Char)] code is inserted into the Find text box after the word *brain* (see figure 4.6).

Figure 4.6
The [*(Many Char)] code is inserted into the Find text box.

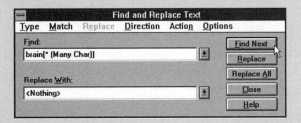

⑧ Click the **F**ind Next button.

WordPerfect begins the search and highlights the first occurrence of the search string.

Using the Replace Feature

You can use the Replace feature with the Find feature. When you use Replace, you enter a **F**ind string and a Replace **W**ith string. You can use the Replace feature to replace a string of text or codes with different text or codes. You also can remove the Find string completely from the document. Using Find and Replace saves you a great deal of editing time.

Replacing a String

To replace the word *generate* with the word *produce,* for example perform the following steps:

1 Position the cursor at the top of the document.

2 Open the **E**dit menu; then choose Find and **R**eplace.

WordPerfect displays the Find and Replace Text dialog box.

3 Type **generate** in the F**i**nd text box.

4 Type **produce** in the Replace **W**ith text box (see figure 4.7).

Figure 4.7
Using the Find
and Replace
Text dialog box
to replace text.

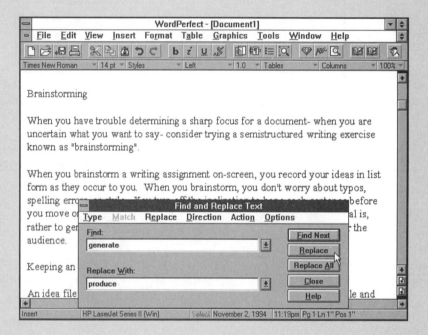

Note: *Enter text for the replacement string exactly as you want it to appear. Include any capitalization and punctuation that is to be entered. If you want to remove text or codes from the document using the Replace feature, leave the Replace **W**ith text box displaying the default of Nothing.*

5 Click the **R**eplace button.

WordPerfect highlights the first occurrence of the search string.

6 Click **R**eplace again to replace the old text with the new text.

7 Continue clicking **R**eplace until the message "generate" Not Found appears. This message indicates that WordPerfect has located the last occurrence of the search string.

8 Click OK.

9 Click **C**lose to return to the document screen.

10 Save the document as **BRAIN.DOC.**

The following options are available in the Find and Replace Text dialog box:

- *Find Next.* Does not replace the highlighted string, but instead finds the next occurrence of the search string.

- *Replace.* Replaces the highlighted string with the replacement string, stopping at each occurrence.

- *Replace All.* Replaces all occurrences of the search string.

Objective 3: Use the Spell Checker

Dictionary
A file named WP{WP}US.LEX, which contains about 115,000 words that WordPerfect uses to check your documents for spelling errors. When checking spelling, WordPerfect ignores all words that are spelled correctly according to this dictionary.

WordPerfect's *Spell Checker* compares each word in a document to the words in the WordPerfect *dictionary*. WordPerfect's 115,000-word dictionary contains a file that lists *common words* (frequently used words) and *main words* (words generally found in a dictionary). WordPerfect's Spell Checker matches each word against its list of common words first. If the Spell Checker doesn't find the word there, the program looks in its dictionary of main words. In addition to WordPerfect's built-in dictionary, you also can create a *supplemental dictionary*, in which you can save words not in the WordPerfect dictionary. You also can add words to a document dictionary that is part of the document and is used only when correcting that document.

The Spell Checker can locate three types of errors in a document:

- Misspellings caused by typing errors

- Double words, such as *the the*

- Irregular capitalization, such as *DAte* or *daTE*.

Because of the Spell Checker's phonetic capability, you can enter a word exactly as it sounds, such as *okashunaly* for *occasionally*. The Spell Checker will find the correct spelling in the dictionary.

Checking a Word, a Page, a Document, or a Selection
WordPerfect can check the spelling of the current word, selected text, a sentence, a paragraph, a page, or an entire document. WordPerfect also can check spelling from the insertion point to the end of the page or document, or check spelling for a specified number of pages beginning with the current page.

Using the Spell Checker

To use the Spell Checker, follow these steps:

1 Open the **T**ools menu; then choose **S**peller.

WordPerfect opens the Spell Checker window, and immediately begins spell checking the document. Any spelling not found in WordPerfect's dictionary will be highlighted. If you want to check only part of your document, wait until the Spell Checker stops and highlights a word.

(continues)

Using the Spell Checker (continued)

2 Use the Check menu to specify how much of the document you want WordPerfect to check. The default setting is the entire document.

3 Choose Start to resume the Spell Check.

WordPerfect begins checking the spelling of each word in the specified section of text.

When selecting the amount of text to check, choose from the following options:

- *Word*. Checks the spelling of the word containing the cursor.

- *Sentence*. Checks the sentence that contains the cursor.

- *Paragraph*. Checks the paragraph that contains the cursor.

- *Page*. Checks the page that contains the cursor.

- *Document*. Checks the spelling of the entire document. This is the default setting.

- *To End of Document*. Checks the spelling from the cursor's position to the end of the document.

- *Selected Text*. Checks the spelling of the highlighted text.

- *Text Entry Box*. Checks the spelling of text that you enter into a text box within a WordPerfect dialog box.

- *Number of Pages*. Displays the Number of Pages text entry box, in which you can specify the number of pages to be checked, beginning with the current page.

Selecting an Alternative Spelling

If the Spell Checker finds a word not included in any of the dictionary lists, WordPerfect highlights the word in the document and offers alternative spellings in the Suggestions list box. The message Not Found, followed by the unknown word, appears near the top of the Spell Checker window. Spell Checker also places in the Replace **W**ith text box the first alternative word listed in the Suggestions list box.

Choosing a New Spelling

To replace the highlighted word in the document with an alternative spelling, follow these steps:

1 Select an alternative spelling from the Suggestions list box by clicking it (see figure 4.8).

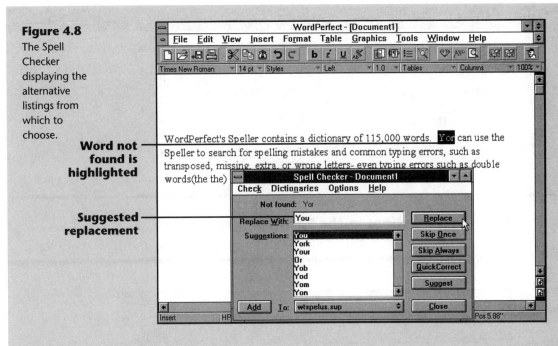

Figure 4.8
The Spell Checker displaying the alternative listings from which to choose.

Word not found is highlighted

Suggested replacement

❷ Click the **R**eplace command button.

WordPerfect replaces the highlighted word with the alternative spelling, and then continues to check the selected text.

Tip

The first alternative spelling is selected automatically when the Suggestions list box appears; simply Replace to insert this alternative spelling into the document.

Using Command Buttons in the Spell Checker Window

If the Spell Checker window does not display the correct spelling, you can use one of the following options:

- Type what you think is the correct spelling in the Replace **W**ith text box, and click the S**u**ggest command button.

- Click Skip **O**nce to have the Spell Checker ignore this particular occurrence of the unknown word in the document.

- Click Skip **A**lways to have the Spell Checker ignore all occurrences of the unknown word in the document.

- Click A**d**d to add the unknown word to the supplementary dictionary.

- Click S**u**ggest to display additional words or phrases.

- Click **C**lose to close the Spell Checker window and cancel the spelling check.

Typing Spelling Changes

If you don't want to choose a suggested alternative, but instead want to type your own editing changes, follow these steps:

1 Type your own changes in the Replace **W**ith text box.

2 Click **R**eplace.

The Spell Checker replaces the highlighted word in the text with the word you typed.

Using Other Options in the Spell Checker Window

You can choose several other options from the O**p**tions pull-down menu in the Spell Checker window. Figure 4.9 shows the Duplicate Words option.

Figure 4.9
The Spell Checker finds duplicate words in the document.

Duplicate words highlighted

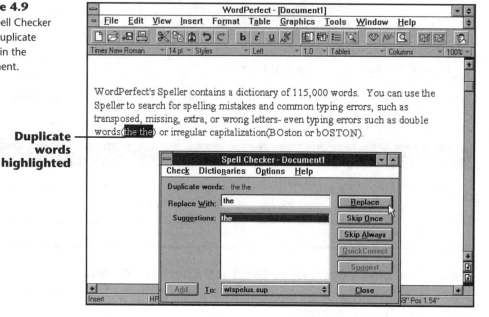

The options available from the O**p**tions pull-down menu include the following:

- *Words with **N**umbers*. When your document contains words with numbers such as *B52* or *RX7*, the Spell Checker stops at each occurrence unless you deselect this option.

- ***D**uplicate Words*. The Spell Checker searches for double words, such as *the the*. When it locates double words, the Spell Checker displays the message Duplicate Words. To delete one of the duplicates, click **R**eplace. You must deselect this option from the O**p**tions menu if you want to ignore duplicate words.

- *Irregular Capitalization*. When locating a word with questionable capitalization, the message `Capitalization` appears, followed by the word in question. To change the capitalization, click the **R**eplace command. You must deselect this option from the O**p**tions menu to ignore occurrences.

- *Auto Replace*. Choose this option to have WordPerfect automatically replace additional occurrences of misspelled words.

Headword

A word in the WordPerfect Thesaurus that contains a list of synonyms and antonyms.

- *Document Dictionary*. This option enables you to create a specialized dictionary that remains in the document itself when you save the document. The next time you spell check the document, WordPerfect uses this dictionary to help with the spell check.

Objective 4: Use the Thesaurus

Antonym

A word that has the opposite or nearly opposite meaning of another word. When you choose a headword in WordPerfect's Thesaurus, you are shown lists of antonyms as well as synonyms.

Synonym

A word that has an identical or similar meaning to another word.

WordPerfect's *Thesaurus* can improve your writing by helping you find alternative choices for many common words in your document. The Thesaurus is similar to the Spell Checker, except that the Thesaurus lists alternative word choices instead of alternative spellings.

The Thesaurus contains approximately 10,000 headwords. *Headwords* are words associated with lists of alternative word choices. If the word you are looking up is a headword, WordPerfect displays a list of *synonyms* (words with identical or similar meanings) and *antonyms* (words with opposite meanings). You can choose one of these words and substitute it for the selected word in the text. If the word you are looking for is not a headword, the message `Word Not Found` appears at the bottom of the dialog box. The Thesaurus can display up to three headwords and their references at one time. You can use the scroll arrows below the headword list box to move from column to column.

Using the Thesaurus to Replace a Word

To replace a word using the Thesaurus, follow these steps:

1 Move the cursor to the word you want to look up in the Thesaurus.

2 Open the **T**ools menu; then choose **T**hesaurus.

WordPerfect displays the Thesaurus dialog box (see figure 4.10).

(continues)

Using the Thesaurus to Replace a Word (continued)

Figure 4.10
The Thesaurus dialog box displaying alternatives for the headword mistake.

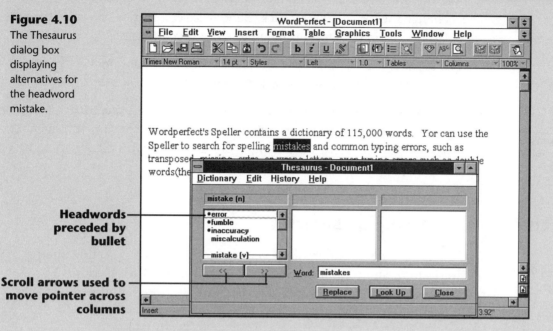

Headwords preceded by bullet

Scroll arrows used to move pointer across columns

❸ Select the alternative word you want to use. The program places it in the **W**ord text box.

❹ Click **R**eplace.

The document reflects the change.

You may not see the exact word you want in the list of alternative words, but you may see a word similar to one you want. To see a list of synonyms and antonyms for an alternative headword, follow these steps:

❶ Double-click any of the words in the list box preceded by a bullet, or select the word and press ↵Enter. (The bullet preceding a word indicates that it is a headword.)

Additional choices appear in the list boxes to the right.

❷ Select one of the alternative words, and then click **R**eplace.

❸ If you do not replace a word, click **C**lose to exit the Thesaurus window.

Note: *Although WordPerfect's SmartSense technology tries to match parts of speech (for example, "bored" replaced by "weary" becomes "wearied"), you always should verify that the replacement is correct grammatically.*

Using the Look Up Option

If the word you are looking for is not a headword in the Thesaurus, the Thesaurus window will be empty, and you will see the message Word not Found in the lower left corner of the Status Bar. To look up alternative words, you must enter a synonym of your own in the **W**ord text box; then click the **L**ook Up command button.

Objective 5: Use the Grammar Checker

WordPerfect for Windows includes *Grammatik*, a powerful grammar checker, which can help you identify and correct errors in writing style, grammar, and sentence structure. Grammatik also can check spelling, as well as adapt to 10 writing styles (informal, memo, speech, documentation, and so on).

When you start Grammatik (by choosing **G**rammatik from the **T**ools menu), you can choose the **P**references menu, which contains the following options for customizing your grammar-checking task:

- *Checking Styles.* Displays the checking styles dialog box, which contains 10 supplied writing styles from which to choose.

- *Environment.* Enables you to select procedural options such as whether to check headers, footers, and footnotes.

The **V**iew menu enables you to learn more about your writing as you proceed. Specific options follow:

- *Parts of Speech.* Lists each word in the current sentence and identifies its part of speech.

- *Parse Tree.* Illustrates graphically how the current sentence is constructed.

- *Statistics.* Displays the Document Statistics dialog box, without correcting any spelling and grammar errors. The Document Statistics dialog box shows a list of grammar-related statistics, such as number of sentences, number of words, average words per sentence, and so on.

4

Using Grammatik

To use Grammatik to check a document, follow these steps:

❶ Open the **T**ools menu; then choose **G**rammatik. WordPerfect displays the Grammatik dialog box and begins checking the document (see figure 4.11).

(continues)

Using Grammatik (continued)

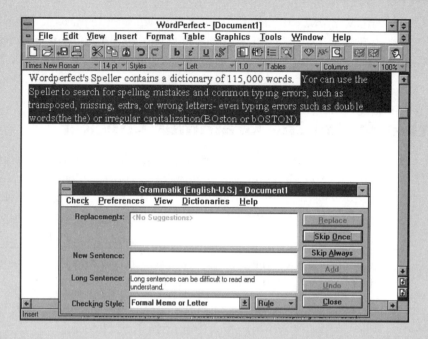

Figure 4.11
The Grammatik
dialog box.

❷ If you want to check something other than the whole document, wait until Grammatik stops. Then open the Che**ck** menu and choose one of the following options: **S**entence, **P**aragraph, **D**ocument (the default), To **E**nd of Document, or Selected **T**ext.

❸ Choose **S**tart to resume checking grammar for the text you specified, using options you set for writing style, grammar, sentence mechanics, and so on.

❹ When you reach the end of the document, choose **Y**es to close Grammatik and return to your document.

When Grammatik encounters an error, it suggests a replacement, shows the replacement in the context of a new sentence, and describes the grammatical problem. You then have the following options for dealing with the problem:

- *Resume.* If you click in the document to make corrections, the **R**esume button appears in the dialog box. Use **R**esume to finish checking your document.

- *Replace.* If you don't leave the Grammatik dialog box, the first button is **R**eplace, which you use to replace your text with the suggested correction.

- *Skip **O**nce.* Enables you to skip past the problem just this one time.

- *Skip **A**lways.* Enables you to skip past the problem any time it occurs throughout the remainder of the document.

- *A**d**d.* Adds misspelled words to your dictionary.

- *Undo.* Undoes a correction you make.

- *Close.* Closes the grammar checker and returns you to your document.

In addition, the Rule pop-up menu enables you to do the following:

- *Turn off.* Turns off a rule so that it doesn't apply while you are checking your document.

- *Turn On.* Turns on a rule.

- *Save Rules.* Enables you to create custom checking procedures, if you turn off or turn on rules.

- *Mark.* Marks the error in the text for correction later.

- *Help.* Provides help for the currently selected grammar problem.

- *Write Error.* Writes the rule and error to disk, along with comments if you want.

Tip

To display information about a specific error, open the Rule pop-up menu and choose **H**elp. Grammatik displays specific information about the error. To return to Grammatik from the Help window, click the **C**lose button or choose E**x**it from the **F**ile menu.

4

Chapter Summary

In this chapter, you learned how to delete hidden codes from the Reveal Codes window and how to use various tools in WordPerfect—including the Spell Checker, the Thesaurus, and Grammatik.

Checking Your Skills

True/False Questions

For each of the following statements, circle *T* or *F* to indicate whether the statement is true or false.

T F **1.** A *string* is a set of characters, or characters and codes, that you can search for by using the Reveal Codes window.

T F **2.** In order to find all occurrences of a set of characters, regardless of the capitalization, you must type in uppercase letters.

T F **3.** You can use the Find and Replace feature to search for hidden codes.

T F **4.** When the Spell Checker encounters an unknown word, the program checks a list of common words, a list of main words, and a list of special words you may have added.

T F **5.** Grammatik contains synonyms and antonyms as alternatives from which to choose.

T F **6.** Hidden codes control how your document is formatted when printed.

T F **7.** Placing a space before and after a word when using the Find feature is the same as choosing **A**ction and then the **W**hole Word option.

T F **8.** You can create a Main dictionary in which you can save words that are not in the WordPerfect dictionary.

T F **9.** Skip **O**nce is a command button in the Spell Checker dialog box.

T F **10.** The scroll arrows found below the headwords list box are used to scroll up and down the list of headwords.

Multiple-Choice Questions

In the blank provided, write the letter of the correct answer for each of the following questions.

___**1.** The Find and Replace feature enables you to search for _____.

  a. a single character

  b. a word or phrase

  c. a sentence

  d. all these answers

___**2.** The dictionary that you create to have WordPerfect's Spell Checker check for words is called the _____.

  a. Main dictionary

  b. Common dictionary

  c. Supplemental dictionary

  d. Extra dictionary

___**3.** You have used the word *justice* incorrectly. You want the opposite meaning of the word. The action most appropriate is _____.

  a. using Grammatik to find out what went wrong

  b. using the Spell Checker to find a related word

  c. using the Thesaurus to identify antonyms

  d. using the Thesaurus to identify related words

___**4.** The words associated with lists of alternative words in the Thesaurus are called _____.

  a. strings

  b. character sets

  c. headwords

  d. codes

___**5.** Wild-card characters are used to search for _____.

    a. antonyms

    b. synonyms

    c. unknown characters

    d. headwords

___**6.** To look up a word in the Thesaurus, you first enter the word in the _____ text box.

    a. **R**eplace

    b. **W**ord

    c. Replace **W**ith

    d. Sugg**e**stions

___**7.** To search for a hidden code with a certain value, use the _____ menu options.

    a. **T**ype, **C**odes

    b. **M**atch, **S**pecific Codes

    c. **T**ype, **S**pecific Codes

    d. **M**atch, **C**odes

___**8.** The **I**nclude Headers and Footers option is included with the _____ dialog box.

    a. Grammar Checker

    b. Spell Checker

    c. Thesaurus

    d. Find and Replace Text

___**9.** The **T**ext Entry Box option is part of the _____ dialog box.

    a. Spell Checker

    b. Grammar Checker

    c. Thesaurus

    d. Find and Replace Text

___**10.** To find more information about a specific grammatical error, choose _____.

    a. **C**hecking Style from the **P**references menu

    b. **P**arts of Speech from the **V**iew menu

    c. **H**elp from the Ru**l**e pop-up menu

    d. none of these answers

4

Fill-in-the-Blank Questions

In the blank provided, write the correct answer for each of the following questions.

1. When you use the Replace feature, you must enter a _____ string as well as a _____ string.

2. WordPerfect enables you to create a _____ dictionary to store words that are not found in the WordPerfect dictionary.

3. The _____ is the wild-card character used to search for many characters.

4. Because of the Spell Checker's _____ capability, you can search for the spelling of a word based on the sound of it.

5. Grammatik is located in the _____ menu.

6. You cannot insert wild-card characters from the _____ when using the _____ option.

7. As you delete codes in the Reveal Codes window, the _____ window reflects your changes.

8. Before deleting a hidden code, place the cursor _____ it.

9. You can choose an * (asterisk) or ? (question mark) from the Find Text dialog box by selecting the _____ option.

10. After you click the **F**ind Next option from the Find and Replace Text dialog box, WordPerfect finds the next occurrence of the search string, but does not _____ what it finds.

Applying Your Skills

Review Exercises

Exercise 1: Using the Grammar Checker

In this exercise, you use the grammar checker to make corrections to a letter. Follow these steps:

1. Open the document LETTER1.DOC.

2. Using Grammatik, follow any suggestions offered by WordPerfect for Windows, if you feel they are appropriate.

3. Save the changes and close the document.

Exercise 2: Finding and Replacing Text

In this exercise, you use the Find and Replace feature to make changes to a document. Follow these steps:

1. Open the document ADDITION.DOC.

2. Replace all occurrences of the word *file* with the word **document**; replace the word *files* with the word **documents**.

Exercise 3: Using the Spell Checker

In this exercise, you use the Spell Checker to make spelling corrections to your document. Follow these steps:

1. Open the LETTER1.DOC file.

2. Activate the Spell Checker.

3. Correct any spelling errors you find.

Exercise 4: Using the Spell Checker and Using Find and Replace

In this exercise, you use the Spell Checker and the Find and Replace feature to make corrections to your document. Follow these steps:

1. Open the JOB.DOC file. Use the Spell Checker to correct the various errors within the document.

2. Using the Find and Replace techniques that you learned, find the word *trigger* and replace it with the word **launch**.

3. Print the file.

4. Save the file as **JOB2.DOC**.

5. Record the steps you used to perform this exercise.

Exercise 5: Deleting Hidden Codes

In this exercise, you delete hidden formatting codes using Reveal Codes. Follow these steps:

1. Delete the Tab codes that precede each paragraph in the JOB2.DOC file. (Hint: Use the Reveal Codes window to view the codes.)

2. Print the file (notice the difference in appearance).

3. Save the file as **JOB2.DOC**.

4. Close the file.

5. Record the steps used to perform this exercise and explain how the text appeared differently after deleting the hidden codes.

Continuing Projects

Project 1: Deleting Hidden Codes, Finding and Replacing Text, and Printing

In this project, you use various editing features, such as Find and Replace, to make changes to your document. Follow these steps:

1. Open the document KEYTERMS. Open the Reveal Codes window and delete the [Tab] codes. Your text will reposition itself. Print a copy of the document.

2. Using the Find and Replace feature, replace the string *WordPerfect for Windows* with *WordPerfect*; then replace *WordPerfect* with *WordPerfect 6.1 for Windows*.

3. Save the document with the changes. Print the document.

Project 2: Spell Checking a Document and Using the Thesaurus

In this project, you use two of WordPerfect's writing tools to correct the content of your document. Follow these steps:

1. Open the document NEWS.DOC.

2. Use the Spell Checker to make any necessary spelling corrections.

3. Use the Thesaurus to find alternative words to use for *overwhelming* and *strategies*.

4. Print the document and save the changes.

Project 3: Using the Spell Checker, Thesaurus, and Grammar Checker

In this project, you use three of WordPerfect's writing tools to make corrections to the content of your document. Follow these steps:

1. Open the TRAINING.DOC file.

2. Use the Spell Checker to correct any errors in the document.

3. Use the Thesaurus to find synonyms for the words *satisfy*, *variety*, and *options*.

4. Use the Grammar Checker to make any necessary changes to the document.

5. Save the file as **TRAIN4.DOC**.

6. Record the steps you used to complete this project.

CHAPTER 5

Formatting Paragraphs and Characters

Formatting refers to the appearance of text in a finished document. As a WYSIWYG word processing program, WordPerfect can display on-screen almost all of the formatting you use in your document.

Formatting occurs on three levels in a WordPerfect document: the document level, the paragraph level, and the character level. In WordPerfect for Windows, you can perform most paragraph and character formatting in the document editing window by using the Ruler and the Power Bar. This chapter introduces you to the various formatting capabilities of WordPerfect for Windows—these include changing margin settings; creating tab settings; and using different types of indentation, alignments, and justification.

Objectives

By the time you finish this chapter, you will have learned to

1. Set Margins

2. Set Tabs

3. Indent Paragraphs

4. Align Text

5. Enhance Text

6. Control Line Breaks

Objective 1: Set Margins

Ruler
An on-screen tool you use to control paragraph and line formatting, such as tab settings and margin settings.

WordPerfect's default margin setting is one inch for the left and the right margins. You can change these settings by using the *Ruler* or the Margins dialog box. In the Margins dialog box, one inch is expressed as 1".

Adjusting the Left and Right Margins by Using the Ruler

If the Ruler is not displayed, open the **V**iew menu and choose **R**uler Bar to display it. The top line of the Ruler indicates the document margins. This part of the Ruler contains cup-shaped boxes that point toward each other, which represent the left and right margin settings. The shaded areas on the left and right side of the bar depict the actual *margins*—the distance between the edge of the paper and the margin setting (see figure 5.1).

To complete the following tutorials, you need to open the document file ADDITION.DOC.

Figure 5.1
Left and right margin settings and the left and right margins are shown on the Ruler.

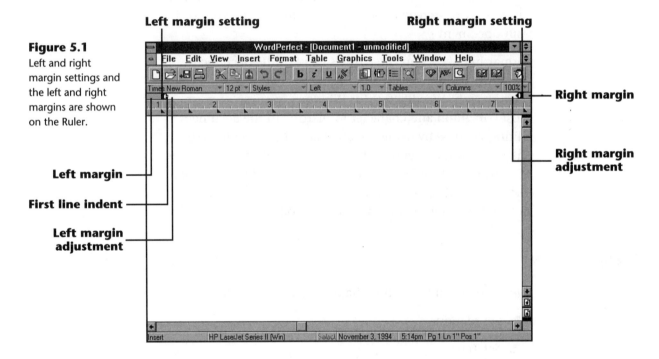

As shown in figure 5.1, for a standard page width of 8 1/2 inches, the WordPerfect default places the left margin setting at the 1-inch mark, and the right margin setting at the 7 1/2-inch mark on the Ruler, which is one inch from the right edge of the paper. Each number on the Ruler represents inches. Each of the vertical lines between the numbers represents a fraction of an inch.

Changing Margins by Using the Ruler

To change the default left margin to 1.5 inches by using the Ruler, perform the following steps:

❶ Display the Ruler Bar by choosing the **V**iew menu; then choose **R**uler Bar.

❷ Position the cursor at the beginning of the document.

❸ Position the mouse pointer over the icon representing the left margin in the Ruler Bar.

❹ Drag the left margin icon to the 1.5-inch mark on the Ruler.

Notice the dotted vertical line that appears on the document as you drag the icon to its new position (see figure 5.2). This represents the new left margin.

Figure 5.2

Dragging the left margin icon to a new setting.

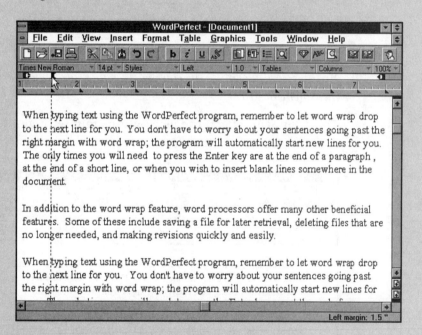

❺ Release the mouse button.

As soon as you reset a margin, WordPerfect immediately reformats the text of your document from the cursor position forward to conform to the new setting.

You can reset the right margin by using the same procedure.

Using the Margins Dialog Box

You also can change the left and right margin settings by typing new values into the **L**eft and **R**ight text boxes in the Margins dialog box.

Changing the Right Margin Using the Margins Dialog Box

To display the Margins dialog box using the Ruler and then change the right margin to 1.5 inches, perform the following steps:

❶ Double-click anywhere in the margin area (the gray portion) of the upper line of the Ruler or on the margin icon.

WordPerfect displays the Margins dialog box (see figure 5.3).

Figure 5.3
The Margins dialog box.

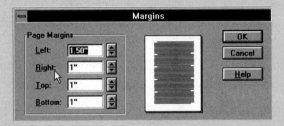

❷ Click in the **R**ight text box, type **1.50**, and then press ⏎Enter or click OK.

Note: *You also can use the counter (increment/decrement arrows) to increase the measurement to 1.5".*

The document reflects the new right margin setting of 1.5 inches at the 7-inch position (see figure 5.4).

Figure 5.4
The right and left margins set at 1.5 inches.

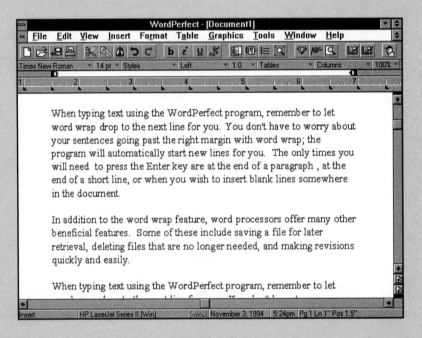

❸ Close ADDITION.DOC without saving the changes. Then move on to the following section.

You also can set left margins by using the Margins dialog box.

Objective 2: Set Tabs

WordPerfect's default Tab Ruler positions left-justified tab stops at half-inch intervals. WordPerfect supports four types of tab settings: Left, Center, Right, and Decimal (see table 5.1).

Table 5.1 Tab Settings Available in WordPerfect for Windows	
Type	**Effect on Text**
Left	Left-justifies text at the tab stop. In Insert mode, WordPerfect indents existing text to the tab stop. The left tab is the default tab setting.
Center	Centers text at the tab stop. An equal number of characters will appear on each side of the tab position. A center tab commonly is used to center column headings in tables.
Right	Right-justifies text at the tab stop. The last character of each line will be aligned.
Decimal	Justifies text on the alignment character (by default, the period) at the tab stop so that any text typed before the period is right-justified, and any text typed after the period is left-justified. A decimal tab often is used to align columns of numbers on the decimal point.

Each type of tab is represented by a different type of marker in the Ruler, and each can include a *dot leader*—a series of periods preceding the tab (see figure 5.5).

5

Figure 5.5

The WordPerfect Ruler with different types of tabs.

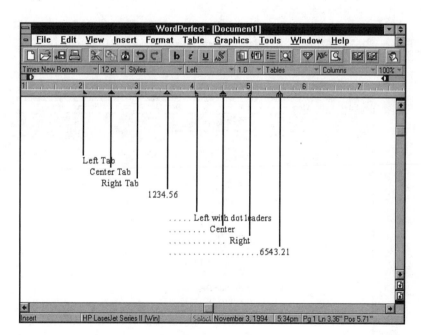

Changing Tab Settings Using the Ruler

To change the default tab settings by using the Ruler, follow these steps:

❶ Place the mouse pointer on the tab you want to change and drag it off the Ruler Bar (see figure 5.6).

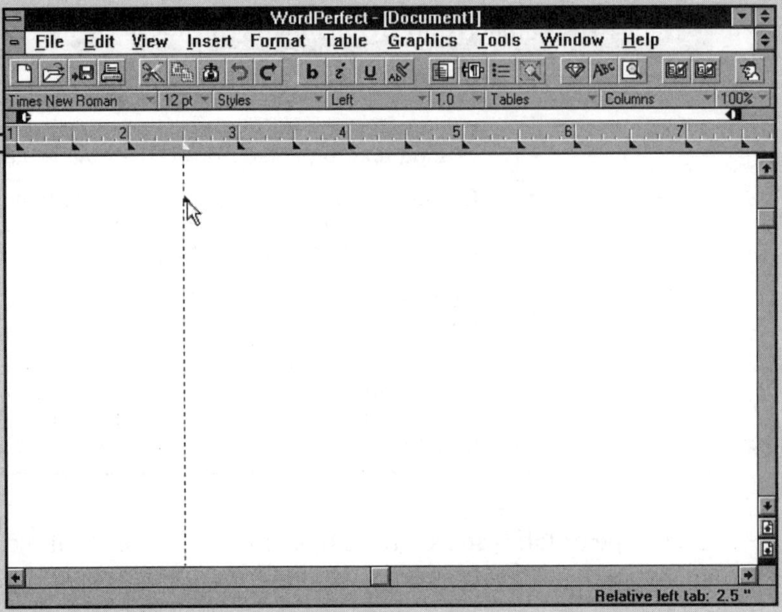

Figure 5.6
Dragging a tab setting off the Ruler.

Numbered area of the Ruler

Tab stop area of the Ruler

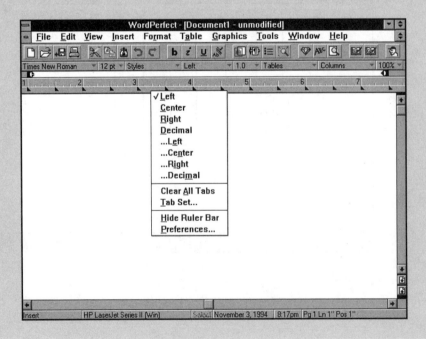

❷ Position the mouse pointer in the bottom row of the Tab Ruler in the line that contains the tab marker. Click the *right* mouse button to display the QuickMenu, which contains the different tab types (see figure 5.7).

Figure 5.7
The Tab Ruler QuickMenu, displaying different tab types.

3 Choose the type of tab you want, with or without dot leaders, from the QuickMenu.

4 Move the mouse pointer to the position on the Tab Ruler where you want to insert the tab, and click the left mouse button.

When you release the left mouse button, the new tab marker appears on the Ruler.

For the following tutorial, open a new document screen with the Ruler Bar displayed.

Creating Additional Tabs

To create additional tabs and place them on the Ruler, perform the following steps:

1 Position the mouse pointer in the Tab Ruler and click the right mouse button to display the QuickMenu.

2 Choose Clear All Tabs from the QuickMenu to remove all the default tab settings from the Ruler Bar.

3 Position the mouse pointer in the Tab Ruler, and click the right mouse button to display the QuickMenu.

4 Choose Right to select a right tab setting. Release the mouse button.

5 Position the pointer at the 1.5" position on the Tab Ruler. (Make sure that the pointer is under the very thin line that separates the tab area from the numbered area.)

6 Click the left mouse button to place a right tab at the 1.5" position on the Tab Ruler.

7 Use this method to insert a center tab at position 2.5", a decimal tab at position 3.5", a left dot-leader tab at position 4.5", and a right dot-leader tab at position 5.5".

Using the Tab Set Dialog Box

Caution

Before you make any changes to the tab settings, make sure that the cursor is positioned where you want to make the changes.

Although you can meet most of your tab-set needs by using the Ruler and the QuickMenu, you also can use the Tab Set dialog box to delete all existing tabs, or to set a series of uniformly spaced tabs across the Ruler.

To display the Tab Set dialog box when the Ruler is displayed, use either of these methods:

- Position the mouse pointer on any tab stop on the Tab Ruler and double-click the left mouse button.

• Click on the Ruler Bar with the **_right_** mouse button to display the QuickMenu and choose **T**ab Set. WordPerfect displays the Tab Set dialog box (see figure 5.8).

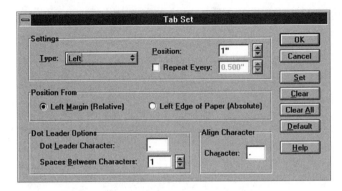

The following tutorials demonstrate how to clear tab stops and to set evenly spaced tab stops using the Tab Set dialog box.

Deleting and Restoring All Existing Tabs

At times, you will want to delete the default tabs in order to insert your own tabs. To delete all tab settings, click the Clear **A**ll command button in the Tab Set dialog box; then click OK (refer to figure 5.8).

To insert new tabs after you have cleared all tab settings, simply point to the positions on the Ruler Bar where you want tabs to appear and click the left mouse button.

If you want to restore deleted default tabs, access the Tab Set dialog box and click the **D**efault command button.

Setting Uniform Tabs

To evenly space tabs across the page, perform the following steps:

❶ Access the Tab Set dialog box (refer to figure 5.8).

❷ Clear all existing tabs by clicking Clear **A**ll.

❸ Enter your first tab position in the **P**osition text box.

For this tutorial, type **2**.

❹ Choose the Repeat **E**very check box to place an x in the box.

❺ In the Repeat **E**very text box, type the amount of space you want between the tabs.

For this tutorial, type **.75** and then click OK. Note: You also can type a fraction (for example, 3/4) and WordPerfect converts it to a decimal.

When you insert evenly spaced tabs, WordPerfect uses all the remaining available tabs. By default, the tabs are placed relative to the current left margin, and are left-aligned. If you want the tab settings to start relative to the edge of the paper, choose Left **E**dge of Paper in the Tab Set dialog box.

Although using the Ruler Bar to set tabs can be quick and easy, sometimes you need precisely positioned tab stops.

Setting Precise Tab Stops

Follow these steps to set tab stops:

❶ Access the Tab Set dialog box.

❷ In the **P**osition text box, enter the amount of space for the new tab that you want to add. Remember that you can use decimals or fractions.

For this tutorial, type **2 1/8**.

❸ Click the **S**et command button.

WordPerfect displays the new tab in the Tab Ruler. Although in the **P**osition box it now says **2.13"**, the real measurement is 2.125" (2 1/8).

❹ Click OK to add the tab to the Ruler and return to the document screen.

Note: *You can continue to add additional tabs by repeating steps 3 and 4 before clicking OK.*

❺ Close the document without saving your changes.

5

Objective 3: Indent Paragraphs

When you use WordPerfect's Tab or Indent feature, the settings in your document control how the text of a paragraph is indented. When you press (Tab⇄) or choose **I**ndent, WordPerfect inserts a hidden code that indents the text to the next available tab setting. Do not use the space bar to indent text in a document, because your text will not align properly when printed.

Indenting Paragraphs by Using Tab

If you want to indent only the first line of a paragraph from the left margin, you can just press (Tab⇄). Each time you press (Tab⇄), the cursor moves to the next tab stop on the Ruler. By default, a left tab is set every five spaces.

To indent existing text using (Tab⇄), toggle on Insert mode and place your cursor immediately before the first letter of the line you want to indent. Then press (Tab⇄).

You can use WordPerfect's Indent feature to indent an entire paragraph instead of just the first line.

Indenting a Paragraph on the Left

To indent an entire paragraph from the left margin, follow these steps:

1 Open the Format menu.

2 Choose Paragraph; then choose Indent.

The cursor moves to the next tab stop, temporarily resetting the left margin. All text you type until you press ⏎Enter is indented to this tab stop (see figure 5.9).

Use the same steps to indent an existing paragraph, but make sure that the cursor is located at the beginning of the paragraph and that the Status Bar indicates that you are in Insert mode.

Figure 5.9
The first paragraph displaying a left indent.

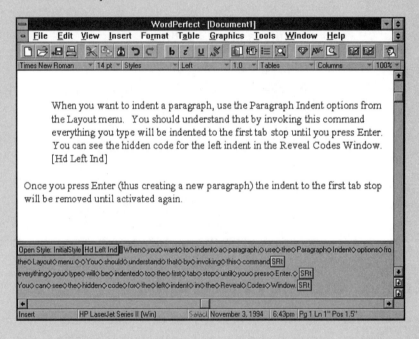

Long quotations within a paper often are indented on both the left and right. When you want to indent text from both margins, choose the **D**ouble Indent option.

Indenting a Paragraph on the Left and Right

To indent a paragraph from both the left and the right margins, follow these steps:

1 Open the Format menu.

2 Choose Paragraph; then choose **D**ouble Indent.

The cursor moves to the next tab stop, and the left and right margins are reset temporarily. All text you type is indented one tab stop on the left and one tab stop on the right until you press ⏎Enter (see figure 5.10).

Figure 5.10
Both right and left margins temporarily reset.

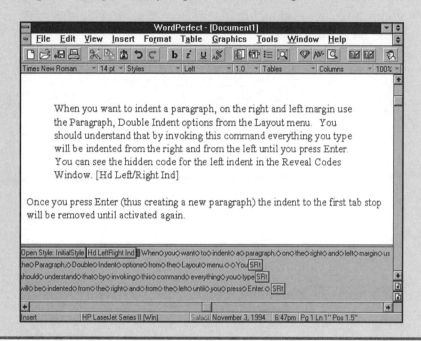

A *hanging indent* places the first line of a paragraph flush with the left margin, and indents all subsequent lines of the paragraph to the first tab stop. Entries in a bibliography frequently use a hanging indent.

5

Creating a Hanging Indent

To create a hanging indent for a new paragraph, perform the following steps:

1 Open a new WordPerfect document screen.

2 Position the cursor at the beginning of a new line.

3 Open the Format menu.

4 Choose Paragraph; then choose Hanging Indent.

5 Type the following text:

This paragraph illustrates the way a hanging indent appears.

Hanging indents are very easy to create when you use WordPerfect 6.1 for Windows.

6 Save the paragraph as **HANGING.TXT**.

(continues)

Creating a Hanging Indent (continued)

To format an existing paragraph with a hanging indent, position the cursor at the beginning of the paragraph. Then open the Format menu, choose Paragraph, and choose Hanging Indent from the submenu that appears. Or, press Ctrl+F7 (see figure 5.11).

Figure 5.11
A paragraph using a hanging indent.

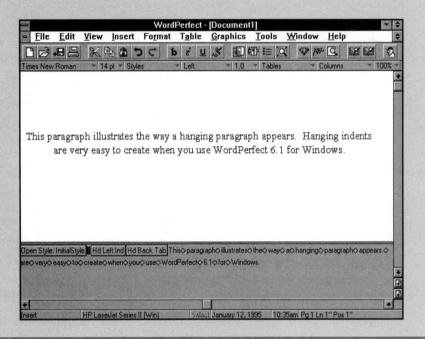

Changing the Type of Justification

Justification determines the way in which the lines in each paragraph are aligned. Table 5.2 describes the five types of justification that WordPerfect supports. Figure 5.12 illustrates the five types of justification.

Table 5.2 Types of Justification Available in WordPerfect	
Option	**Effect on Text**
Left	Justifies text on the left margin, leaving a ragged right margin. Left is the default justification for all new documents.
Right	Justifies text on the right margin, leaving a ragged left margin.
Center	Centers all lines of text.
Full	Justifies text on the left and right margins, except the last line of the paragraph.
All	Justifies text on the left and right margins, including the last line of the paragraph. Enables you to evenly space letters in a title or a heading between the left and right margins.

Figure 5.12
A document showing five paragraphs, each formatted with a different type of justification.

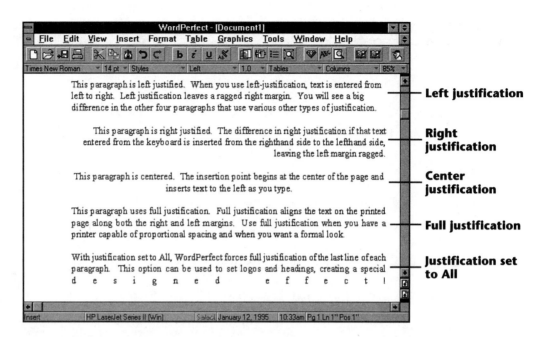

Left justification

Right justification

Center justification

Full justification

Justification set to All

Changing Justification

To change the type of justification in a document, follow these steps:

❶ Position the mouse pointer on the Justification button on the Power Bar.

Note: *As you move the mouse across the buttons of the Power Bar, the top line of the screen indicates what each button represents.*

❷ Click on the Justification button, and a drop-down list of justification choices appears.

❸ Click on the justification option you want.

WordPerfect realigns the text according to the justification used.

Tip

To apply a justification type to only one section of text, select the section of text before using these steps.

Objective 4: Align Text

Report titles or headings, and other short lines of text often are formatted using special justification features. With WordPerfect, you can choose to center a line of text between the margins, center text on a specific point in a line, or align the text flush with the right margin.

Centering Text between Margins

To center a heading between the left and right margins of the HANGING.TXT document, perform the following steps:

1 Place the cursor on the first line of the document before the word *This*, and press ↵Enter.

2 Move the cursor to the top of the document, and then open the Format menu.

3 Choose **L**ine; then choose **C**enter.

The cursor moves to the center of the page.

4 Type the heading **Chapter I** and press ↵Enter.

Notice that the text is inserted on both sides of the center point as you type.

To center an existing line of text, position the cursor at the beginning of the line, and then execute steps 2 and 3.

Aligning Flush Right

You easily can align individual lines of text with the right margin when using WordPerfect. This technique is useful when you want the *last* character of each line to align at the right margin, as in a date in a business letter (see figure 5.13).

Figure 5.13
A return address.

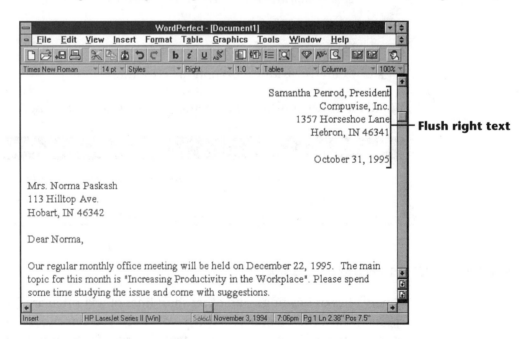

Flush right text

Aligning Text Flush Right

To align the date flush right as you type it, perform the following steps:

1 Position the cursor at the top of the document.

2 Open the Format menu.

3 Choose Line, and then choose Flush Right.

The cursor moves to the right margin.

4 Type **October 31, 1995** and press ⏎Enter.

Notice that the copy moves from the right to the left as you type.

5 Close the document without saving these changes.

To right-align existing text, simply position the cursor at the beginning of the desired line; then execute steps 2 and 3.

The Decimal Align feature most often is used to align numbers on the decimal point. Numbers often look best when they are aligned along the decimal points, especially if all the numbers in the column do not have the same number of digits. In some instances, you may want to align text along another character, such as a dollar sign.

5

Aligning Text on a Decimal or Other Character

To align text on a decimal or other alignment character, follow these steps:

1 Set a decimal tab stop where desired.

2 Position the cursor at the beginning of a blank line.

3 Press Tab↹ to move the cursor to the position where you set the decimal tab stop.

4 Type the text that precedes the alignment character (usually the decimal point).

All text moves to the left of the decimal tab stop until you type the alignment character.

5 Type the alignment character (such as the period), followed by any text that follows.

All text typed after the alignment character appears to the right of the tab stop.

Objective 5: Enhance Text

Font

A collection of characters with an identifiable type-face, such as Courier or Times Roman. In WordPerfect, you can assign fonts from the Power Bar, the **F**ont menu, or the Font dialog box.

One method of enhancing text is to use various *fonts*. In WordPerfect, you can adjust the font, size, and appearance (or attribute) of text. You can choose from *proportionally spaced* fonts (different characters take up different amounts of horizontal space on the line) or *monospaced* fonts (each character takes up the same amount of space on the line).

WordPerfect uses point size to determine basic character height. A *point* is the fundamental measure of type. Because 72 points equal one inch, 72-point Times Roman characters, for example, are approximately one inch tall. The higher the point number, the larger the type. Most documents use 10- or 12-point type for printing.

The printer you use determines, to a large extent, the number of fonts available to you in WordPerfect. When you begin a new document, WordPerfect uses the font designated as the initial font for the printer. When you choose a new printer, this initial font usually changes. You can enhance text by using different attributes such as boldface, italics, and underline.

Open a new document window to complete the following tutorials.

Choosing a Font

To choose a font for a document, perform the following steps:

❶ Position the cursor at the top of the document.

❷ Open the Fo**r**mat menu and choose **F**ont.

The Font dialog box appears (see figure 5.14).

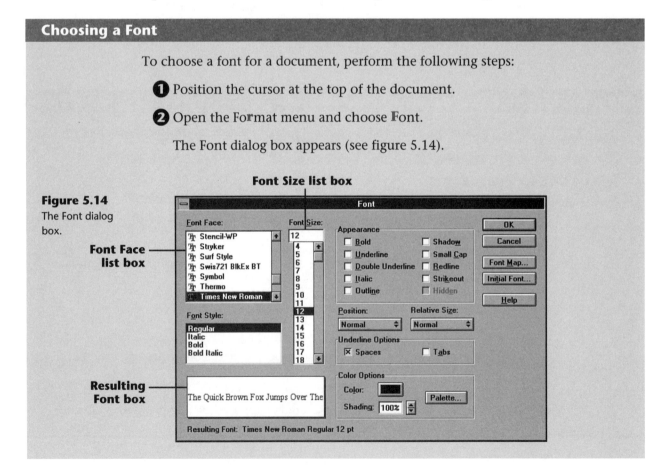

Figure 5.14
The Font dialog box.

❸ Choose the font you want to use from the Font Face list box.

You can preview your chosen font in the Resulting Font box. The sample text also reflects any modifications you make to the point size or appearance attributes.

❹ To change the size of your new font, type the desired point size in the Font Size box or choose a size from the Font Size list box.

❺ To add attributes to the font, choose the options you want from the Appearance, Position, and Relative Size boxes.

❻ When you are satisfied with the appearance of the sample text in the Resulting Font box, click OK to apply the changes.

❼ Type the following text into your document window:

This is the x font type (in place of the *x*, substitute the name of the font you have chosen).

You can choose several different fonts, using the same sentence to illustrate each (see figure 5.15).

Figure 5.15
Samples of different Windows and WordPerfect fonts.

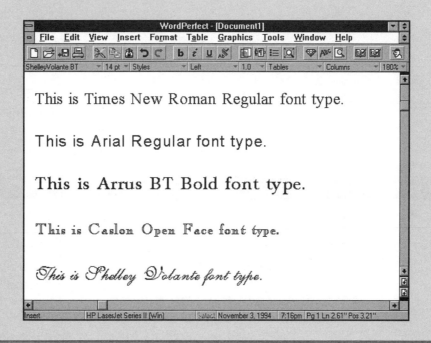

You can apply different fonts and attributes to new or existing text. To change existing text, you first must select the text you want to modify before opening the Font dialog box. Then execute the steps outlined in the "Choosing a Font" tutorial.

Applying Attributes to Text

You may want to enhance a heading with boldface type or indicate the title of a periodical or book by using italics. You can apply these types of attributes to your text as you enter the text or after you enter text.

Adding Attributes to Text Using the Toolbar

To make the text in your document boldface, underlined, or italic, perform the following steps:

1. Highlight the sentence you typed in the "Choosing a Font" tutorial.

2. Click on the Bold icon on the Toolbar. Alternatively, you can press Ctrl+B.

3. Open the Format menu; then choose Font.

4. Click the mouse button to deselect the text and to see the boldface text in your document.

5. Select the sentence again and click the Bold icon on the Toolbar to remove the boldface attribute.

Use the procedures outlined in this tutorial to apply underline (use the Underline icon), or italics (use the Italics icon). Note, however, that your choices are limited by the capabilities of your printer.

You also can assign attributes to text before you type by clicking on the Bold, Italic, or Underline icon before typing text into the document.

Removing Attributes

To remove attributes applied to the text, follow these steps:

1. Select the text for which you want to remove an attribute.

2. Open the Font dialog box by choosing Format, Font (or press F9).

3. Remove any attributes that currently are applied to the text, which are indicated in the Font dialog box by an x or are filled with gray. Click on that attribute or highlight the attribute and the x should disappear. Press ↵Enter.

Using the Font Dialog Box for Attribute Changes

In addition to using the Toolbar and shortcut keys, you can add attributes such as bold, italic, and underline by using the Font dialog box. You also can apply other attributes to selected text, such as superscript and subscript.

Changing Attributes by Using the Font Dialog Box

To apply attributes using the Font dialog box, follow these steps:

1 Select the text you want to change.

2 Access the Font dialog box by opening the Format menu and choosing Font; or press F9. WordPerfect displays the Font dialog box (see figure 5.16).

Figure 5.16
You can use the Font dialog box to apply appearance attributes to your text.

Appearance options

Appearance preview box

Position (subscript/superscript)

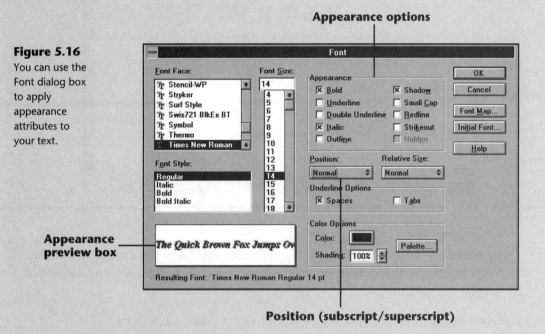

3 In the Appearance area, attributes that already are in effect are checked. You can check other attributes (for example, Shadow), or uncheck others if you don't want them.

4 Below the Appearance area is the Position button. Click on this button and hold down the mouse button. WordPerfect offers the option of applying the *Superscript* attribute (text that is smaller and positioned above the current text line) or the *Subscript* attribute (text that also is smaller, but positioned below the current line), as shown in figure 5.17. Highlight the attribute you want and release the mouse button.

5 You also can choose other attributes for just your selected text, including font and size, *relative size* of the font (smaller or larger than the surrounding text), and even the color of the text.

6 After you choose all the attributes you want to apply to your selected text, click OK.

(continues)

Changing Attributes by Using the Font Dialog Box (continued)

Figure 5.17
Text with
various font
attributes
added.

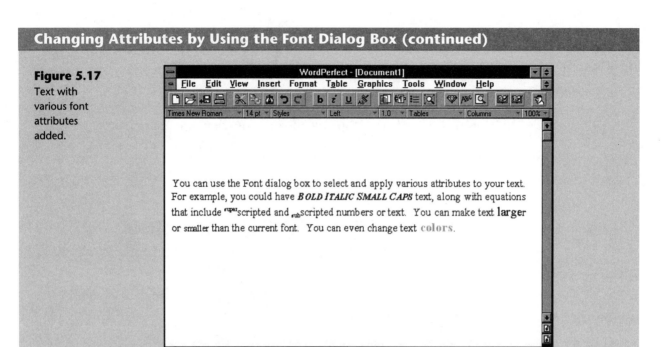

Changing the Line Spacing

By default, WordPerfect uses single spacing for each new document you create. You can change this default by increasing or decreasing the line spacing by half-line increments.

Open the ADDITION.DOC file to complete the following tutorial.

Changing Line Spacing by Using the Power Bar

To change the line spacing from single spacing to double spacing by using the Power Bar, follow these steps:

❶ Click the Line Spacing button on the Power Bar and hold down the left mouse button until the pop-up menu containing line spacing options appears.

> **Tip**
>
> As you move the mouse across the buttons of the Power Bar, the top line of the screen indicates what each button represents.

❷ Drag down the list until the number *2* is highlighted.

❸ Release the mouse button to put the line spacing into effect. The button on the Power Bar now reflects the changed spacing.

The line spacing code [Ln Spacing] is inserted into the document at the location of the cursor. (You can see the code in the Reveal Codes window.)

The code affects any text typed from this point to the end of the document, or until WordPerfect encounters another [Ln Spacing] code.

4 Close the document without saving the changes.

Using the Other Option for Line Spacing

The **O**ther option (also located in the pop-up menu) activates the Line Spacing dialog box. You can set line spacing to precise values in increments as small as one thousandth of an inch.

Using the Line Spacing Dialog Box

To increase and decrease line spacing in 1/10-line increments, follow these steps:

1 Click the Line Spacing button on the Power Bar, and choose **O**ther from the pop-up menu.

WordPerfect displays the Line Spacing dialog box (see figure 5.18).

Figure 5.18
The Line Spacing dialog box.

2 To increase or decrease the line spacing, click the up or down arrow to the right of the **S**pacing text box until the text box contains the line spacing you want.

3 Click OK.

To use a line spacing other than 1 (single spacing), 1.5, or 2 (double spacing), you must set the line spacing from the Line Spacing dialog box.

Converting Text to a Different Case

Choosing Con**v**ert Case from the **E**dit menu makes converting text to all upper-case or lowercase easy. When using the Convert Case feature to change text to all lowercase letters, the following rules apply:

- WordPerfect does not lowercase *I* or words starting with *I*, followed by an apostrophe, such as *I'm* or *I'll*.

- WordPerfect does not lowercase the first letter of the first word that follows a period in the selected text. (WordPerfect assumes that a capital letter following a period marks the beginning of a new sentence.)

5

Changing Text to Upper- or Lowercase

To convert text to all uppercase or all lowercase, follow these steps:

1 Select the text you want to convert.

2 Choose Edit; then choose Convert Case.

WordPerfect displays the following options:

- *Uppercase.* Converts all letters in the selected text to uppercase.

- *Lowercase.* Converts all letters in the selected text to lowercase.

- *Initial Capitals.* Formats each word with an initial capital letter. Words that normally are not capitalized in a title are not affected.

3 Choose the option you want; WordPerfect makes the changes for you.

Adding Footnotes and Endnotes to Your Document

If you want to show that what you say is reliable and based on fact, you can document what you write by using footnotes or endnotes. WordPerfect makes using such notes very easy by automatically numbering, formatting, and placing the notes in your document. All you have to do is provide the information.

Footnotes, by default, are placed at the bottom of the page on which they occur, separated from the text by a two-inch line, and numbered with a superscript note number.

Using Footnotes

To create a footnote, follow these steps:

1 Position the cursor at the point where you want to insert a footnote.

2 Open the Insert menu, choose Footnote, and then choose Create from the submenu that appears. WordPerfect displays the Footnote Feature Bar just below the Power Bar, and positions the cursor at the bottom of the page, preceded by a separator line and a footnote number (if this is your first footnote, the number of the footnote is 1).

3 Type the text of your footnote. Do not press `↵Enter` when you finish typing (see figure 5.19).

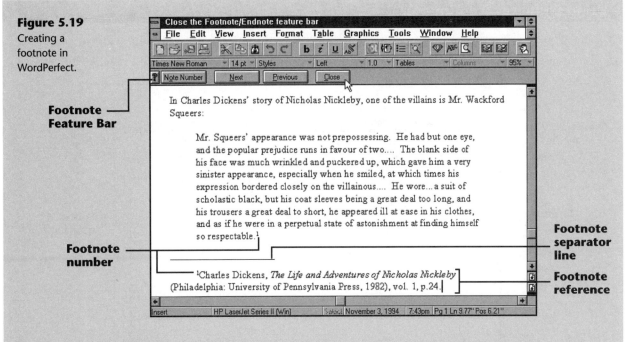

Figure 5.19
Creating a footnote in WordPerfect.

Footnote Feature Bar

Footnote number

Footnote separator line

Footnote reference

❹ Click **C**lose from the Feature Bar or click in the body of your text to exit from the Footnote editing area.

That's all there is to it! The next footnote you create is numbered 2, the one after that is numbered 3, and so on. If you delete a footnote or insert a footnote between existing notes, WordPerfect renumbers all footnotes so that they appear in the proper sequence. Better yet, WordPerfect reserves just the right amount of space at the bottom of the page for the footnotes that appear on that page.

Endnotes came about because footnotes were too hard to format on a typewriter. Endnotes accomplish the same thing as footnotes, but are harder for the reader to follow, because they appear at the end of a document. WordPerfect removes this reason for using endnotes, but some publishers and some professors still require endnotes rather than footnotes.

Using Endnotes

To create endnotes instead of footnotes, follow these steps:

❶ Position the cursor at the point where you want to insert an endnote.

❷ Open the **I**nsert menu, choose **E**ndnote, and choose **C**reate from the submenu that appears. WordPerfect moves to the end of your document and inserts an endnote number.

❸ Press ⟨Tab⟩ to insert a tab, or insert an indent, and type the text of your endnote.

❹ Click **C**lose from the Endnote Feature Bar, or click the mouse in the body of yourtext.

(continues)

Using Endnotes (continued)

Because endnotes appear at the end of the document, you may want to create a separate, final page for your endnotes. Do this by going to the end of your document (press `Ctrl`+`End`), and creating a new page by pressing `Ctrl`+`⏎Enter` (see figure 5.20).

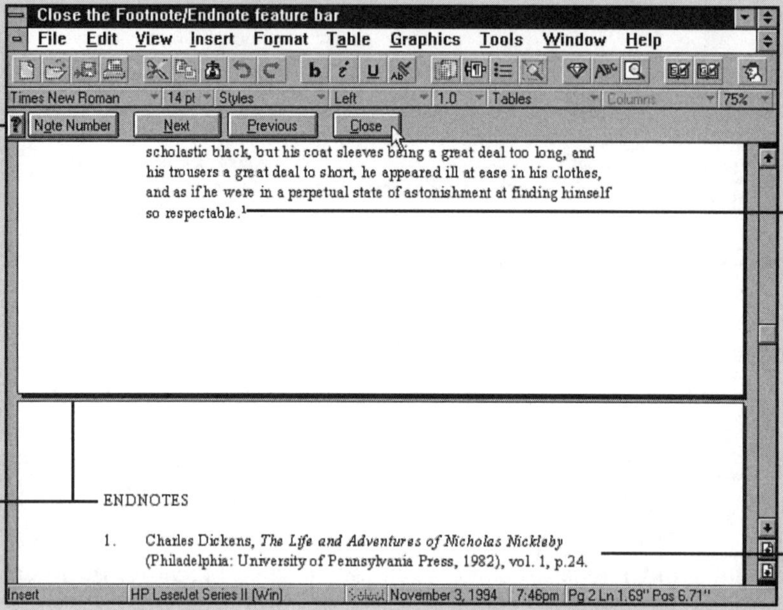

Figure 5.20
Endnotes are added at the end of the document.

Endnote Feature Bar

Page break and title added by user

Endnote number

Endnote reference

Note: *Footnotes and endnotes are visible only when working in Page mode (you can open the View menu and choose Page). If you don't want your endnotes or footnotes to get in the way, simply open the View menu and choose Draft.*

Formatting Text with Bullets and Numbers

Bullets are special characters that mark items in a list. You can insert a single bullet, or you can instruct WordPerfect to insert a new bullet each time you press `⏎Enter` to start a new paragraph. WordPerfect can automate the task of formatting paragraphs with bullets or numbers. If you specify paragraph numbering, for example, WordPerfect numbers each new paragraph when you press `⏎Enter`.

Use the current document screen, or open a new document screen to complete the following tutorial.

Inserting Bullets and Numbers

To insert bullets into a list, perform the following steps:

❶ Open the **I**nsert menu and choose Bullets & **N**umbers.

WordPerfect displays the Bullets & Numbers dialog box (see figure 5.21).

Figure 5.21
The Bullets & Numbers dialog box.

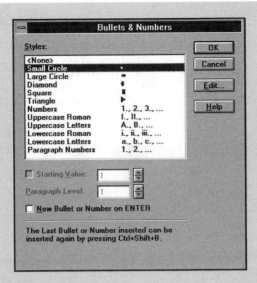

2 From the **S**tyles list, highlight the Triangle bullet.

3 Choose **N**ew Bullet or Number on ENTER to instruct WordPerfect to insert a new bullet each time you press ⏎Enter to begin a new line.

Note: *If you want to increment numbers, choose Starting **V**alue and type or use the increment/decrement buttons to insert a new starting number.*

4 Click OK to return to the document window.

5 Type the following lines, pressing ⏎Enter after typing each of the first two lines. Do not press ⏎Enter after typing line 3.

   1994 earnings boosted by favorable tax deduction

   Approval for rate increase

   Cost of capital reduced by finance program

WordPerfect inserts the selected bullet before each entry.

6 To turn off the Insert Bullets and Numbers option, open the Bullets & Numbers dialog box, deselect any selected options, and then click OK to return to the document.

The WordPerfect Character feature includes many useful and decorative characters that are not directly available from the keyboard, such as math symbols and foreign language characters.

Inserting Special Characters

To use the Character feature, follow these steps:

1 Open the **I**nsert menu and choose **C**haracter.

WordPerfect displays the WordPerfect Characters dialog box (see figure 5.22).

Figure 5.22
The WordPerfect Characters dialog box.

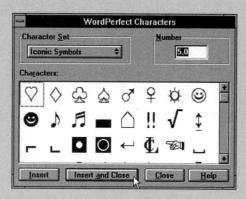

2 Choose Character **S**et, and then click the up- or down-arrow keys to see the available sets of characters in the pop-up list.

In the Cha**r**acters box, WordPerfect displays the available characters for the character set you choose.

3 To insert a character from the Cha**r**acters box, point to the character and click the left mouse button.

WordPerfect places a box around the selected character.

4 To insert the selected character and keep the WordPerfect Characters dialog box open, click the **I**nsert button.

5 To insert the character and close the WordPerfect Characters dialog box, choose Insert **a**nd Close.

Inserting the Current Date in a Document

You easily can insert the current date in a document by performing the following steps:

1 Position the cursor in the document where you want the date to appear.

2 Double-click the Date Text button on the Status Bar.

The current date is inserted at the current cursor position.

> **Tip**
>
> The current date is generated by the system's internal clock. If the date is set incorrectly on the system, the date may not be correct. You can reset the date by using the DOS DATE command.

Formatting Text with QuickFormat

You can use WordPerfect's *QuickFormat* feature to copy formatting from one paragraph to another paragraph. You can copy just fonts and attributes, or you can copy complete paragraph styles.

Using QuickFormat to Format Text

To use QuickFormat to copy attributes and margins from one paragraph to another, follow these steps:

1 Move the cursor into the paragraph that contains the formatting attributes you want to copy.

2 Open the Format menu and choose QuickFormat. Or, click the QuickFormat button on the Toolbar.

The QuickFormat dialog box appears (see figure 5.23).

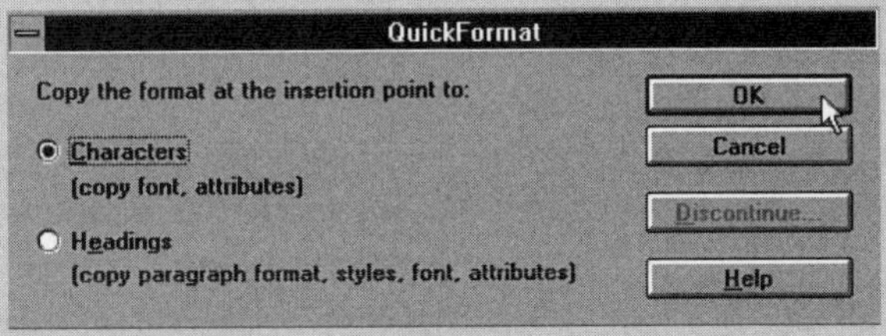

Figure 5.23
The QuickFormat dialog box.

3 Choose Characters to copy only the fonts and attributes found at the current location of the cursor.

4 Click OK.

The cursor changes to a paint roller icon.

5 Drag the paint roller icon across the text you want to reformat to apply the copied styles.

Objective 6: Control Line Breaks

WordPerfect offers several features to help you control how and when a line breaks in a paragraph. The most commonly used method is the Hyphenation feature. You can use this feature to hyphenate words and reduce the raggedness of the right margin when your document is left-justified or reduce the amount of white space between words when using full justification.

Keeping Text Together with Hard Spaces

WordPerfect generally breaks the end of a line at the space between the last word that will fit and the next word. In some cases, however, you may want to keep two words together, such as a date (December 11, 1995). To prevent words from separating on different lines, you can enter a hard space between the pair of words to bind them together.

Entering a Hard Space

To enter a hard space, follow these steps:

1 Open the Format menu and choose **L**ine.

2 Choose **O**ther Codes.

The Other Codes dialog box is displayed (see figure 5.24).

Figure 5.24
The Other Codes dialog box with the Hard Space option selected.

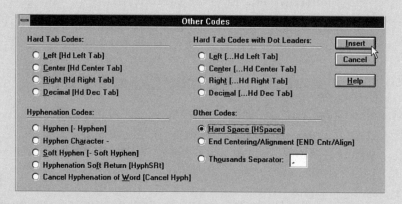

3 Click the Hard S**p**ace option button.

4 Click **I**nsert to insert a hard space in the document.

Tip

You also can insert a hard space by pressing Ctrl + Spacebar.

Hyphenating Text Manually

You can manually hyphenate words by entering any of the following types of hyphens supported by WordPerfect:

- *Hard Hyphen.* Press ⊟ to separate compound words that always require hyphenation, such as *self-defense* and *mother-in-law.* Use a hard hyphen when you don't care whether word wrap separates the words on different lines. Hard hyphens always are visible in the document and always are printed.

- *Dash Character.* Press Ctrl+⊟ to bind hyphenated words into one unit so that WordPerfect wraps the entire unit to the next line when it extends beyond the right margin. Use dash characters with text that always should stay together on a line, such as dates (07-05-95) or products (Lotus 1-2-3).

- *Soft Hyphen.* Press Ctrl+⬆Shift+⊟ to indicate where a word should be hyphenated when that word extends beyond the right margin. When the word does not extend beyond the right margin, the hyphen is not visible and is not printed. WordPerfect inserts this type of hyphenation when you use the automatic Hyphenation feature.

By default, WordPerfect's Hyphenation feature is turned off; words are wrapped to the next line rather than hyphenated.

Turning On the Hyphenation Feature

To turn on hyphenation in order to control line spacing, follow these steps:

❶ Move to the beginning of the document you want to hyphenate.

❷ Open the Format menu and choose Line; then choose Hyphenation.

WordPerfect displays the Line Hyphenation dialog box (see figure 5.25).

Figure 5.25
The Line Hyphenation dialog box.

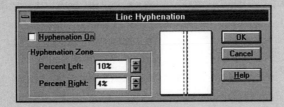

❸ Turn on hyphenation by choosing the Hyphenation On check box.

❹ Click OK.

You can use the Hyphenation feature in two ways. You can turn on the Hyphenation feature and make hyphenation decisions as you type the text of a document; or you can enter all the text first and then go to the beginning of the document, turn on Hyphenation, and scroll through the document to hyphenate it.

5

Chapter Summary

In this chapter, you learned many ways to format paragraphs and characters in WordPerfect for Windows by using the Ruler and dialog boxes. You also learned how to use the hyphenation options, as well as how to use text attributes and line spacing.

Checking Your Skills

True/False Questions

For each of the following statements, circle *T* or *F* to indicate whether the statement is true or false.

T F **1.** A *font* is a collection of characters with an identifiable typeface.

T F **2.** Font sizes are measured in points. Sixty points equal one inch.

T F **3.** To create your own tabs, you first must delete the default tabs or drag them off the Ruler.

T F **4.** Text must be selected (highlighted) before you can align it.

T F **5.** By choosing the Line Spacing option from the Power Bar, you can select precise measurements.

T F **6.** The shaded areas on the left and right side of the Ruler Bar represent the distance between the edge of the paper and the margin setting.

T F **7.** When automatic hyphenation is turned on, WordPerfect inserts a soft hyphen to indicate where a word should be hyphenated if that word extends beyond the right margin.

T F **8.** You must carefully number each of your footnotes.

T F **9.** When you use a decimal tab, text typed to the left of the decimal point is right justified, and text typed to the right of the decimal point is left justified.

T F **10.** You can enter the current date by double-clicking the date on the Status Bar.

Multiple-Choice Questions

In the blank provided, write the letter of the correct answer for each of the following questions.

___ **1.** To change a margin on the Ruler, you _____.

    a. drag the numbers on the Ruler Bar

    b. drag the icons representing the left and right margins

    c. drag the gray areas

    d. drag the dotted line

___ **2.** The Repeat Every option for Tab settings appears _____.

    a. on the Tab pull-down menu

    b. on the QuickMenu

    c. in the Tab Set dialog box

    d. none of these answers

___ **3.** _____ types of justification are available in WordPerfect for Windows.

    a. Four

    b. Six

    c. Five

    d. Three

___ **4.** By default, endnotes are placed _____.

    a. at the end of the document

    b. at the bottom of the current page

    c. at the end of the current paragraph

    d. at the end of the chapter

___ **5.** You use the _____ command to place a return address at the right margin of a document.

    a. **H**anging Indent

    b. **F**lush Right

    c. **C**enter

    d. none of these answers

___ **6.** To set precise increments for tab stops, use the _____.

    a. Ruler Bar

    b. Tab Set dialog box

    c. Tab QuickMenu

    d. all these answers

___ **7.** Hanging indents often are used in _____.

    a. report titles

    b. return addresses

    c. bibliographies

    d. none of these answers

5

___ **8.** To cause a ragged right margin, you use the _____ type of justification.

    a. right

    b. left

    c. center

    d. all these answers

___ **9.** The Superscript option is found under the _____ option in the Font dialog box.

    a. Underline

    b. Relative Size

    c. Position

    d. Appearance

___ **10.** The measurement used to determine basic character height is called _____.

    a. font size

    b. proportional size

    c. monospaced size

    d. point size

Fill-in-the-Blank Questions

In the blank provided, write the correct answer for each of the following questions.

1. The _____ feature enables WordPerfect to determine when words should be split at the end of a line.

2. Different characters take up different amounts of horizontal spacing in a _____ font.

3. The QuickFormat option uses an icon that looks like a _____.

4. A _____ is a character that is printed in a smaller point size above the normal line of text.

5. If you want to change all lowercase letters to uppercase, you use the _____ _____ option.

6. _____ _____ can be used to align columns.

7. You can adjust line spacing by using the Line Spacing button on the _____ _____.

8. Subscript text is shown _____ the baseline of regular text.

9. The _____ option activates the Line Spacing dialog box.

10. QuickFormat enables you to copy _____, _____, or _____ from one paragraph to another.

Applying Your Skills

Review Exercises

Exercise 1: Changing the Format of a Document

In this exercise, you use the margin, spacing, and justification features to change the layout of an existing document. Follow these steps:

1. Open the LETTER1.DOC file. Change the left and right margins to 2 inches, and change the line spacing to double spacing.

2. Add the following return address and date flush right to the first four lines of the document:

   Compuvise, Inc.

   1357 Horseshoe Lane

   Hebron, IN 46341

   November 1, 1995

3. Print the document and don't save the changes.

Exercise 2: Setting Tabs

In this exercise, you set tabs to align data in your document:

1. Set a left tab at 1.5 inches, a right tab with dot leaders at 3.5 inches, a center tab at 4.5 inches, and a decimal tab (dollar sign included) at 6.5 inches.

2. Type the following data. Use tabs to align each entry with the tabs you just created:

   Jim, Mary, Cameron, $2500.00

   Add three more lines of data, using names and dollar amounts of your own choosing.

3. Print the document. Do not save the document.

Exercise 3: Changing Fonts and Case

In this exercise, you practice changing fonts, changing text attributes, and converting the case of selected words. Follow these steps:

1. Type the following sentences exactly as each appears.

   This is the Shelley Volante font, size 20, with italicized lettering.

   This is Arial font, size 19, with boldfaced and double-underlined lettering.

   This is Commercial Script font, size 21, with normal appearance.

2. Apply to each sentence the attributes stated in that sentence, using the named fonts if they are available with your system. If not, substitute an available font and change the name in the sentence.

3. Print the document.

4. In the second sentence, convert all the lowercase letters to uppercase.

5. Print the document again.

6. Save the document as **FONT.DOC**.

Exercise 4: Using Formatting Procedures to Modify the Layout of a Document
In this exercise, you use formatting procedures such as margins, line spacing, indenting, and working with hidden codes to modify the layout of your document. Follow these steps:

1. Open the file JOB1.DOC.

2. Place the current date at the 4.5" position on the first line of the letter and press ⏎Enter.

3. Directly above the salutation of the letter, insert the following information:

> **Ms. Cindy Ziegley**
>
> **Director of Advertising**
>
> **Fashion Step Shoes**
>
> **1110 Signpost Dr.**
>
> **Fort Wayne, IN 46322**

4. Press ⏎Enter twice.

5. Indent the first sentence of each paragraph to the first default tab stop.

6. Italicize and double underline the words *Fort Wayne Gazette*.

7. Italicize *Brown's Sporting Goods*, *Telenex Communications*, *Kay-Mart Office Supplies*, and *Stay in Style Clothing Stores*.

8. Set the right margin to 1.25".

9. Set the line spacing to 1.5".

10. Delete the [HRt] code between each paragraph.

11. Enter the following closing two lines down from the last sentence at the 4.5" position:

> **Sincerely,**
>
>
> **Cameron Mark**

12. Save the document as **JOB3.DOC**.

13. Print the file.

14. Record the steps used to perform this exercise.

Exercise 5: Aligning Text in a Document

In this exercise, you align text using centering, dot leaders, and bullets. You also use other formatting procedures such as line spacing. Follow these steps:

1. Type the following memo:

> **current date**
>
> **MEMO**
>
> **TO: James Penrod**
>
> **FROM: Georgeanne Drake**
>
> **RE: NEW PRODUCT ITEMS**
>
> **Please inform the sales staff that on November 3, 1994, the following new products will be available for purchase:**
>
> **Wash & Clean Shampoo   9.95**
>
> **Wash & Clean Conditioner   5.95**
>
> **Hair Styling Combs   1.59**
>
> **Information about these new products can be found in the 1995 Spring Catalog. Please make sure all sales representatives who are listed with your division have a current copy of the catalog.**

2. Center the word *MEMO* and bold it.

3. Insert the current date flush right two lines above the line on which *MEMO* is positioned.

4. Place dot leaders between the names of the products and the prices.

5. Use a decimal tab for the price.

6. Make the list of products a bulleted list.

7. Bold the list.

8. Set line spacing to 1.5" for items in the list.

9. Save the document as **MEMO.DOC**.

10. Print the file.

11. Record the steps you used to perform this exercise.

Continuing Projects

Project 1: Using Indents and Fonts

In this project, you format a list of key terms in a large font. Open the KEYTERMS.DOC document and make the following changes:

1. Change all words being defined to boldface and double underlined, and change the point size to 25.

2. Indent the paragraphs from the left once.

3. Save the document as **KEYTERMS.DOC**

Project 2: Adding Information to a News Release

In this project, you add information to a news release, including bulleted paragraphs.

1. Open the NEWS.DOC file. Add the following text to the bottom of the document:

   > **Robert Matter became the Sales District Manager for the Los Angeles branch on February 15, 1995. Owner of R.J. Matter & Associates, Mr. Matter brings to the Los Angeles branch a wide range of business and community experience.**
   >
   > **Robert's innovative techniques for developing disk catalogs have brought great success to the many companies who use his products. We hope to be able to utilize his talents to their full capacity in the near future.**
   >
   > **The items Mr. Matter will be addressing this month for Compuvise are:**
   >
   > **Increase sales performance by staff**
   >
   > **Provide greater tracking of profits**
   >
   > **New database for Accounting Department**

2. At the top of the document, center the heading *Compuvise Company News*. Make the text boldface, and use a font type that is different from the body text font. Make the point size 15.

3. Double space the entire document.

4. Insert a tab at the beginning of each paragraph.

5. Use the Bullets & Numbers dialog box to number the problems being addressed by Mr. Matter.

6. Save and print the document.

Project 3: Editing the Training Document

In this project, you edit the format of the training document, including fonts, margins, spacing, and tab settings. You also use dot leaders. Follow these steps:

1. Open TRAIN3.DOC.

2. Separate each paragraph with a double space.

3. Delete the second sentence of the last paragraph.

4. Make the second paragraph the last paragraph.

5. Set justification to Full.

6. Change the right margin to 1.50".

7. Change all text to a 15 point size.

8. Change the last sentence of the last paragraph to read:

> **Please feel free to call any one of our convenient locations for information regarding class content as well as special group discount rates.**

9. After the last sentence, press ⏎Enter two times.

10. Set a left tab at 2 inches, and a left dot leader tab at 5 inches.

11. Enter the following information at the new tab settings:

Phoenix, Arizona	**(415) 788-1640**
Tampa, Florida	**(615) 455-2727**
Indianapolis, Indiana	**(219) 317-5002**
Chicago, Illinois	**(708) 815-5669**

12. Save the file as **TRAIN5.DOC.**

13. Print the file.

5

CHAPTER 6

Formatting Pages

Chapter 5 discusses formatting documents at the paragraph and character levels. Formatting at the paragraph level affects the layout of each paragraph of text; and formatting at the character level affects the font, size, and type styles assigned to individual characters and words.

This chapter examines formatting at the page level. When formatting at the page level, you are concerned primarily with the overall layout of the page and any recurring elements in the design. In this chapter, you learn how to choose paper size and type; how to add headers, footers, and page numbers; and how to control page breaks in a document.

Objectives

By the time you have finished this chapter, you will have learned to

1. Choose Paper Definitions
2. Change Margins and Center Text Vertically
3. Work with Headers and Footers
4. Number Pages
5. Control Page Breaks

Objective 1: Choose Paper Definitions

A *paper definition* includes information on the size of the paper, paper type (the name assigned to the paper definition), the location of the paper in the printer (continuous, bin, or manual feed), and the orientation of the printing on the page (portrait or landscape). WordPerfect comes with several predefined forms, including standard, labels, and envelopes, which can be used with most printers. Paper definitions are directly related to the printer you are using and therefore are limited to that printer's capabilities.

WordPerfect's default paper size is standard, which uses 8 1/2-by-11-inch paper in *portrait mode* (where text runs parallel to the shorter width of the paper). If you want to use a different paper size or intend to change the orientation to *landscape mode* (where text runs parallel to the longer width of the paper), you can choose a different paper size for your document, using a predefined size, or using a size you create yourself.

Some of the most frequently used options in the Size list follow:

Letter	8 1/2 inches by 11 inches
Legal	8 1/2 inches by 14 inches
Executive	7 1/4 inches by 10 1/2 inches
A4	210 mm by 297 mm
B5	182 mm by 257 mm
Envelope # 10	4 1/8 inches by 9 1/2 inches

To complete the following tutorials, open the ADDITION.DOC file.

Choosing a Paper Size

To choose a paper size for a document, perform the following steps:

❶ Position the cursor at the top of the page where you want the new paper size to take effect.

❷ Open the Format menu, choose **P**age, and then choose Paper **S**ize.

WordPerfect displays the Paper Size dialog box with a list of paper definitions (see figure 6.1).

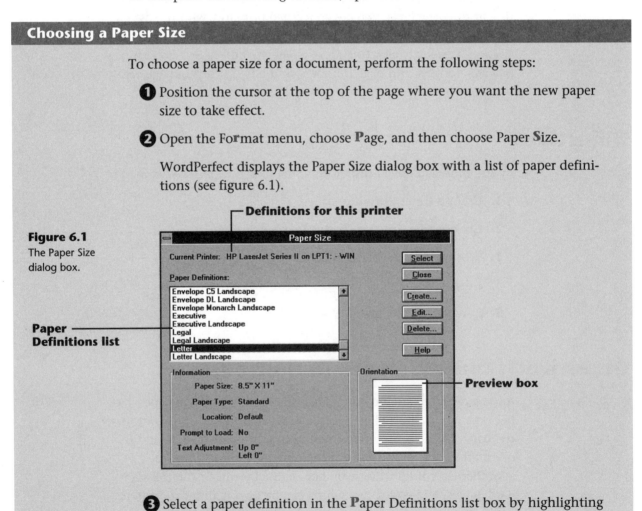

Figure 6.1
The Paper Size dialog box.

Definitions for this printer

Paper Definitions list

Preview box

❸ Select a paper definition in the **P**aper Definitions list box by highlighting the definition. Preview your choice in the Orientation box.

4 Click the **S**elect command button to put the new paper size into effect and return to the document.

You can create your own paper size definition by using the Create Paper Size dialog box. WordPerfect has several paper types you can choose from. These types include Standard, Bond, Letterhead, Labels, Envelopes, Transparency, Cardstock, Glossy Film, Clay Based, and Other. After you choose a WordPerfect paper type, you can base your paper definitions on one of the predefined sizes or specify your own size.

Defining a New Paper Definition

To create a new paper definition, perform the following steps:

1 Open the **F**ormat menu, choose **P**age, and then choose Paper **S**ize.

WordPerfect displays the Paper Size dialog box.

2 Click the **C**reate command button.

WordPerfect displays the Create Paper Size dialog box (see figure 6.2).

Figure 6.2
The Create
Paper Size
dialog box.

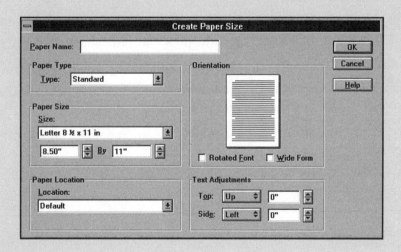

3 Choose one of the predefined paper types from the **T**ype drop-down list.

4 Type a unique name for the new paper type in the **P**aper Name text box.

5 To change the paper size, choose one of the predefined sizes in the **S**ize pop-up list.

6 If you choose the User Defined Size option, enter a customized paper size by typing a width and length in the **B**y text boxes. (You also can scroll through these measurements.)

(continues)

Defining a New Paper Definition (continued)

7 Choose an option in the Text Adjustments area to change where printing begins on a page. If information is formatted to print in an area that is considered an unprintable zone (such as certain margin areas), you must shift the information on the page to print in the specified margin.

To adjust where the printing starts in relation to the top edge of the paper, choose the **U**p or **D**own option from the **T**op pop-up list; then enter the distance in its text box on the right. To adjust where printing begins in relation to the left side of the paper, choose **L**eft or **R**ight from the Sid**e** pop-up list, and then enter the distance in its text box.

8 To print in landscape mode with vertical paper orientation, place a check in the Rotated **F**ont box. You use this option when using a printer that can rotate the fonts on a page (such as a laser printer). To print in landscape mode in the landscape (wide) paper orientation, choose **W**ide Form. Look at the orientation sample box to view these options graphically.

9 To change the paper location, choose **L**ocation and an option from the pop-up list.

10 Click the OK button.

WordPerfect returns you to the Paper Size dialog box and adds the new definition to the list of paper definitions in the **P**aper Definitions list box.

11 You can choose the new definition by highlighting it from the list box and clicking **S**elect, or you can return to your document without selecting a new definition by clicking **C**lose.

12 Close ADDITION.DOC without saving your changes.

Note: *When you define a new paper definition, it applies only to the current printer being used. If you change printers and want to use the same paper definition for another printer, you must redefine the paper definition for the new printer.*

Choosing Envelope Definitions

WordPerfect's Envelope option enables you to create new envelope definitions or customize existing envelope definitions (see figure 6.3). Open the Fo**r**mat menu and choose En**v**elope to display the Envelope dialog box.

The following options are available in the Envelope dialog box:

- *Add/A**d**d*. Adds the address displayed in the **R**eturn Addresses or **M**ailing Addresses list to a stored list of addresses you frequently print on envelopes. The program lists the first line of each address in the box below the Addresses box. To choose an address from this list, select it and press ⏎Enter.

- *Return Addresses* and *Mailing Addresses*. Enables you to type a return address or a mailing address in the appropriate space. WordPerfect shows the position of the return address in the sample envelope window. You can store this address for future use by clicking the **A**dd or the A**d**d button.

- *Delete/Delete.* Enables you to delete addresses from the lists of return addresses or mailing addresses.

- *Print Return Address.* Select this check box if you want to print the return address; remove the x if you want to omit the return address.

- *Envelope Definitions.* Enables you to select a new envelope definition from the drop-down list.

- *Create New Definition.* Displays the Create Envelope Definition dialog box, where you can specify a new envelope paper size, type, and location, as well as the envelope printer orientation.

- *Print Envelope.* Prints the envelope and returns to the document window.

- *Append to Doc.* Moves the insertion point to the end of the current document, inserts a hard page break, and inserts the envelope definition and text. This option is useful when you want to save an envelope definition with a document.

- *Options.* Displays the Envelope Options dialog box where you can adjust the position of the mailing and return addresses, and specify whether you want to print a postal bar code.

Note: *The font used for the envelope is the same font that currently is used in the associated letter. You can change the envelope font type and size to something more attractive or readable by clicking the **F**ont/Fo**n**t button in the Envelope dialog box. The font you select becomes the default envelope font until you change it.*

WordPerfect can read the address from a letter on-screen and then print the address on the envelope, as explained in the following tutorial.

6

Figure 6.3
The Envelope dialog box displaying a graphic of the automatically addressed envelope.

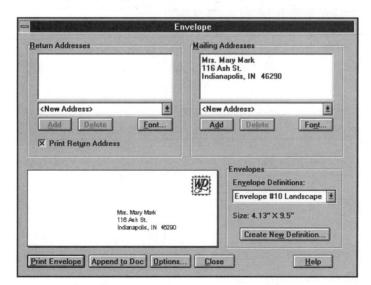

Addressing an Envelope Automatically

To have WordPerfect automatically address an envelope for LETTER1.DOC, perform the following steps:

❶ Open the LETTER1.DOC file.

❷ Position the cursor on or above the address in the letter.

❸ Open the Format menu and choose Envelope.

WordPerfect displays a preview envelope in the bottom left corner of the Envelope dialog box to show you how the printed envelope will look (refer to figure 6.3).

❹ Click Close to return to the document window.

❺ Close LETTER1.DOC without saving any changes.

If you plan to bind your document, you can specify a binding offset to control the way the document prints on each side of a double-sided sheet. A *binding offset* increases the margin on one side to leave room for inserting the pages into a binder. You can indicate whether this offset should apply to the left, right, top, or bottom edge of the paper.

Specifying a Binding Offset

To apply a binding offset, follow these steps:

❶ Open the Format menu, choose Page, and then choose Binding Duplex.

WordPerfect displays the Binding/Duplexing Options dialog box (see figure 6.4).

Figure 6.4
The Binding/ Duplexing Options dialog box.

❷ Choose a Binding Width location: Left (default), Right, Top, or Bottom.

❸ Enter the amount of binding offset (measured in inches) by typing it in the Amount text box or by scrolling through the list. Then click OK to return to the document window.

Objective 2: Change Margins and Center Text Vertically

By default, WordPerfect sets all four page margins (left, right, top, bottom) at one inch. As you learned in Chapter 5, "Formatting Paragraphs and Characters," you can use the Ruler to change the left and right margins. To change the top and bottom margins, however, you must use the Margins dialog box.

Open BRAIN.DOC to complete the following tutorials.

Changing Top and Bottom Page Margins

To change the top and bottom page margins of a document, perform the following steps:

❶ Position the cursor on the page where you want the new margins to take effect.

❷ Open the Format menu and choose Margins.

The Margins dialog box appears (see figure 6.5).

Figure 6.5
The Margins dialog box.

❸ To change the top margin, choose the Top text box; then enter the new value. For this tutorial, type **2**.

❹ To change the bottom margin, choose the Bottom text box; then enter the new value. For this tutorial, type **1.50**. Notice that the changes are reflected in the sample graphics box.

Note: *If your document contains more than one page, you must move the cursor to the beginning of the document to change the margins for the entire document.*

❺ Click OK to put the new margins into effect and return to the document.

6

Centering text between the top and bottom margins of a page is easy in WordPerfect. You can use this technique when you create a title page that vertically centers the title, byline, and a few lines of explanatory text, for example.

Centering Text Vertically

To center text vertically, follow these steps:

❶ Position the cursor on the area of the page that contains the text you want to center vertically.

❷ Open the Format menu, choose **P**age, and choose **C**enter from the submenu that appears.

The Center Page(s) dialog box appears (see figure 6.6).

Figure 6.6
The Center Page(s) dialog box.

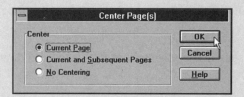

❸ Choose Current **P**age to center just the page containing the cursor. Choose Current and **S**ubsequent Pages to center all pages from the current page forward, or choose **N**o Centering to turn off page centering.

For this tutorial, choose Current **P**age.

❹ Click OK to put the centering into effect and return to the document window.

Tip

In order for the text to be centered correctly, the text should not include extra hard returns at its beginning or end.

Objective 3: Work with Headers and Footers

Header
Text that is printed automatically at the top of every page of the document.

Footer
Text that is printed automatically at the bottom of every page of the document.

A *header* is information (text or graphics) that prints at the top of every page. A *footer* is information that prints at the bottom of every page (see figure 6.7). WordPerfect inserts one blank line between the text on the page and the header or footer. Typical header or footer information includes the chapter or section title, page number, and revision dates and times. Header or footer text can consist of several lines; WordPerfect adjusts the text to make the necessary space for them. You also can suppress the header or footer from appearing on every page.

Figure 6.7

A document page that uses a header and a footer.

Header A ⎯⎯⎯   Page number ⎯⎯⎯

Birkie, The Wayward Sheltie   Page 1

Birkie, The Sheltie Movie Star

Shetland Sheepdogs have a long history of performing, although admittedly most of that history is fulfilling such tasks as herding livestock. Well, meet Birkie, the star performer in the Walt Disney production television movie *The Little Shepherd Dog of Catalina*!

This is the story of a champion Shetland Sheepdog who becomes lost on Catalina Island, off the coast of California. Luckily for him, the dog finds his way to a farm that offers him a new home. Here, the dog's natural herding instinct is recognized by Bud Parker, a farm hand. Bud trains Birkie in herding and the two soon become inseparable.

In the meantime, the dog's real owner on the mainland of California discovers Birkie's whereabouts. When he comes upon Birkie, the heroic little dog is busy trying to prevent an Arabian stallion from falling off a cliff to his death. After witnessing this encounter, the dog's real owner decides to let Birkie stay in his new home.

Birkie, whose real name is Gaywyn Sandstorm (Shane for short) is a registered Shetland Sheepdog who is owned by Carol Snip in St. Louis, Missouri. He is the grandson of two Sheltie greats, Ch. Maipsh Great Scot on his sire's side, and Ch. Kawartha's Matchmaker on his dam's side.

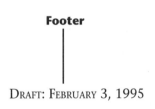

Footer

DRAFT: FEBRUARY 3, 1995

You can create two different headers (Header A and B) and two different footers (Footer A and B) in the same document. Although both Headers A and B and Footers A and B can appear on every page, generally one will go on odd pages and the other on even pages, facing each other. Generally, the shorter the headers and footers, the better.

Note: *You cannot see the headers and footers in a document when you are in Draft view, but you can see them in Page view.*

When you create a header or a footer, WordPerfect displays a special Feature Bar below the Power Bar (see figure 6.8).

Figure 6.8

The Header/Footer Feature Bar is displayed below the Power Bar.

Header/Footer Feature Bar

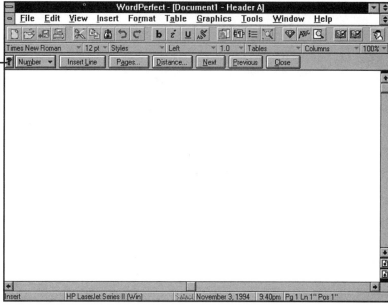

This Feature Bar provides buttons for the following options:

- *Number.* Inserts a page number, section number, chapter number, or volume number into a header or footer.

- *Insert Line.* Creates a graphics line from margin to margin in a header or footer.

- *Pages.* Places headers or footers on odd pages only, even pages only, or every page.

- *Distance.* Sets the distance between the text and the header or footer.

- *Next.* Places the cursor at the next header or footer.

- *Previous.* Places the cursor at the preceding header or footer.

- *Close.* Closes the Header/Footer Feature Bar and returns you to the document window.

Creating a Header or Footer

To create a header or footer, perform the following steps:

❶ Position the cursor on the page where you want the header or footer to appear. If you want the header or footer to appear on all pages, move the cursor to the beginning of the document.

❷ Open the Format menu and choose Header/Footer.

The Headers/Footers dialog box appears (see figure 6.9).

Figure 6.9
The Headers/
Footers dialog
box.

③ Indicate whether you are creating your first header (Header **A**), second header (Header **B**), first footer (**F**ooter A), or second footer (**F**ooter B) by choosing the appropriate option button in the Select area.

For this tutorial, choose Header **A**.

④ Click **C**reate.

WordPerfect displays the Header/Footer Feature Bar below the Power Bar (refer to figure 6.8).

⑤ Click **P**ages in the Header/Footer Feature Bar.

WordPerfect displays the Pages dialog box (see figure 6.10).

Figure 6.10
The Pages dialog
box.

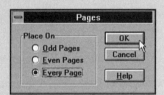

⑥ Choose the E**v**ery Page option button and click OK.

⑦ Type the header text, and place any graphics you want to appear in the header or footer in the document screen.

For this tutorial, type **Brainstorm Document** and press (Tab⇆).

⑧ To insert a page number into the header, click the Nu**m**ber button in the Header/Footer Feature Bar and then choose **P**age Number from the drop-down menu.

⑨ Click **C**lose in the Feature Bar to remove the Header/Footer Feature Bar and return to the document window.

Editing a Header or Footer

To change the text or appearance of text in a header or a footer, perform the following steps:

❶ Open the Fo**r**mat menu; then choose **H**eader/Footer.

(continues)

6

Editing a Header or Footer (continued)

The Headers/Footers dialog box appears (refer to figure 6.9).

② Choose the header or footer you want to edit; then click the **E**dit command button.

For this tutorial, choose Header **A**.

The Feature Bar appears, enabling you to make any necessary editing changes to the header or footer.

③ Change the word *Document* to **Report**.

④ Click **C**lose to record the changes and close the window.

Tip

You quickly can display the Header/Footer Feature Bar by displaying Reveal Codes (pressing Alt+F3,) and double-clicking the header's or footer's hidden code.

Turning Off a Header or Footer

To avoid printing a particular header or footer at some point in the document, follow these steps:

① Position the cursor somewhere on the first page you want to print without the header or footer.

② Open the Fo**r**mat menu and then choose **H**eader/Footer.

③ Click **D**iscontinue from the Headers/Footers dialog box. The dialog box disappears and the header/footer no longer appears.

Objective 4: Number Pages

WordPerfect's Page Numbering feature enables you to place the page number at the top or bottom margin so that the page number is flush with the left margin, right margin, or centered. When copying a document on both sides of the page, you can specify that the page numbers alternate between left and right for even and odd pages. You also can use the Page Numbering feature to change the starting page number, change the page text or accompanying symbol type, force a page to be odd or even, or insert the current page number somewhere in the text on that page.

Adding and Formatting Page Numbers

To use the Page Numbering feature, perform the following steps:

1 Position the cursor somewhere on the page where you want page numbering to begin. To number the entire document, position the cursor at the beginning of the document.

2 Open the Format menu, choose **P**age, and choose **N**umbering from the submenu that appears.

The Page Numbering dialog box is displayed (see figure 6.11).

Figure 6.11
The Page Numbering dialog box.

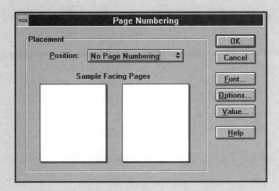

3 By default, No Page Numbering is chosen. To start page numbering, choose one of the options in the **P**osition pop-up list: Top **L**eft, Top **C**enter, Top **R**ight, **A**lternating Top, **B**ottom Left, B**o**ttom Center, Bo**t**tom Right, or Alt**e**rnating Bottom.

As soon as you choose an option, WordPerfect illustrates the page number position in the Sample Facing Pages area in the dialog box.

For this tutorial, choose any option you want. Try several options to see how each appears in the Sample Facing Pages area.

4 Choose B**o**ttom Center and click OK.

Tip

When you are assigning page numbers to a document that is going to be printed on both sides of the paper and stapled in an upper corner, choose the **A**lternating Top option so that the staple will not hide the number of the page.

You can begin page numbering at any page in the document; the change takes effect from that page forward. You can choose to start the new page numbering on a new page, a new chapter, or on volume numbers. Chapter and volume numbers enable you to number larger portions of your document.

Setting a New Number for a Page

To set a new number for a page, perform the following steps:

1 Position the cursor on the page where the numbering is to begin.

2 Open the Format menu, choose Page, and then choose Numbering from the submenu that appears.

3 Click the Value command button from the Page Numbering dialog box.

The Numbering Value dialog box appears (see figure 6.12).

Figure 6.12
The Numbering
Value dialog
box.

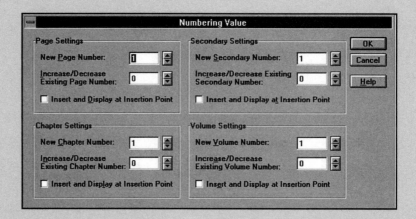

4 Choose New Page Number in the area for Page, Chapter, Secondary, or Volume Settings; then type the starting page number, or scroll to a new page number in the text box.

For this tutorial, type 2 in the New Page Number box in the Page Settings area.

5 Click OK to return to the Page Numbering dialog box.

Changing the Numbering Style

You can change the way numbers appear—for example, from Arabic to Roman numerals—by doing the following:

1 From the Page Numbering dialog box, click the Options command button.

WordPerfect displays the Page Numbering Options dialog box (see figure 6.13).

Figure 6.13
The Page
Numbering
Options dialog
box.

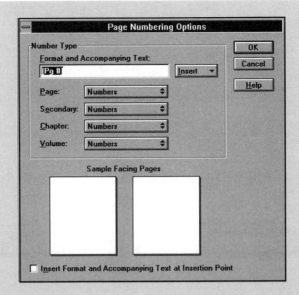

2 Choose a numbering style from the pop-up list for **P**age, **S**econdary, **C**hapter, or **V**olume and then click OK to return to the Page Numbering dialog box.

For this tutorial, access the pop-up list for **P**age, and choose one of the page numbering styles; then click OK to return to the Page Numbering dialog box.

3 Click OK to return to the document window.

Removing Page Numbering

To remove page numbering from your document, you first must locate the Page Numbering hidden code and delete it. Follow these steps:

1 Position the insertion point at the beginning of the page where your page numbering begins (usually on the first page).

2 Access Reveal Codes by pressing Alt+F3.

3 Locate the [Pg Num Pos:] code and delete it by using the mouse to drag the code out of the Reveal Codes window. You also can use the keyboard to position the cursor before or after the code and then use Del or Backspace to delete the code.

Stopping Page Numbering

To stop page numbering at a certain page in the document, follow these steps:

1 Position the cursor on the page where you want the numbering to stop.

(continues)

Stopping Page Numbering (continued)

2 Access the Page Numbering dialog box by choosing For**m**at, **P**age, **N**umbering.

3 Choose the **N**o Page Numbering option from the **P**osition list.

4 Click OK.

Note: *To see how page numbers will look when printed, you must be in Page view; page numbers are not displayed in Draft view.*

Suppressing Page Numbering for a Single Page

To suppress page numbering, headers, or footers for a single page, perform the following steps:

1 Position the cursor somewhere on the page where you want to suppress the page number, header, or footer.

2 Open the For**m**at menu, choose **P**age, and choose **S**uppress from the submenu that appears.

WordPerfect displays the Suppress dialog box (see figure 6.14).

Figure 6.14
The Suppress dialog box.

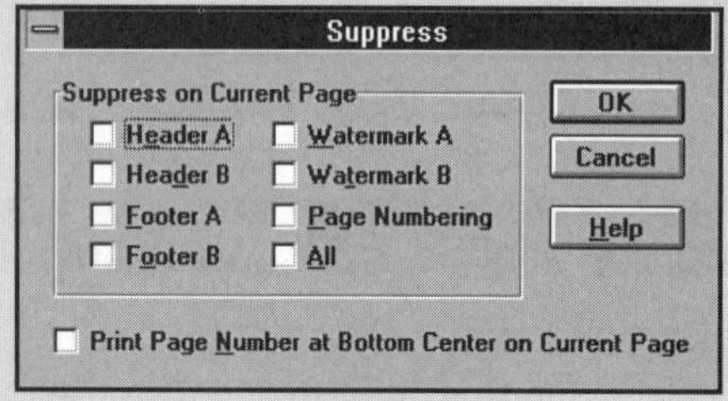

3 In the Suppress on Current Page area, place an x in all check boxes for page formatting features you don't want to print in the page.

For this tutorial, check H**e**ader A and **P**age Numbering.

4 Click OK to return to the document.

Objective 5: Control Page Breaks

Soft page break
A page break that WordPerfect automatically inserts into a document.

WordPerfect indicates page breaks on-screen as solid single or double lines in the document window. A *soft page break* is inserted automatically when you have typed enough lines to fill a page. The program uses the current paper size and top and bottom margins to determine where a soft page break occurs. You can insert a *hard page break* manually wherever you want to begin a new page. The program uses a single line to represent a soft page break and a double line for a

Hard page break
A page break that you manually insert into the document.

hard, or manual, page break in Draft mode. In Page mode, both types of page breaks appear as a thick, solid line.

To force a page break—for example, at the beginning of a new section in a report or after a title page—insert a hard page break.

Inserting and Deleting Hard Page Breaks

To insert a hard page break into the BRAIN.DOC file, perform the following steps:

1 Position the cursor at the place in the document where you want the new page to start.

For this tutorial, place the cursor before the letter *K* in the word *Keeping*.

2 Press `Ctrl`+`↵Enter`.

WordPerfect inserts a hard page break.

To delete the hard page break you just inserted, perform these steps:

1 Open the Reveal Codes window and locate the [HPg] code.

2 Place the cursor in front of the [HPg] code and press `Del`.

3 Close BRAIN.DOC without saving changes.

WordPerfect enables you to protect your work from unwanted page breaks at the time you enter the text. The text then stays together regardless of how the page breaks are adjusted as you edit the document.

6

Using Block Protect to Keep Text Together on a Page

To keep text together with the Block Protect feature, follow these steps:

1 Select (highlight) the text that should appear on the same page.

2 Open the Format menu, choose **P**age, and then choose **K**eep Text Together.

The Keep Text Together dialog box appears (see figure 6.15).

(continues)

Using Block Protect to Keep Text Together on a Page (continued)

Figure 6.15
The Keep Text Together dialog box.

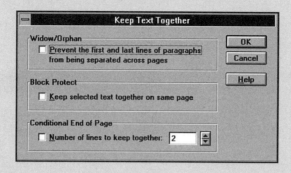

3 Choose **K**eep Selected Text Together on the Same Page.

4 Click OK to return to the document window.

You also can keep text together by specifying the number of lines to keep together. WordPerfect groups the specified lines so that they don't break between pages.

Using Conditional End of Page

To stop certain lines from breaking between pages, follow these steps:

1 Count the number of lines that should remain together on the same page.

2 Move the cursor to the line immediately above the lines you want to keep together.

3 Open the Fo**r**mat menu, choose **P**age, and then chose **K**eep Text Together to display that dialog box.

4 Choose **N**umber of Lines to Keep Together.

5 Enter the number of lines that should be kept together.

6 Click OK to return to the document window.

Orphan
The first line of a paragraph that appears alone at the bottom of a page.

Widow
The last line of a paragraph that appears alone at the top of a continuation page.

Using Widow/Orphan Protection

You can use the Widow/Orphan Protection feature to prevent single lines from being "stranded" at the top or bottom of a page. In WordPerfect, a paragraph's first line alone at the bottom of a page is an *orphan*; a paragraph's last line alone at the top of a page is a *widow*.

Turning on Widow/Orphan Protection

To turn on the Widow/Orphan Protection feature, follow these steps:

1 Position the cursor at the place in the document where you want to prevent widows and orphans. To prevent widows and orphans from appearing in the entire document, move the cursor to the beginning of the document.

2 Open the Format menu, choose Page, and then choose Keep Text Together.

3 In the Keep Text Together dialog box, place an x in the Prevent the First and Last Lines of Paragraphs from Being Separated across Pages box.

4 Click OK to return to the document window.

5 To turn off Widow/Orphan protection at a certain place in the document, open the Keep Text Together dialog box and remove the x from the Prevent the First and Last Lines of Paragraphs from Being Separated across Pages box.

WordPerfect inserts a `[Wid/Orph:off]` code that turns off Widow/Orphan protection.

Chapter Summary

In this chapter, you learned about page formatting features, including how to change the paper size and top and bottom margins, how to insert headers and footers, how to number pages, and how to control page breaks.

6

Checking Your Skills

True/False Questions

For each of the following statements, circle *T* or *F* to indicate whether the statement is true or false.

T F **1.** You can set the top and bottom margins by using the Ruler.

T F **2.** Text runs horizontally in portrait mode.

T F **3.** The **S**elect command for paper sizing is found on the **L**ayout menu.

T F **4.** Headers and footers can contain both text and graphics.

T F **5.** By default, WordPerfect does not place page numbers in a document.

T F **6.** Hard page breaks are created automatically by WordPerfect.

T F **7.** *Labels* are predefined forms that are included with the WordPerfect program.

T F **8.** You are limited to using WordPerfect's paper type when defining a new paper definition.

T F **9.** The **A**dd/A**d**d option in the Envelope dialog box enables you to add mailing addresses and return addresses.

T F **10.** Headers and footers can be seen in Draft view and not in Page view.

Multiple-Choice Questions

In the blank provided, write the letter of the correct answer for each of the following questions.

___**1.** In order to see the way a header or footer will appear in a document, you must activate _____.

    a. the **S**how Options command

    b. Page view

    c. the Reveal Codes window

    d. Draft view

___**2.** To insert a hard page break, you press _____.

    a. Ctrl+Break

    b. Ctrl+End

    c. ↵Enter

    d. Ctrl+↵Enter

___**3.** You use the _____ feature to prevent a single line from being stranded at the top or bottom of a page.

    a. Conditional End of Page

    b. Widow/Orphan Protection

    c. Block Protect

    d. Page Break

___**4.** WordPerfect controls page breaks automatically with _____.

    a. hard page breaks

    b. hard returns

    c. soft page breaks

    d. special characters

___**5.** You can suppress the _____ formatting options on a single page.

    a. header

    b. footer

    c. page number

    d. all these answers

___**6.** Page level formatting is concerned with all of the following except
_____.

    a. recurring elements in the design

    b. paper size and type

    c. type styles assigned to individual words

    d. controlling page breaks

___**7.** The default margins of WordPerfect are set at _____.

    a. 1" for top, bottom, left, and right

    b. 2" top and bottom, 1" left and right

    c. 1.25" left and right, 1" top and bottom

    d. none of these answers

___**8.** The Number option on the Header/Footer Feature Bar enables you to
insert _____.

    a. page numbers

    b. chapter numbers

    c. volume numbers

    d. all these answers

___**9.** The **D**istance option on the Header/Footer Feature Bar enables you to
_____.

    a. place headers and footers on odd pages only

    b. place headers and footers on even pages only

    c. set the amount of space between the header and the footer

    d. set the amount of space between the text and the header or footer

___**10.** To change the appearance of a page number from Arabic to Roman,
you choose an option from the _____ dialog box.

    a. Page Number

    b. Number Value

    c. Page Number Options

    d. all these answers

6

Fill-in-the-Blank Questions

In the blank provided, write the correct answer for each of the following questions.

1. A _____ is information printed at the bottom of every page.

2. _____ and _____ modes are types of page orientation available in WordPerfect for Windows.

3. To center text vertically for more than one page of a document, you must choose the _____ _____ option.

4. When you are creating the header or footer and want it to appear on all pages, you must position the cursor at the _____ of the document.

5. You quickly can display a header or footer in the Header/Footer editing screen by double-clicking the header's or footer's _____ _____.

6. Formatting occurs at _____ levels in WordPerfect.

7. In WordPerfect, a paragraph's first line alone at the bottom of a page is a/an _____; a paragraph line alone at the top of a page is a/an _____.

8. A picture in the _____ box reflects the different choices of paper definitions as you go through them.

9. The _____ _____ _____ option is useful when you want to save an envelope definition with a document.

10. The _____ _____ dialog box is used when centering text vertically.

Applying Your Skills

Review Exercises

Exercise 1: Creating and Printing an Envelope

Practice creating and printing an envelope by following these steps:

1. Create an envelope for the LETTER1.DOC file. Use the following to include a return address:

   DataProtect, Inc.

   771 W. Hampton Ave.

   New York, NY 10077

2. Print the envelope.

Exercise 2: Using Basic Layout Formatting

Practice setting top and bottom margins, centering a page, and printing by following these steps:

1. Create a title page using the following specifications:

    Set the top margin at 2 inches; set the bottom margin at 2 inches.

2. Type the following lines, double spacing between them:

    Your Name (insert your own name here)

    SmartStart: WordPerfect 6.1 for Windows

    Tutorial 2

3. Center the page when finished.

4. Print the document.

Exercise 3: Adding Document Navigation Features to a Document

In this exercise, you create a page break, insert a header and footer, number pages, and print the pages. Follow these steps:

1. Retrieve the ADDITION.DOC file.

2. Insert hard page breaks between the paragraphs, create a header and footer to appear on the pages, number the pages, and print both pages.

3. Save the document as **ADD1.DOC**.

Exercise 4: Creating an Envelope

Follow these steps to create an envelope:

1. Append an envelope to the JOB3.DOC file you created in Chapter 5.

2. Save the file as **JOB4.DOC**.

3. Print the document and the envelope.

Exercise 5: Adding Headers and Footers to a Document

In this exercise, you add a second header and a second footer to a document that already contains a header and a footer. Be careful that your headers/footers don't print on top of each other.

Open ADD1.DOC and do the following:

1. Delete the hard page breaks in the document.

2. Add a header B that includes the name of your school.

3. Add a footer B that includes the current time.

4. Remove the page numbers from the document.

5. Save the document as **ADD2.DOC** and print it.

Continuing Projects

Project 1: Creating a Title Page

In this project, you create a title page for your key terms list, using hard page breaks and centering the title page. Follow these steps:

1. Create a title page for the document KEYTERMS.

2. Include a centered, two-line title and a two-line byline. Also include the date.

3. Vertically center the entire title page.

Project 2: Designing Headers and Footers and Inserting Page Breaks

In this project, you add headers and footers to your key terms list and insert page breaks for each chapter.

Open the KEYTERMS document. Modify the document by adding the following:

1. Header A: **KEY TERMS**

2. Footer A: **Page** # (insert page number after the # symbol).

3. Create a new page for each of the following chapter terms by inserting a hard page break after each one:

   Header

   Information that prints automatically at the top of every page.

   Footer

   Information that prints automatically at the bottom of every page.

   Soft Page Break

   A page break that occurs automatically. A soft page break appears on-screen as a single line.

   Hard Page Break

   A page break you insert manually to force a break at a certain point in the document. A hard page break appears on-screen as a double dashed line.

   Orphan

   In WordPerfect, a paragraph's first line at the bottom of a page.

   Widow

   In WordPerfect, a paragraph's last line at the top of a page.

4. After adding the preceding text, print the document and save it as **KEYTERMS.DOC**

Project 3: Creating a Summary of *WordPerfect 6.1 for Windows SmartStart*

In the following project, you create a document that includes a title page and a one-paragraph summarization of each chapter covered so far in *WordPerfect 6.1 for Windows SmartStart.* The document should include the following specifications:

1. Create a title page vertically centered. The title page should include the heading *Text Book Summary* followed by *Yourname* on the second line and your *Classname* on the third line. The title should have a larger font size than the text on the second and third lines. Bold and underline the first line of the heading. All three lines should be centered horizontally. Bold, but do not underline, the second and third lines of text.

2. Pages following the title page should have margins set at 1.25" on the right and left, and default margins at the top and bottom.

3. On the following pages, write a short summary of each chapter covered so far in the SmartStart. Each chapter paragraph should be preceded by its own subheading that is bold, underlined, and flush with the left margin. Double space after each subhead.

   Paragraphs should be indented to the first tab stop to the right and single spaced. Insert a hard page break after each paragraph.

4. Create a header and footer that begins on the first page following the title page:

   Header A:: **Text Book Summary** in bold and italics.

   Footer A:: **Page** # centered in Roman Numeral style. Page number should begin with the number **2**.

5. Print the document and save it as **SUMMARY.DOC**

6

Chapter 7

WordPerfect's Customizing Features

WordPerfect for Windows offers many functions to help you customize the way in which the program interacts with you, including the capability to automate some of the things you do with macros. In addition, WordPerfect provides many of the same file-maintenance capabilities that Windows usually handles. As a result, you can perform such tasks as deleting, renaming, and copying files from within the WordPerfect program.

This chapter focuses on features that can help you make your system easier to work with and more specific to your needs.

Objectives

By the time you finish this chapter, you will have learned to

1. Work with Print Options

2. Enter Document Summary Information

3. Understand QuickList

4. Use File Management Options

5. Use Preferences to Change Defaults

6. Customize the Way Files Are Displayed

7. Use QuickCorrect to Correct Errors as You Type

8. Use Macros to Customize and Speed Up Your Work

Objective 1: Work with Print Options

With WordPerfect, you can print all or part of any document you create. You can print selected text, a range of pages, or the entire document. You also can print more than one copy of a document in a single step. Many of the options available for printing are found in the Print dialog box. By default, WordPerfect prints a single copy of the full document.

For the following tutorial, open the KEYTERMS document.

Printing the Current Page or Entire Document

To print the current page or entire document, perform the following steps:

1 Open the document that you want to print or, if multiple documents are open, activate the window displaying the document you want printed.

2 Open the File menu and choose Print.

The Print dialog box is displayed (see figure 7.1).

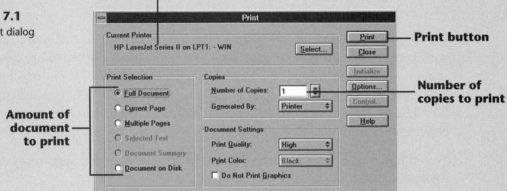

Figure 7.1
The Print dialog box.

3 At the top of the Print dialog box, WordPerfect shows the name of the current printer. To switch to a different printer, click the Select button and specify the name of the new printer.

4 To print the current page only, choose the Current Page radio button. Full Document, which prints the entire document, is the default.

5 To print multiple copies, enter a new value in the Number of Copies text box. For this tutorial, enter 2 for the number of copies to be printed. You also can use the counter control arrows to the right of the box to increase or decrease the number of copies.

6 To generate multiple copies of a document with the pages of the document collated during printing, change the setting in the Generated By drop-down list to Printer. Even if your printer doesn't have the capability to collate, selecting this option still prints multiple pages faster on a laser printer.

7 To begin printing, click the Print command button.

After you choose Print, WordPerfect displays a message box informing you of the page or pages being sent to the Windows Print Manager. To cancel printing, you must click the Cancel button in this message box before the program sends all the pages to the Print Manager. As soon as the message box is gone, you can resume working in WordPerfect.

Specifying a Range of Pages to Print

You can specify different print ranges by using the Multiple Pages dialog box. The following table demonstrates several print ranges that you can enter in the Multiple Pages dialog box, and the pages that are printed.

Print Range Entered	Pages Printed
3	3
2,4,6	2, 4, and 6
1 5	1 and 5
2-	Starting at page 2, to the end of the document
2-4	2 through 4

Printing Certain Pages

To specify particular pages of a document to print, perform the following steps:

❶ From the Print dialog box, choose **M**ultiple Pages, and then click the **P**rint command button.

The Multiple Pages dialog box appears.

❷ In the **P**age(s)/Label(s) text box, enter the pages you want printed. The program defaults to All, but for this tutorial type **1,3,4** to print only pages 1, 3, and 4.

❸ Click the **P**rint command button.

Close the KEYTERMS document without saving it before going on to the next objective.

Objective 2: Enter Document Summary Information

7

Document Summary

A brief description of the contents and vital statistics about a document, which can help you quickly identify and locate the document later.

In WordPerfect for Windows, you can add summary information to any document you create. The summary helps you identify the contents of a document at a glance and find documents quickly. *Document summaries* can include a descriptive or long file name (up to 251 characters), a descriptive file type, the original creation date, the date of the last revision, and the names of the author and typist. You also can record other distinctive information about the file, such as an account number, keywords, and an abstract of the file's contents. In addition, WordPerfect can extract information from your document and insert it into the corresponding document summary fields.

Creating a Document Summary

To create a document summary for the LETTER1.DOC file, perform the following steps:

1 Open LETTER1.DOC so that it is the active document.

2 Open the File menu and choose Document Summary.

The Document Summary dialog box appears (see figure 7.2).

Figure 7.2
The Document Summary dialog box.

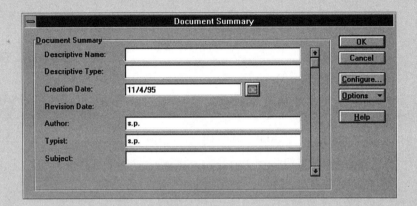

3 In the Descriptive Name text box, enter a file name containing as many as 251 characters to describe the letter.

4 In the Descriptive Type text box, enter descriptive information about the type of file (up to 68 characters). You can use *business letter*, for example, as a type for this document.

5 In the Creation Date text box, enter a new creation date. The current date and time are entered automatically when you create the document summary, but you can change either entry by typing a new date or time following the same pattern (hyphens between the parts of the date, colon between the hours and minutes, and *a* for a.m. and *p* for p.m.).

6 Type your name or initials in the Author text box.

7 Click OK to save the document and return to the document window.

Other entries in the Document Summary dialog box follow:

- *Revision Date.* WordPerfect automatically inserts the date and time when you create a document summary and choose **O**ptions, **E**xtract Information from Document. To update this information, you must choose **O**ptions, **E**xtract Information from Document again from the Document Summary dialog box.

- *Author.* Enter the name or initials of the document's author.

- *Typist.* Enter the name or initials of the document's typist.

- *Subject.* Enter up to 250 characters on the subject of the document. If the document already contains this information following the heading RE: in the document, you can copy this text by positioning the insertion point in the Subject text box and then choosing **O**ptions, **E**xtract Information from Document.

To view the following document summary fields, press Tab⇄ or use the scroll bar to bring the fields onto the screen:

- *Account.* Enter an account name or number, up to 160 characters, assigned to the document.

- *Keywords.* Enter keywords that can be used to locate the document quickly, using QuickFinder in the Open File or Insert File dialog box.

- *Abstract.* Enter a synopsis of the document's contents. You can have WordPerfect copy the first 400 characters of the document into the Abstract text box by choosing **O**ptions, **E**xtract Information from Document.

At times, you may want just the specific information on a particular document instead of the document itself. The following tutorial shows you how to get this information.

Printing a Document Summary

To print only the document summary, perform the following steps:

1 Open the **F**ile menu and choose Document Summar**y**.

The Document Summary dialog box appears (refer to figure 7.2).

2 Click the **O**ptions button, and then choose **P**rint Summary from the drop-down list.

Printing a Document Summary and a File

To print the document summary along with the file, perform the following steps:

1 Open the **F**ile menu and choose **P**rint.

WordPerfect displays the Print dialog box.

2 Click the **O**ptions button.

3 Select the Print **D**ocument Summary check box.

4 Click OK.

5 Click **P**rint to begin printing the document with the summary information.

7

Objective 3: Understand QuickList

QuickList
A feature that enables you to assign a descriptive alias to à directory to help you quickly locate its contents.

By using *QuickList*, you easily can identify the directories that contain the document files you frequently need and use. You can assign a descriptive title to any directory or single file to save you from having to remember and type long subdirectory path names. QuickList does not limit you to the standard DOS file-naming practice of eight characters or fewer. You can make the titles for files as long and descriptive as needed.

Creating a QuickList

To create a QuickList of frequently used files, perform the following steps:

1 Choose a WordPerfect command that uses a Filename list box, such as choosing **O**pen from the **F**ile menu.

2 From the Open File dialog box, click the Quick**L**ist command button. The QuickList pop-up menu appears.

3 Choose Show **B**oth to display both the **Q**uickList box and the **D**irectories box in the Open File dialog box (see figure 7.3).

Figure 7.3
The Open File dialog box displaying the QuickList and Directories boxes.

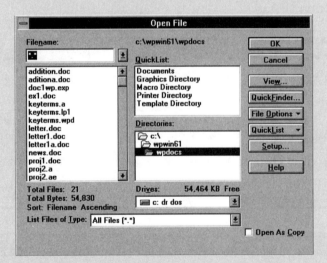

4 Click the Quick**L**ist command button and choose **A**dd Item from the pop-up menu.

The Add QuickList Item dialog box appears (see figure 7.4).

For this tutorial, you will create a QuickList for the ADDITION.DOC file.

5 In the Directory/**F**ilename text box, type **addition.doc** as the file name (refer to figure 7.4).

6 In the **D**escription text box, type **classwork** as the name of the QuickList item.

Figure 7.4
The Add
QuickList Item
dialog box.

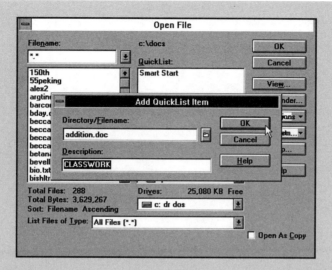

⑦ Click OK to return to the Open File dialog box, where the CLASSWORK
item is displayed in the QuickList box.

Note: *You also can give an entire directory of files a new descriptive name by typing
the name of the directory in the Directory/Filename text box.*

Editing a QuickList

To change the contents of an existing QuickList item or to change the descriptive title, follow these steps:

❶ From the QuickList list box in the Open File dialog box, select the QuickList
item that you want to change. For this tutorial, choose CLASSWORK and
then click the QuickList command button.

WordPerfect displays the QuickList pop-up menu.

❷ Choose Edit Item.

WordPerfect displays the Edit QuickList Item dialog box.

❸ Type **wordwrap.doc** in the Directory/Filename text box to change the
contents of the QuickList item.

❹ Type **exercise files** in the Description text box to change the name of the
QuickList item (see figure 7.5).

(continues)

7

Editing a QuickList (continued)

Figure 7.5
The Edit
QuickList Item
dialog box.

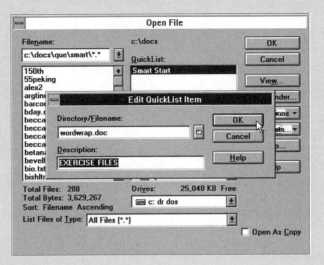

⑤ Click OK to return to the Open File dialog box.

The new changes are displayed in the QuickList box in the Open File dialog box.

Deleting a QuickList Item

To remove an existing QuickList item from the QuickList box, perform the following steps:

❶ From the Open File dialog box, select the QuickList item that you want to delete. For this tutorial, choose EXERCISE FILES; then click the QuickList command button.

❷ Choose Delete Item.

WordPerfect for Windows displays a message box for you to confirm the deletion of the EXERCISE FILES item from the QuickList (see figure 7.6).

Figure 7.6
A message box
asking you to
confirm the
deletion of a
QuickList item.

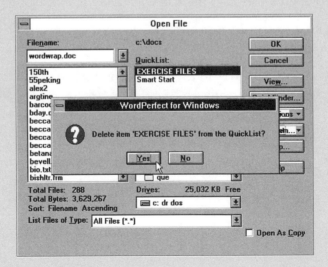

❸ Click **Y**es to confirm the deletion and return to the Open File dialog box.

The item EXERCISE FILES is removed from the QuickList box.

The following options are available when you first click the Quick**L**ist command button from the Open File dialog box:

- *Show* **Q**uickList. Replaces the **D**irectories list box with a **Q**uickList list box displaying any QuickLists you have defined.

- *Show* **D**irectories. The default setting, which displays a directory tree in the **D**irectories list box.

- *Show* **B**oth. Reduces the default **D**irectories list box to a smaller size and adds a **Q**uickList list box above it.

Displaying Files with QuickList

To display files using the QuickList feature, perform the following steps:

❶ Choose a WordPerfect command that uses a Directories and Files dialog box, such as **F**ile, Save **A**s; **F**ile, **O**pen; or **I**nsert, **F**ile.

❷ Make sure that the QuickList box is displayed. If not, click Quick**L**ist, and then choose Show **Q**uickList or Show **B**oth.

❸ In the **Q**uickList list box, double-click the descriptive name of the directory or file you want to list in the File**n**ame list box. For this tutorial, double-click the Graphics Directory item in the **Q**uickList list box.

The File**n**ame list box displays only files that are found in the Graphics directory. WordPerfect displays the entire directory path in the File**n**ame box, and all the files in that directory in a list box below the directory path (see figure 7.7).

Figure 7.7
The entire
directory path
with associated
files is displayed.

**Files in the
selected
directory**

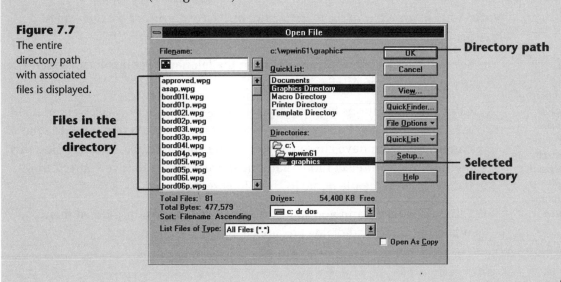

Directory path

**Selected
directory**

7

(continues)

Displaying Files with QuickList (continued)

4 Select the file you want to use from the list box, or enter the new file name in the Filename text box.

5 Click the appropriate command button, such as OK.

Close the Open File dialog box and return to a blank screen before completing the next set of tutorials.

Objective 4: Use File Management Options

WordPerfect simplifies common file-maintenance chores, such as copying, moving, renaming, or deleting files. You can perform any of these tasks by using the File **O**ptions drop-down list box that is located in the Open File, Insert File, and Save As dialog boxes. Choosing File **O**ptions from any of these dialog boxes activates a drop-down menu of file-management choices (see figure 7.8).

Figure 7.8
The drop-down menu of file-management choices.

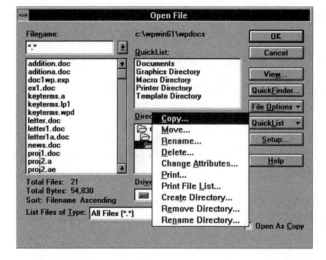

Note: *You can use either of the following two methods to carry out the commands from the File **O**ptions pull-down menu.*

Warning
When making copies of files from one drive location to another, make sure that the drive location to which the file(s) are being copied is large enough to store the information.

- Select the name of the file or files from the File**n**ame list box in the Open File, Insert File, or Save As File dialog box.

  Click the File **O**ptions button. From the drop-down menu, select a command. When the associated dialog box appears for the selected command, the file name(s) that you have chosen appear in the File**n**ame text box. By using this method, you can select more than one file at a time and save yourself from having to type the file name in the File**n**ame text box.

- Choose the command you want from the File **O**ptions drop-down menu. When the associated dialog box appears, type the file name.

The steps for the following tutorials assume that you have used the highlighting method for choosing the desired file name(s) from the list box. You will use the Open File dialog box to access the File **O**ptions menu.

Copying a File

To copy a file by using the File **O**ptions drop-down menu, follow these steps:

❶ In the Open File dialog box, select LETTER1.DOC from the file list box.

❷ Click the File **O**ptions command button, and then choose **C**opy.

WordPerfect displays the Copy File dialog box. The **T**o and **F**rom text boxes display the default path, directory, and file name of the LETTER1.DOC file.

❸ In the **F**rom text box, type the name of the new file name or directory that you want to copy. For this tutorial, keep the default name that is listed.

❹ In the **T**o text box, type **letter1a.doc** in place of LETTER1.DOC to place a copy of LETTER1.DOC in the default directory (see figure 7.9).

Figure 7.9
The Copy File dialog box.

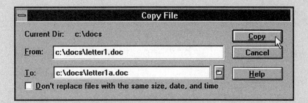

❺ Choose **D**on't Replace Files with the Same Size, Date, and Time; to avoid copying files that are identical to the files they would replace.

❻ Click **C**opy to perform the copy and return to the Open File dialog box.

The LETTER1A.DOC file is displayed in the file list box in the Open File dialog box.

Deleting a File

To delete a file using the File **O**ptions drop-down list, perform the following steps:

❶ Highlight the LETTER1A.DOC file in the file list box.

❷ Click the File **O**ptions command button and choose **D**elete.

WordPerfect displays the Delete File dialog box with the selected file included in the text box (see figure 7.10).

(continues)

7

Deleting a File (continued)

Figure 7.10
The Delete File dialog box.

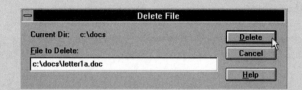

Warning
Be careful when using the Delete command. WordPerfect does not prompt you before deleting the file.

3 Click **D**elete to delete the selected file or directory and return to the Open File dialog box.

The LETTER1A.DOC file is removed from the file list in the Open File dialog box.

Printing a List of Files

To print a list of files using the File **O**ptions pull-down list, perform the following steps:

1 Choose Print File **L**ist.

The Print File List dialog box appears (see figure 7.11).

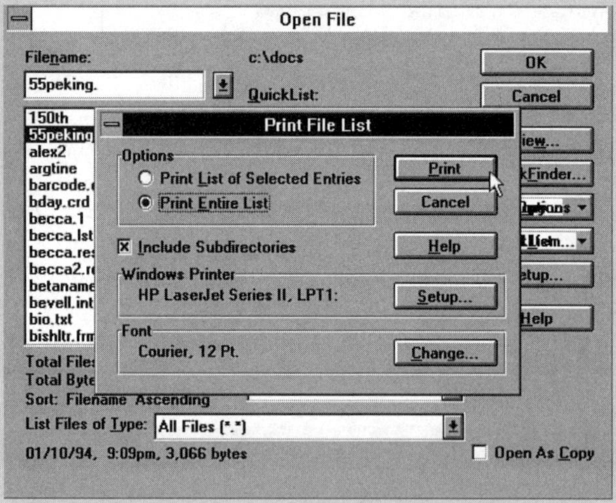

Figure 7.11
The Print File List dialog box.

2 If you choose more than one file for the file list, WordPerfect chooses the Print **L**ist of Selected Entries option button.

3 If you don't choose any files in the File**n**ame list box, or choose just one, WordPerfect defaults to the Print **E**ntire List option.

4 Click **P**rint to begin printing after making either selection.

Creating a Directory

To create a new subdirectory using the File **O**ptions pull-down list, follow these steps:

1 Choose Cre**a**te Directory.

WordPerfect displays the Create Directory dialog box (see figure 7.12).

Figure 7.12
The Create Directory dialog box.

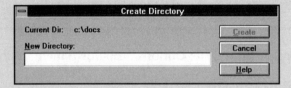

2 Type the name and path for the new directory in the **N**ew Directory text box.

3 Click **C**reate to return to the preceding dialog box.

Removing a Directory

To remove a subdirectory using the File **O**ptions pull-down list, do the following:

1 Choose R**e**move Directory.

The Remove Directory dialog box appears with the current directory listed in the **D**irectory to Remove text box (see figure 7.13).

Figure 7.13
The Remove Directory dialog box.

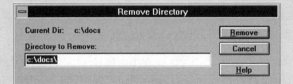

2 Accept the current directory name in the **D**irectory to Remove text box, or type the name of the directory you want removed.

3 Click **R**emove.

If the directory contains files, WordPerfect displays a message box warning that the specified directory contains files. You must click **Y**es to confirm the removal of the directory, or **N**o to stop the operation.

(continues)

7

Removing a Directory (continued)

If the directory contains subdirectories, WordPerfect displays a message box warning that the specified directory contains files and subdirectories. You must choose **Yes** to confirm the removal of the directory, or **No** to stop the operation.

4 Click **Yes** to remove files from directories or subdirectories from within directories, or choose **No** to cancel the process.

Additional options in the File **O**ptions drop-down menu follow:

- *Print*. Prints a selected file.

Archive Attribute
Causes a file to be backed up the next time you run a backup program.

- *Change Attributes*. Enables you to change the attributes of a file. You can use the **R**ead-Only option to save a file and prevent yourself or others from making changes to the file. The *Archive option* (the default) saves the file as an archived file.

- *Move*. Enables you to move a file from one location (drive, directory) to another.

Objective 5: Use Preferences to Change Defaults

You can customize many WordPerfect program features by using the **P**references option on the **E**dit menu. The features activated by this command enable you to change the program *defaults*—the way WordPerfect behaves and displays information every time you use the program. The changes you make in the Preferences dialog box affect the documents you create in the future--not just the current document. The following sections explain how to customize some of the more frequently used WordPerfect features.

You can customize many aspects of WordPerfect's screen display with the options in the Display Preferences dialog box, as shown in the following tutorial.

Customizing the Status Bar

To change the way information appears in the Status Bar, perform the following steps:

1 Open the **E**dit menu and choose P**r**eferences.

WordPerfect displays the Preferences dialog box (see figure 7.14).

Figure 7.14
The Preferences
dialog box.

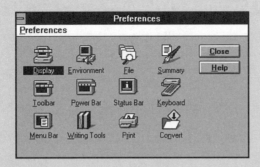

② Choose **P**references, St**a**tus Bar from the menu, or double-click the St**a**tus Bar icon.

The Status Bar Preferences dialog box appears (see figure 7.15).

Figure 7.15
The Status Bar
Preferences
dialog box.

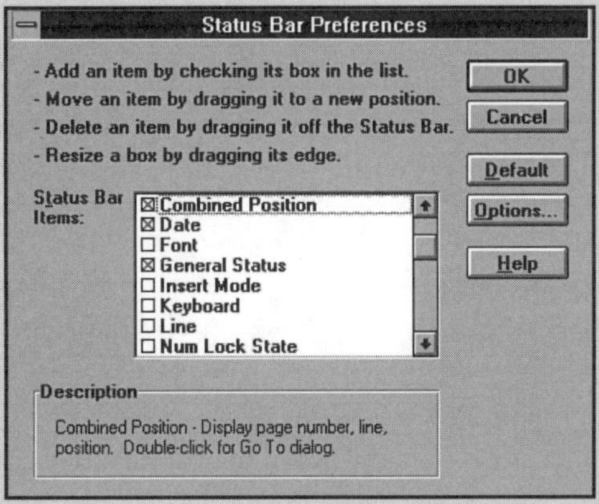

③ To add new items to the Status Bar, place an x next to the desired options in the St**a**tus Bar Items list box by clicking the check box beside the item. To remove an option, click the box again so that the x is removed.

④ To resize an item on the Status Bar, position the mouse pointer on one of the item's edges. When the pointer is a double-headed arrow, drag to the left or right to decrease or increase the item's size. The Status Bar Preferences dialog box must be displayed when you do this.

⑤ To rearrange the items on the Status Bar, drag the item's outline with the mouse to the new position.

⑥ To change the appearance of information in each item or the item itself on the Status Bar, click the **O**ptions button.

⑦ Select a new font or font size; then click OK to return to the Status Bar Preferences dialog box.

⑧ Click OK to see the changes take effect.

⑨ To return the Status Bar to the default setting, click the **D**efault button in the Status Bar Preferences dialog box.

7

Displaying the Ruler Bar in All Document Windows

To make WordPerfect automatically display the Ruler Bar in all document windows that you open, perform the following steps:

1 Open the **E**dit menu; then choose P**r**eferences.

WordPerfect displays the Preferences dialog box.

2 Choose **P**references, **D**isplay from the menu; or double-click the **D**isplay icon.

WordPerfect displays the Display Preferences dialog box.

3 Click the **R**uler Bar option button.

The bottom half of the Display Preferences dialog box displays options for the Ruler Bar command button (see figure 7.16).

Figure 7.16
The Display Preferences dialog box with the Ruler Bar option button selected.

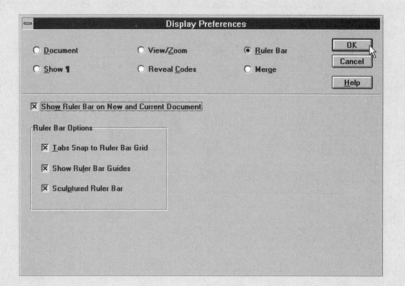

4 Choose Sho**w** Ruler on New and Current Document so that an x appears in the check box.

5 Click OK to return to the document screen.

Displaying the Reveal Codes Window in All Document Windows

To make WordPerfect automatically display the Reveal Codes window in all document windows that you open, perform the following steps:

1 Open the **E**dit menu, choose P**r**eferences, and then choose **D**isplay.

WordPerfect displays the Display Preferences dialog box.

2 Click the Reveal **C**odes option button.

3 Click Show Reveal Codes on New and Current Document so that an x appears in the check box (see figure 7.17).

Figure 7.17
The Display Preferences dialog box with the Reveal Codes option button selected.

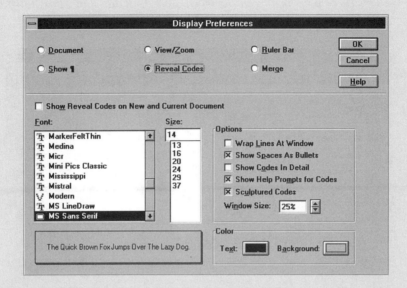

You also can modify such things as the font and font size shown in the codes by placing an x in the appropriate check box.

Objective 6: Customize the Way File Names Are Displayed

You can customize the way WordPerfect for Windows displays file names in the Open File dialog box. You can sort files in a number of different ways, for example, show only certain elements of the file listing, or place the elements in custom columns. The following list describes the different options available after clicking the **S**etup button in the Open File dialog box (see figure 7.18).

Figure 7.18
The Open/Save As Setup dialog box.

The Open/Save As Setup options follow:

- *Show*. From this option, you can choose **F**ilename Only; Filename, **S**ize, Date, Time; **D**escriptive Name, Filename; or **C**ustom Columns.

Note: *If you choose **C**ustom Columns, WordPerfect displays the file name, size, date, and time in the Open File dialog box. You then can rearrange the order of the columns by dragging the column titles with the mouse (see figure 7.19). The Show Column **La**bels check box, located in the Open/Save As Setup dialog box, must be checked in order to reorder the columns.*

Figure 7.19
The File**n**ame list box displaying files in custom columns.

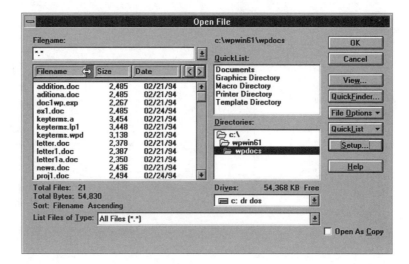

- *Sort **B**y*. Tells WordPerfect how to sort the file display. Then choose **F**ilename, **E**xtension, **S**ize, **D**ate/Time, Descriptive **N**ame, or Descriptive **T**ype as the basis of the sort.

- *Sort **O**rder*. Enables you to choose **A**scending (the default) or **D**escending to have WordPerfect sort files accordingly.

- *Change **D**efault Directory*. Makes a directory selected in the Open File dialog box's **D**irectories list box the default directory.

- *List Files of **T**ype*. Displays a specific file type--for example, to display only files with a DOC extension. All Files is the default setting.

Objective 7: Use QuickCorrect to Correct Errors as You Type

The QuickCorrect feature enables you to automatically correct mistyped words and spelling errors. Or, you can use it to expand abbreviations for words. To have the QuickCorrect feature make corrections for you, you first must identify your most commonly misspelled words in the QuickCorrect dialog box.

Identifying Misspelled Words

To identify words in the QuickCorrect dialog box, follow these steps:

1 Choose **T**ools; then choose **Q**uickCorrect.

The QuickCorrect dialog box appears (see figure 7.20).

Figure 7.20
The QuickCorrect dialog box.

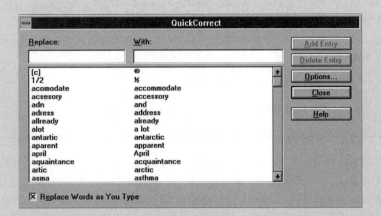

2 In the **R**eplace text box, type a word that you find yourself often misspelling. For this tutorial, type the word **prorgam**.

3 In the **W**ith text box, type the correct spelling of the word. Type **program**.

4 Click **A**dd Entry.

5 Activate the R**e**place Words as You Type check box.

6 Click **C**lose.

To see how the QuickCorrect option works, type the following sentence on a blank document screen:

```
The prorgam details are unclear at this time.
```

As you type the incorrect spelling and press Spacebar the misspelled word is corrected automatically.

Expanding an Abbreviation Using QuickCorrect

To demonstrate how you can use QuickCorrect to expand abbreviations automatically in a document, perform the following steps:

1 Choose **T**ools; then choose **Q**uickCorrect.

The QuickCorrect dialog box appears.

2 In the **R**eplace text box, type **DOS**. *DOS* is the abbreviation for the *disk operating system*.

3 In the **W**ith text box, type **Disk Operating System**.

4 Click **A**dd Entry.

5 Make sure the R**e**place Words as You Type option is activated, and then click **C**lose.

(continues)

Expanding an Abbreviation Using QuickCorrect (continued)

Add the following sentence to the same document screen you used for the preceding tutorial:

```
The DOS was installed at 1:00 p.m.
```

The abbreviation *DOS* is changed to *disk operating system.*

Note: *Try to avoid QuickCorrect abbreviations that you often use as normal abbreviations in your documents. If you really want to type* DOS, *for example, QuickCorrect will insist on expanding it to* Disk Operating System. *Instead, choose an abbreviation you probably will not use, such as* OS. *Also, don't forget to delete abbreviations you no longer want to use.*

Using Other QuickCorrect Options

QuickCorrect helps speed typing in several other ways. From the QuickCorrect dialog box, click **O**ptions to see the QuickCorrect Options dialog box (see figure 7.21).

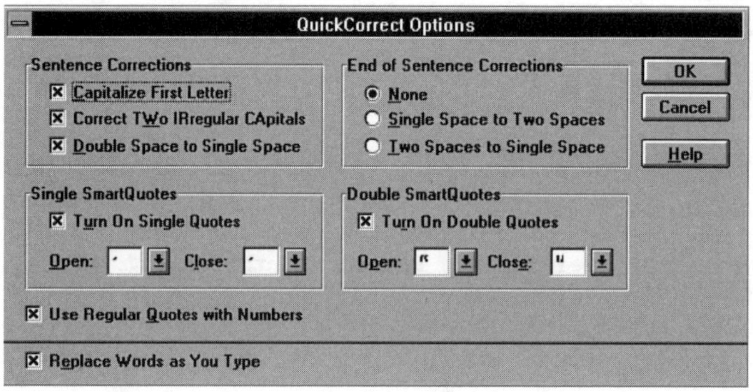

Figure 7.21
The QuickCorrect Options dialog box.

Here, you can choose whether to use the following features:

- ***C**apitalize First Letter.* After certain punctuation marks, and at the beginning of a paragraph, QuickCorrect capitalizes the first letter.
- *Correct T**W**o IRregular CApitals.* If you mistakenly type *REsume*, for example, QuickCorrect corrects it to *Resume*.
- ***D**ouble Space to Single Space.* Except between sentences, if you mistakenly type two spaces, QuickCorrect deletes the second space.
- *End of Sentence Corrections.* By default, QuickCorrect makes no changes at the end of a sentence. You can choose to change one space to two, or two spaces to one, however.
- *SmartQuotes.* If you choose Single or Double SmartQuotes, QuickCorrect places typographically correct quotation marks at the beginning and end of quotations. You also can choose to use regular quotation marks along with numbers (for example, 10").

Tip

If you want to override a QuickCorrect correction, don't backspace and type it again, or QuickCorrect will simply recorrect it. Instead, move your cursor to the left and edit the correction. Then return to your original cursor position and continue typing.

Objective 8: Use Macros to Speed Your Work

The QuickCorrect feature you learned in the preceding section is an example of using just a few keystrokes to create many keystrokes. Macros do exactly the same thing, except that they produce more than just text. Macros also can obtain input from the user, and execute commands such as selecting a font or formatting a paragraph.

Suppose that you have a series of keystrokes and formatting commands you use repeatedly. Rather than typing and executing commands over and over again, you can record what you do in a macro and then play it back, saving you time and effort.

Recording a Simple Macro

To record your company's name in boldface type, follow these steps:

❶ Begin recording the macro by choosing **T**ools, **M**acro, **R**ecord; or press Ctrl+F10. WordPerfect displays the Record Macro dialog box (see figure 7.22).

❷ In the File**n**ame list box, type the name of your macro file, using up to eight characters. Here, for example, type **logo**. WordPerfect supplies the extension WCM. Click **R**ecord.

Figure 7.22
Begin recording a macro by first supplying a file name.

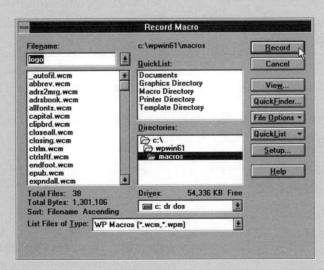

(continues)

Recording a Simple Macro (continued)

> **Tip**
>
> Keep your macro names as short as possible, because you must type this name later when you use it; you want to reduce, not increase, the number of keystrokes you type.

❸ You now can type or format whatever you want. Press Ctrl+B, for example, to turn on boldface type. Then type the name of your company: for example, **Megabucks Corporation**.

❹ Make sure that the spelling and formatting are correct. Then choose **T**ools, **M**acro, **R**ecord again; or press Ctrl+F10. This stops the macro recording process.

WordPerfect saves the macro information in a macro file (for example, type **logo.wcm**) in your MACROS directory (for example, C:\WPWIN61\MACROS).

Playing a Macro

To play back a macro you (or someone else) has recorded, simply choose **T**ools, **M**acro, **P**lay; or press Alt+F10. Then type the name of the macro (for example, **logo**) and click OK. WordPerfect duplicates exactly what you recorded in the macro as many times as you play it. If you made a mistake in a simple macro, simply record the macro again.

In addition to simple macros you create yourself, WordPerfect comes with more than 35 very useful prerecorded macros. To see a list and descriptions of these macros, choose **M**acros from the **H**elp menu. Then choose Additional Help, and finally WordPerfect Macros. Some of the more interesting and useful macros follow:

- *CLOSING.* Creates a closing to a letter or memo.

- *ENDFOOT.* Converts all endnotes to footnotes.

- *FOOTEND.* Converts all footnotes to endnotes.

- *PAGEXOFY.* Places *Page x of y* (or another pagination format) at a specified position on the page.

- *PGBORDER.* Helps you choose a fancy border for your document pages.

- *PLEADING.* Creates pleading lines and numbers in a legal document.

- WATERMRK. Enables you to choose a watermark (a light gray background graphic) for your document, such as *Confidential*, *Top Secret*, and so on.

Note: *WordPerfect also enables you to program your own macros, taking advantage of the capability to solicit user input via customized dialog boxes, and to perform tasks based on decision-making processes such as IF/THEN sequences. To learn more about programming your own macros, explore the **M**acros topic on the **H**elp menu.*

Chapter Summary

In this chapter, you learned the many ways in which to customize WordPerfect features. You learned how to change options when printing, how to enter document summary information, how to use the QuickList and Preferences features, and how to change the display of file listings in the Open File dialog box.

Checking Your Skills

True/False Questions

For each of the following statements, circle *T* or *F* to indicate whether the statement is true or false.

T F **1.** To print multiple pages, the range of numbers must be in sequential order.

T F **2.** You can set and change default options that determine the way WordPerfect for Windows works by choosing the **P**references option from the **T**ools menu.

T F **3.** The QuickList feature enables you to print numerous copies of documents quickly.

T F **4.** Many of the features included with the Preferences option also can be executed from the DOS system prompt.

T F **5.** You can sort files in ascending or descending order by using commands from the File **O**ptions pop-up menu.

T F **6.** When multiple documents are open, you first must activate the document window of the document you want printed.

T F **7.** You can resume working in WordPerfect while a document is printing.

T F **8.** You can create a QuickList for a single file or a set of files.

T F **9.** When you delete a file, WordPerfect displays a warning box before it performs the deletion.

T F **10.** The QuickCorrect feature is a complex macro that is used to expand abbreviations.

7

Multiple-Choice Questions

In the blank provided, write the letter of the correct answer for each of the following questions.

___**1.** The primary reason for filling in the Document Summary information is to _____.

    a. sort files

    b. keep a log of all documents you have created

    c. identify and find the document more easily

    d. satisfy legal requirements if you are a doctor or lawyer

___**2.** The File **O**ptions menu can be found in all of the following dialog boxes *except* for the _____ dialog box.

    a. Save As

    b. Open File

    c. Copy File

    d. Insert File

___**3.** In order to print a listing of files, you must access the _____.

    a. File **O**ptions menu

    b. Print dialog box

    c. Document Summary dialog box

    d. Quick**L**ist button

___**4.** To prevent yourself and others from making changes to a document, you use the _____ command.

    a. Save **A**s

    b. **A**rchive

    c. **R**ead-Only

    d. **R**ename

___**5.** To display reveal codes in all open document windows, choose _____ from the Preferences dialog box.

    a. **E**nvironment

    b. **P**ower Bar

    c. **D**isplay

    d. S**t**atus Bar

___**6.** To substitute one file name for another, choose the _____ option.

    a. Copy

    b. Options

    c. Rename

    d. Replace

___**7.** The **M**ove command is found on the _____ button in the Open Dialog box.

    a. View

    b. Setup

    c. File **O**ptions

    d. QuickFinder

___**8.** The _____ options are located under the **S**etup option in the Open File dialog box.

    a. Sort **B**y

    b. Change **D**efault Directory

    c. List Files of **T**ype

    d. all these answers

___**9.** QuickCorrect does not _____.

    a. perform initial capitalization after certain punctuation

    b. insert opening and closing quotation marks

    c. correct all spelling errors

    d. expand user-defined abbreviations

___**10.** You can use a WordPerfect macro to _____.

    a. format a table

    b. re-create a closing to a letter

    c. convert endnotes to footnotes

    d. all these answers

Fill-in-the-Blank Questions

In the blank provided, write the correct answer for each of the following questions.

1. When you want to resize an item on the Status Bar, the mouse pointer must be a _____ _____ _____ before you can increase or decrease the item.

2. The **K**eywords option is found in the _____.

3. To assign descriptive titles to files or directories, you use _____.

4. To change the appearance of information on the Status Bar, click the _____ button.

5. When using the _____ command, you must be careful, because WordPerfect does not prompt you before performing the task.

6. You should be sure to place page numbers in _____ order when printing multiple pages.

7. To generate multiple copies of pages collated, you must change the setting in the _____ _____ drop-down list.

8. To print from page 5 to the end of a document, type a print range of _____.

9. To have the **D**irectories list box and a **Q**uickList displayed, choose the _____ _____ option.

10. You can use WordPerfect's special programming language to write _____, which you then use to perform specific tasks.

Applying Your Skills

Review Exercises

Exercise 1: Creating a Directory and Copying Files

In this exercise, you create a new subdirectory and copy files to it. Follow these steps:

1. Create a directory called WORKFILS using the File **O**ptions drop-down menu.

2. Copy all the tutorial files that you have done so far into this directory.

Exercise 2: Creating a QuickList

In this exercise, you create a QuickList of the files you copied to the WORKFILS directory. Follow these steps:

1. Using the QuickList feature, create a title for the WORKFILS directory.

2. Use the descriptive title of **tutorials done in Wordperfect 6.1 for Windows**.

Exercise 3: Customizing the Status Bar

Follow these steps to customize the elements displayed on the Status Bar:

1. Customize the Status Bar by choosing a new font and new font size.

2. Rearrange the items on the Status Bar to new positions.

3. Record the steps used to accomplish this exercise.

Exercise 4: Creating a Document Summary

In this exercise, you create and print a document summary for an existing document. Follow these steps:

1. Create a document summary for the MEMO.DOC file you created in Chapter 5.

2. Fill in the Descriptive Name text box using a description of your own, and the Author text box using your name. Use the current date for the Creation Date, and for the Subject text box, use the information that follows the *RE:* (regarding) sentence in the MEMO.DOC file by choosing Extract Information from Document from the Options pop-up menu.

3. Print MEMO.DOC and the document summary information for it.

Exercise 5: Customizing the Filename Listing

In this exercise, you customize the order and type of information displayed in the Open File dialog box Filename list.

Reorder the display of columns in the Open File dialog box using the following specifications:

1. Customize the Filename list display by removing all but the Filename, Extension, and Date columns.

2. Change the Filename list display so that it is sorted by Date in Descending order (from last to first).

3. Record the steps used to perform this exercise.

Exercise 6: Making the Ruler Bar Always Display

By default, WordPerfect does not always display the Ruler Bar. Follow these steps to practice changing the default so that the Ruler Bar displays on all documents.

1. Perform the steps to have the Ruler Bar appear in all documents.

2. Record the steps used in this exercise.

Continuing Projects

Project 1: Working with a Document Summary

Follow these steps to add text to an existing file, to create a document summary, and then to print just the document summary:

1. Add the following paragraphs to the NEWS.DOC file:

   Mary Foist was recently promoted on April 5—from Accounting Clerk to Accounting Supervisor. Mary has played an important role in updating the accounting system over the past six months and has been a faithful employee in good standing with the company for the past five years.

   We are sure that with Mary's dedicated attitude and passion for hard work, we will benefit from her role as Accounting Supervisor.

This year's annual golf outing will be held at Foxmore Hills on July 5, 1995. The day's activities will include

6:30 a.m. Breakfast at the Foxmore Lounge

7:30 a.m. Tee off time

Noon   Tent lunch served and prizes given at the 9th hole

You can purchase tickets for this event from the Human Resources Department between the hours of 9:00 a.m. and 5:00 p.m., Monday through Friday. We are hoping for a great turnout this year, so be sure to reserve your spot on the list for a great day of fun in the sun.

2. Save the information, and then create a document summary for the NEWS.DOC file. This document is going to be a company newsletter, so use your own judgment as far as giving it a description.

3. When you have finished, print only the document summary information.

Project 2: Printing Part of a Document

In this project, you print only certain selected pages of the KEYTERMS document.

Open the KEYTERMS document, and print the document using the following specifications:

1. Print a copy of pages 2 through 5 of the document by using the Multiple Pages option.

2. Print only pages 1, 3, and 6 of the document by using the Multiple Pages option.

3. Print two copies of the full document by using the Number of Copies option.

Project 3: Using Document Summary and Custom Printing Options

In this project, you add a document summary to an existing document, print only selected pages, and print the document summary.

Open the SUMMARY.DOC file created in Chapter 6 and do the following:

1. Place the cursor at the top of page 3 and print two copies of the current page.

2. Begin printing at page 2 to the end of the document.

3. Create a document summary for the SUMMARY.DOC file and include the following in the appropriate text boxes:

Descriptive Name: **Book Report on College Text**

Creation Date and Time: **1/25/95 3:00p.m.**

Author: **Your name**

Typist: **Instructor's name**

Abstract: Enter a synopsis of the document's contents by choosing **E**xtract Information from Document from the **O**ptions pop-up menu.

4. Print only the document summary information.

7

CHAPTER 8

Merging Documents

Merge
To assemble a document by inserting variable data into a fixed format.

The *Merge* feature (often referred to as *mail merge*) represents one of WordPerfect's most versatile tools. You use the Merge feature to insert variable information into a standard format. In this chapter, you learn to use the Merge feature to create personalized form letters, to address envelopes, and to create mailing labels.

Objectives

Record
A collection of fields containing related information pertaining to a single entity, such as the record for a particular company or person.

By the time you finish this chapter, you will have learned to

1. Create Files to Merge

2. Create a Form File

3. Merge Form and Data Files

4. Address Envelopes

5. Create Mailing Labels

Objective 1: Create Files to Merge

Form file
A skeleton document containing the fixed format into which data items are merged.

A merge operation involves two files: a *form file* (primary file) and a *data file* (secondary file). The form file is a skeleton document containing merge codes and text that remains the same for each copy of the document produced by the merge operation.

Data file
A file containing the variable data or individual data items that are merged into the form file.

The data file consists of variable information, which is organized into fields and records. An example of a data file is an employee list. All the information relating to one employee within the data file is called a *record*. Each record contains data items, called *fields*. Fields in the employee list can include such information as first name, last name, company, address, city, state, and ZIP code.

By matching the merge codes you have placed in both the form and data merge files, WordPerfect determines which fields in the data file are used and where the information is inserted in the form file during the merge process. When combined with the form file, each record in the data file produces a different document.

Field
A basic unit of information that makes up a record in a secondary merge file. Each field contains the same type of information.

When creating a data file, you must make sure that every record in the file has the same number of fields and that the fields are in the same order in all records. At times, you may not have information to include in a field for a record; however, you still must include the field in the record even though the field is blank. If you skip a field in a record because of missing information or if you mix up your entries and place them in the wrong fields, WordPerfect will merge incorrect information into the form file.

Creating a Text Data File

To create a text data file, perform the following steps:

1 Open a new document window.

2 Open the **T**ools menu and choose **M**erge.

WordPerfect displays the Merge dialog box (see figure 8.1).

Figure 8.1
The Merge dialog box.

Data button

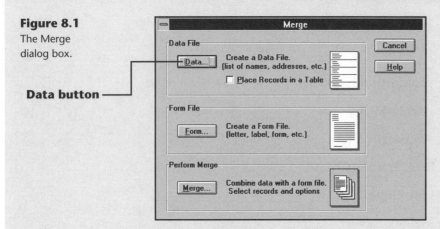

3 To create a text data file, make sure that the **P**lace Records in a Table check box is not marked.

4 Click the **D**ata button to open the Create Data File dialog box.

WordPerfect displays the Create Data File dialog box (see figure 8.2, which also displays data used in this tutorial).

Figure 8.2
The Create Data File dialog box.

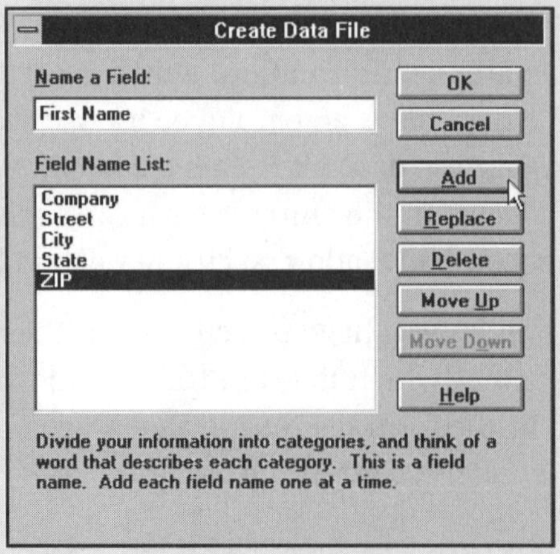

❺ Type the name for the first field in the **N**ame a Field text box.

For this tutorial, type **Company** and click the **A**dd button or press ⏎Enter.

WordPerfect inserts the name into the **F**ield Name List box.

❻ Type **Street** as the name for the next field, and click **A**dd.

❼ Continue to type the field names into the text box. For this tutorial, type the following field names, and press ⏎Enter after each entry:

City

State

ZIP

First Name

❽ When you finish entering all the fields, click the OK button to close the Create Data File dialog box.

WordPerfect displays the Quick Data Entry dialog box that you use to enter the records for the new data file (see figure 8.3). This dialog box contains a text box for each field you have defined.

Figure 8.3
The Quick Data Entry dialog box.

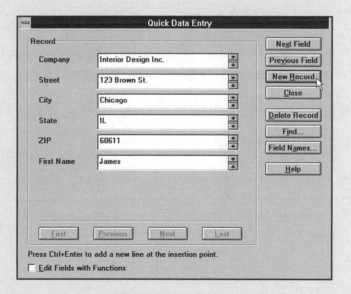

To enter data for your records into the Quick Data Entry dialog box, type the information for each field into its corresponding text box, as demonstrated in the next tutorial.

8

Entering Information in a Data File

To enter individual record information into the data file, follow these steps:

1 Type **Interior Design Inc.** in the Company text box.

2 Press ⏎Enter or click the Next Field button to move to the next line.

3 Type **123 Brown St.** in the Street text box and press ⏎Enter.

4 Type **Chicago** in the City text box and press ⏎Enter.

5 Type **IL** in the State text box and press ⏎Enter.

6 Type **60611** in the ZIP text box and press ⏎Enter.

7 Type **James** in the First Name text box, and then press ⏎Enter or click New Record to clear the text boxes so that you can make the entries for the next record.

8 Enter the following information in the appropriate fields for the next three records:

Company	**Computerland Inc.**	**ABC Company**	**Fashion Trends**
Street	**711 Madison St.**	**301 North Pl.**	**6550 Oak St.**
City	**San Francisco**	**Valparaiso**	**Phoenix**
State	**CA**	**IN**	**AZ**
ZIP	**94107**	**46383**	**66343**
First Name	**Bob**	**Jason**	**Norma**

9 When you finish entering the information for these records, click the Close button.

WordPerfect asks whether you want to save the changes to disk.

10 Choose Yes and save the file as **CUST.DAT**.

The data file and the Merge Feature Bar are displayed in the document window (see figure 8.4).

Figure 8.4
WordPerfect displays the data file and Merge Feature Bar in the document window.

Merge Feature Bar

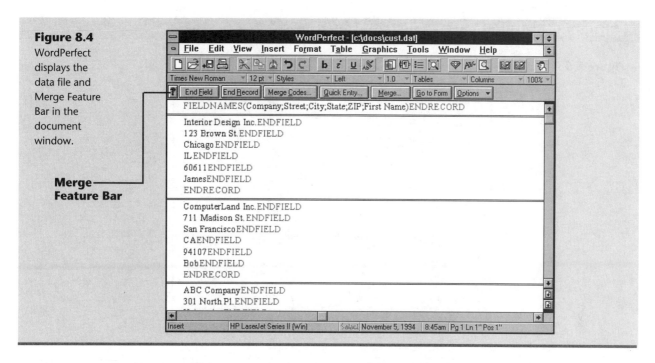

You can edit existing records by using the Quick Data Entry dialog box, as shown in the next tutorial.

Editing Records in the Data File

To edit an existing record, perform the following steps:

❶ Click the **Q**uick Entry button on the Merge Feature Bar.

The Quick Data Entry dialog box appears (refer to figure 8.3).

❷ Use the **F**irst, **P**revious, **N**ext, and **L**ast buttons along the bottom of the dialog box to move through the records in the data file.

❸ Click the **Fi**nd button at the right of the dialog box to locate a specific record in the data file by searching for specific information in one of its fields.

WordPerfect displays the Find Text dialog box (see figure 8.5).

(continues)

8

Editing Records in the Data File (continued)

Figure 8.5
The Find Text
dialog box.

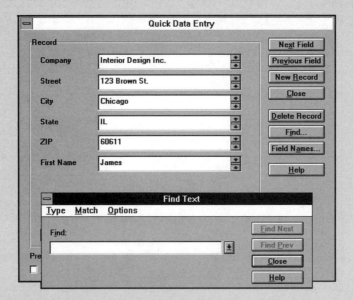

❹ Enter the text for which you want to search. For this example, type **301 North Pl.** in the Find box.

❺ Choose Options from the dialog box menu; choose **B**egin Find at Top of Document, and then click the **F**ind Next button.

In the Quick Data Entry dialog box, WordPerfect displays the first record containing text that matches the search text.

❻ Press Tab to move to the Street field.

❼ With the Street text box highlighted, type **444 North Pl.** to change the address for this record.

❽ Click New **R**ecord.

❾ To find another record with the same text, choose Find from the Quick Data Entry dialog box.

WordPerfect displays the Find Text dialog box containing the record information for which you last searched.

❿ Click the **F**ind Next button in the Find Text dialog box.

When WordPerfect cannot find another match, a message box appears stating that the text is not found.

⓫ Click Ok

⓬ Click the **C**lose button in the Quick Data Entry dialog box after making any editing changes.

WordPerfect records the changes and displays a message box asking whether you want to save your changes to disk.

⑬ Click **Y**es. WordPerfect displays the Save Data File As dialog box. Click OK.

WordPerfect displays another dialog box warning you that you are about to replace an existing data file with the modified file.

⑭ Click **Y**es again to save the changes.

⑮ Open the **F**ile menu and choose **C**lose to return to a blank document screen.

Objective 2: Create a Form File

The form file contains the document text plus FIELD merge codes that indicate which data items are to be used from the data file. In addition to the FIELD codes, you may want to insert the DATE merge code into the form file so that when you perform the merge, WordPerfect replaces the DATE code with the current date.

Creating a Letter Form File

To create a letter form file to be merged with the data file, perform the following steps:

❶ Open the **T**ools menu; then choose **M**erge.

WordPerfect displays the Merge dialog box (refer to figure 8.1).

❷ Click the **F**orm button.

The Create Form File dialog box appears (see figure 8.6).

Figure 8.6
The Create Form File dialog box.

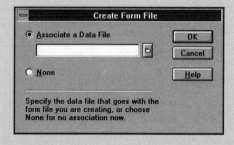

❸ In the **A**ssociate a Data File text box, enter the file name of the data file that you will be using. For this tutorial, type **cust.dat** and click OK.

A new document screen appears, into which you will enter the fields and text of your form letter.

(continues)

8

Creating a Letter Form File (continued)

> **Tip**
>
> If the data file is located somewhere other than the current drive and directory, you must enter the entire path name where it can be found in the **A**ssociate a Data File text box.

4 Position the cursor at the top of the document.

5 Insert the DATE code into the text of the form letter by clicking the **D**ate button on the Merge Feature Bar.

6 Press ⏎Enter twice to skip a line and position the cursor where you want to begin entering additional information.

7 Click the **I**nsert Field button on the Merge Feature Bar to access the Insert Field Name or Number dialog box (see figure 8.7).

Figure 8.7
The Insert Field Name or Number dialog box.

Merge Feature Bar

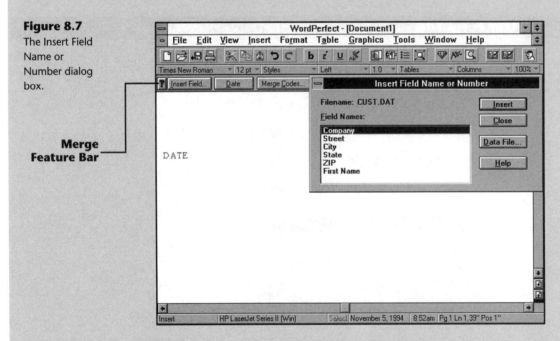

8 Highlight the Company field, click the **I**nsert button, and press ⏎Enter.

WordPerfect inserts a FIELD merge code at the cursor's position in the form document. This FIELD code contains the name of the field. Pressing ⏎Enter moves the insertion point to the next line.

9 Insert the field codes for Street, City, State, and ZIP, as shown in figure 8.8. Type a comma and a space after the City field code, and a space after the State field code.

After you insert the ZIP field code, press ⏎Enter twice to insert a blank line.

Figure 8.8
The form file for a standard form letter.

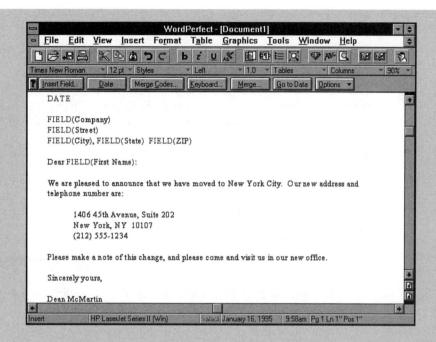

Note: *When placing codes in the form file, remember that you must insert any spaces or punctuation needed to separate the fields.*

Tip

In the event that the Insert Field Name or Number dialog box obscures some portion of your document, you can move it to a different location on-screen by dragging its Title Bar.

---

⑩ Type **Dear**, insert the First Name field code, and then type : (a colon).

Press ⏎Enter twice to insert a blank line. Then type the remainder of the letter, as shown in figure 8.8.

⑪ When you are finished typing the letter, click Close to exit the Insert Field Name or Number box.

⑫ Open the File menu and choose Close.

WordPerfect asks whether you want to save the file.

⑬ Click Yes and save the file as **CUST.FRM**.

Objective 3: Merge Form and Data Files

After you have created the form and data files, you can perform the merge. You can merge the files to the current document, to a new document window, directly to the printer, or to an existing disk file. By default, the program separates the merged documents with hard page returns, prints one copy of each merged document, and leaves a blank line in the merged document when it encounters an empty field in a record.

Performing a Typical Merge

To merge the data file and form file, follow these steps:

1 Open the File menu and choose Open.

2 Enter the name of the form file you want to use in the merge operation. For this tutorial, type **cust.frm** as the file name to open.

3 Click OK.

4 From the Merge Feature Bar, click Merge.

WordPerfect displays the Merge dialog box.

5 Click the Merge button.

WordPerfect displays the Perform Merge dialog box (see figure 8.9).

In this dialog box, you indicate the files you want to merge, and choose the merge options.

Figure 8.9
The Perform Merge dialog box.

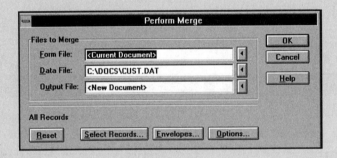

6 Check the files listed in the Files to Merge text boxes. If the file names are incorrect, you can type the correct form file name, data file name, and output file name. For this tutorial, the names should appear as they do in figure 8.9.

7 Click OK to close the Perform Merge dialog box and perform the merge.

WordPerfect displays a Please Wait message, indicating which records are being merged.

8 Examine the merged documents in the new document window by scrolling toward the beginning of the document.

9 To save the merged documents, open the File menu and choose Save. Save the file as **MERGED.DOC**.

Tip

If the file you are merging is a large document, you may want to send it directly to the printer instead of sending it to the screen. Large files that are merged and sent to the screen use up a great deal of memory, which can be a problem if your computer has a limited amount of memory.

The following options are available in the Perform Merge dialog box:

- *Form File.* `<Current Document>` The current active document will be used as the form file unless otherwise specified using a different file name.

- *Data file.* The file name of the data file that is to be used with the current form file. If you associated a data file with the form file you list, the name of the data file appears.

- *Output File.* `<New Document>` You can merge files to the current document or to a new document, directly to the printer, or to an existing disk file (which you can print at a later time).

- *Select Records.* Limits the merge to certain records by marking records or specifying conditions.

- *Envelopes.* Creates envelopes as you merge your document. The envelopes are added to the end of the merged file.

- *Options.* Controls the appearance of the merged file. You can separate each merged document with a page break, for example, specify the number of copies of each record in the data file to print, and eliminate blank lines when there is a blank field in the data file.

- *Reset.* Clears any changes you made to the original merge defaults. If you select only certain records for a merge, for example, **R**eset causes the merge to select all records once again.

Selecting Records to Merge

You can select certain records from a data file to be used in the merge operation. You can mark the records individually, designate a range of records, or specify a selection condition that must be met before the records are used.

8

Marking Records Individually

To select records individually for a merge by using the marking method, follow these steps:

① Open the **T**ools menu and choose **M**erge.

The Merge dialog box appears.

② Click the **M**erge button.

(continues)

Marking Records Individually (continued)

❸ Choose Select Records.

WordPerfect displays the Select Records dialog box (see figure 8.10).

Figure 8.10
The Select Records dialog box with the Mark Records option selected.

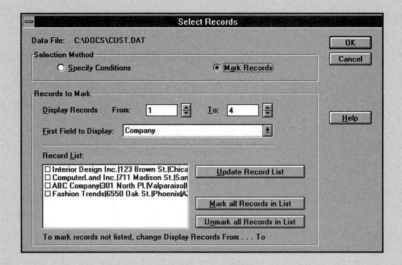

❹ Choose the Mark Records option.

The Select Records dialog box displays part of the first set of records in the Record List box.

❺ In the Record List box, select the records that you want to include in the merge by clicking the inside of the boxes to place an x in them.

❻ To control which records are displayed when making your selections, enter the starting record number in the Display Records From text box. Enter the ending record number in the To text box.

❼ In the First Field to Display list box, select the field name from the drop-down list to change the first field displayed in the Record List box.

❽ Click Update Record List to show the range of records and the first field displayed.

After selecting the records you want to include, click OK.

Selecting a Range of Record Numbers

To select a range of record numbers to include in a merge operation, follow these steps:

❶ Open the Perform Merge dialog box by choosing Merge from the Tools menu, and then clicking the Merge button.

2 Click **S**elect Records.

The Select Records dialog box appears and the **S**pecify Conditions option is selected by default.

3 Choose **R**ecord Number Range.

4 Enter the first record number to include in the **D**isplay Records From text box, and the last record number to include in the **D**isplay Records **T**o text box.

5 Click OK.

Objective 4: Address Envelopes

You easily can address an envelope for each merged letter you create. When you use the Envelope feature with a merge, WordPerfect attaches an envelope to each merged letter that is generated.

Addressing Envelopes for Merged Letters

To create addressed envelopes for the letters, follow these steps:

1 Click the **E**nvelopes button in the Perform Merge dialog box.

WordPerfect displays the Envelope dialog box (see figure 8.11).

Figure 8.11
The Envelope dialog box.

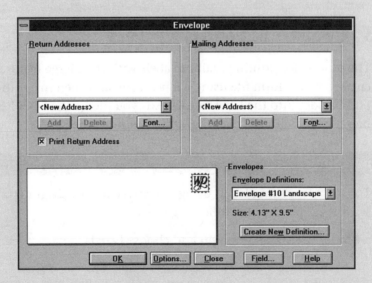

2 Type a new return address in the **R**eturn Addresses box or select a previously added address from the drop-down list.

(continues)

Addressing Envelopes for Merged Letters (continued)

❸ To select a new font for the return address, click the Font button.

WordPerfect displays the Address Font dialog box.

❹ Select the font type, font size, font appearance, and font color.

❺ Position the insertion point in the Mailing Addresses box.

❻ Click the Field button to insert the FIELD codes needed to generate the mailing labels from the records in the data file.

You also can select a new font for the mailing addresses if you want.

❼ Examine the sample box to see whether the envelope is correct.

❽ To choose the size and type of envelope, choose the Envelopes Definitions text box. You can select a definition from the drop-down list or create one of your own with the Create New Definition button.

❾ When finished, click OK to close the envelope dialog box and return to the Perform Merge dialog box.

❿ Click OK in the Perform Merge dialog box.

Scroll through the merged document to see the envelopes appended at the end of the document.

Objective 5: Create Mailing Labels

The process for printing mailing labels with the Merge feature requires that you create a merge form file using a label form, and then insert the appropriate FIELD codes into the label form. Next, you merge the label form containing the merge codes with the data file, and then print the results.

Printing Mailing Labels

To generate mailing labels using the Merge feature, begin at a clear document screen and perform the following steps:

❶ Open the Layout menu and choose Labels.

WordPerfect displays the Labels dialog box (see figure 8.12).

Figure 8.12
The Labels
dialog box.

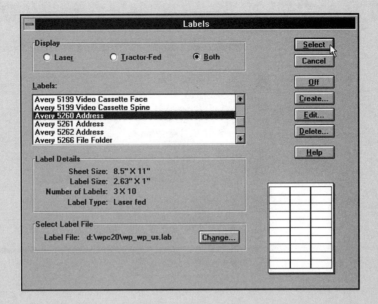

2 Highlight a label definition from the **L**abels list box, and then click **S**elect. For this tutorial, choose Avery 5260 Address for the label definition.

Notice the graphical depiction of the labels on the right side of the box.

3 Open the **T**ools menu and choose **M**erge; then click **F**orm from the Merge dialog box.

WordPerfect displays the Create Merge File dialog box.

4 Click OK to use the label form in the current document window.

5 In the **A**ssociate a Data File text box in the Create Merge File dialog box, type the name of the data file you will use when generating the labels during the merge. For this tutorial, type **cust.dat**.

6 To create the mailing addresses, click the **I**nsert Field button on the Merge Feature Bar.

WordPerfect displays the Insert Field Name or Number dialog box.

7 Select the field you want to insert into the **F**ield Names list box, and then click **I**nsert.

8 Finish inserting the FIELD codes for the labels as shown in figure 8.13, and then click **C**lose.

(continues)

8

Printing Mailing Labels (continued)

Figure 8.13
The label form containing the FIELD codes needed to generate the mailing addresses during the merge.

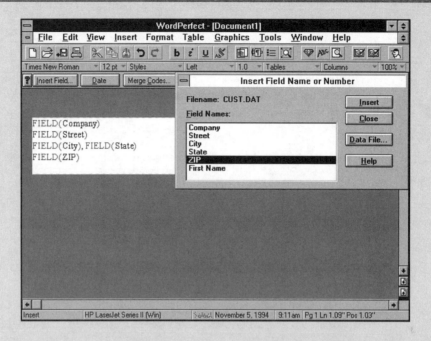

⑨ Open the File menu and choose Save. Save this label form as **cust.lab**.

⑩ Click the Merge button on the Merge Feature Bar to merge the label form with the associated data file.

⑪ Click the Merge button to open the Perform Merge dialog box.

⑫ Click OK to start the merge.

The labels then are generated from the merge to the screen.

Chapter Summary

In this chapter, you learned about WordPerfect's Merge features. You learned how to merge a data file and a form file and how to select only certain records for the merged file. You also learned how to address envelopes for merged documents and how to create mailing labels.

Checking Your Skills

True/False Questions
For each of the following statements, circle *T* or *F* to indicate whether the statement is true or false.

T F **1.** The merge operation requires a data file and a form file.

T F **2.** The data file contains fixed text and graphics along with merge codes.

T F **3.** Each record in a data file contains a number of fields.

T F **4.** You can create mailing labels and address envelopes from the data file that you create.

T F **5.** All records used in a merge must contain the same fields, even if a field contains no information.

T F **6.** If you accidentally mix up entries and place them in incorrect fields, WordPerfect straightens them out before performing a merge.

T F **7.** You enter information for individual records in the Create Data File dialog box.

T F **8.** Field merge codes indicate which data items are to be used from the data file.

T F **9.** WordPerfect inserts a blank line in a merged document when encountering an empty field in a record.

T F **10.** Large merged files can use up a great deal of your computer's memory.

Multiple-Choice Questions

In the blank provided, write the letter of the correct answer for each of the following questions.

___**1.** _____ is *not* a field in a record of the data file.

    a. Company

    b. First name

    c. John Doe

    d. Address

___**2.** A merge operation requires _____.

    a. a list file and a data file

    b. a list file and an address file

    c. an address file and label file

    d. a form file and a data file

___**3.** The methods used for record selection in a merge operation include selecting by _____.

    a. condition

    b. range of record numbers

    c. marking individual records

    d. all these answers

8

___**4.** The **M**erge command is found on the _____ menu.

    a. **E**dit

    b. **T**ools

    c. **I**nsert

    d. **L**ayout

___**5.** The Merge Feature Bar contains all the following options _except_ _____.

    a. **Q**uick Entry

    b. **O**ptions

    c. **G**o To Form

    d. **C**lose

___**6.** You use the _____ option in the Perform Merge dialog box to eliminate a blank line in a merged document.

    a. **D**ata File

    b. **O**utput File

    c. **O**ptions

    d. none of these answers

___**7.** After creating a merge form file using a label form, you insert _____ into the label form.

    a. data codes

    b. field codes

    c. records

    d. none of these answers

___**8.** The New **R**ecord command button is found in the _____.

    a. Quick Data Entry dialog box

    b. Merge Feature Bar

    c. Find Text dialog box

    d. Create Data File dialog box

___**9.** To select certain records by marking them for a merge, you first must open the _____ dialog box.

    a. Merge

    b. Perform Merge

    c. Select Records

    d. Insert Field Name or Number

___**10.** When you want to address an envelope for each merged letter, you use the _____ dialog box, which contains the **E**nvelopes command button.

    a. Envelopes

    b. Perform Merge

    c. Select Records

    d. none of these answers

Fill-in-the-Blank Questions

In the blank provided, write the correct answer for each of the following questions.

1. The Merge feature often is referred to as the _____ _____ .

2. Each field in a data file contains the same _____ of information.

3. A form file is defined as a _____ document.

4. Each record in a data file produces a _____ _____.

5. The Merge dialog box includes options to create a _____ _____, create a _____ _____, and _____ them together.

6. In the Create Data File dialog box, you enter the _____ _____.

7. The Quick Data Entry dialog box is used to enter the _____ for the new data file.

8. The **Fi**nd command button is located in the _____ _____ dialog box.

9. WordPerfect automatically replaces the Date code with the_____ _____.

10. The **A**ssociate a Data File text box is used when creating a _____ or _____ _____.

Applying Your Skills

Review Exercises

Exercise 1: Creating a Data File

In this exercise, you create a simple data file of five records. Follow these steps:

1. Use a list of five friends to create a data file that includes the following fields:

   Name

   Address

   City

   State

   ZIP

   Phone

2. Save the file as **FRIENDS.DAT**.

Exercise 2: Creating a Form File

In this exercise, you create a simple form file that uses the data you created in exercise 1. Follow these steps:

1. Insert the following data fields, codes, and text into a new document:

   {Date}

   {Name}

   {Address}

   {City}, {State} {Zip}

   Call me at {Phone}.

2. Save the form document as **FRIENDS.FRM.**

Exercise 3: Merging

Merge the data file and form file in exercises 1 and 2 and print it.

Exercise 4: Creating and Merging a Cover Letter

In this project, you use the JOB3.DOC file as the form letter to be used in a merge. Follow these steps:

1. Insert the following field codes for the return address portion of the letter:

COURTESY	**Ms., Mrs., or Mr.**
FNAME	**First Name**
LNAME	**Last name**
TITLE	**Position title**
COMPANY	**Company name**

ADDRESS	Company Address
CITY	City
STATE	State
ZIP CODE	ZIP Code

2. Following the word *Dear*, insert the **COURTESY**, **FNAME**, and **LNAME** field codes again.

3. In the first sentence of the first paragraph, insert a field code of **NEWSPAPER** for the name of the newspaper the ad was listed in.

4. Name the form file **COVERLET.FRM**.

5. Use the following records for the data file:

COURTESY	Mr.	Mrs.
FNAME	John	Holly
LNAME	Doe	Sams
TITLE	President	Director Human Resources
COMPANY	Signpost Inc.	Addco Advertising
ADDRESS	2457 Wabash Rd.	3375 Park Ln.
CITY	Tampa	Scottsdale
STATE	FL	AZ
ZIP CODE	62341	23241
NEWSPAPER	Tampa Tribune	Scottsdale Herald

COURTESY	Mr.	Ms.
FNAME	James	Charlotte
LNAME	Irwin	Vale
TITLE	Vice President	Asst. Director
COMPANY	Lakeshore Adds	Advertise Mart
CITY	Hebron	Palos Hills
STATE	IN	IL
ZIP CODE	46341	60160
NEWSPAPER	Hebron Daily News	Chicago Sun Times

8

The Newspaper name should be in italics and underlined when printed on the form letter.

6. Name the data file **COVER.DAT**.

7. Merge the data file and form file together and name the merged file **CVRLETTR.MRG**.

8. Address envelopes for each merged letter of the CVRLETTR.MRG file.

Continuing Projects

Project 1: Creating a Data File and a Form File, and Merging the Files

To create a data file and a form file, and then merge the files, follow these steps:

1. Create a data file consisting of five people you know.

2. Create a form letter inviting those five people to a birthday party.

3. Merge the files to produce an invitation for each person.

4. Print a copy of the merged letters.

5. Address envelopes for each person and print them.

Project 2: Creating Mailing Labels

In the preceding project, you addressed envelopes for the recipients of your letter. For this project, create address labels for packages you intend to send them.

Project 3: Adding Merge Codes to an Existing Document

Use the TRAIN5.DOC file you created in Chapter 5 to create a form letter to use in a merge. Follow these steps:

1. You will insert the following field codes in the TRAIN5.DOC file:

   FNAME

   CURRENT DATE

2. Edit the TRAIN5.DOC file and include the following:

   At the top of the TRAIN5.DOC file, add a salutation of *Dear FNAME* (you will insert the various names provided in the FNAME field).

   On the same line at the right margin, insert the field code to print the current date. Leave the remainder of the TRAIN5.DOC file as it is.

   Save the new form file as **TRAIN.FRM**.

3. Use the following data for the data file. Produce an individual form letter for each of the following names:

   Cindy

   Mary K.

   Linda

   Cameron

   Georgeanne

   Sally

   Jim

   Pete

4. Save the data file as **TRAINING.DAT** and print it.

5. Mark the following records to be included in the merge and produce an individual form letter for only these records:

Pete

Jim

Georgeanne

Mary K.

6. Name the merged file **TRAIN.MRG**.

7. Print the merged letters.

8

Chapter 9

Working with Text Columns and Tables

With WordPerfect, you easily can set up columns and add them to your documents. In this chapter, you learn how to define newspaper and parallel columns, enter text into them, and adjust them using the Ruler.

Objectives

By the time you finish this chapter, you will have learned to

1. Define Text Columns

2. Enter and Edit Text in Columns

3. Adjust Text Column Widths Using the Ruler

4. Create a Table

5. Format a Table

Objective 1: Define Columns

WordPerfect for Windows supports four types of columns:

Newspaper columns
Text flows from the top of a column to the bottom of the column and then wraps to the top of the next column.

- *Standard newspaper columns.* Text flows down the first column and then wraps at the bottom of the page and starts the next column. These types of Columns are used in newsletters, magazine articles, or brochures (see figure 9.1).

- *Balanced newspaper columns.* The columns wrap when necessary to make sure that they always line up with each other at the top and bottom (see figure 9.2).

Figure 9.1
Newspaper columns created by selecting the Columns command.

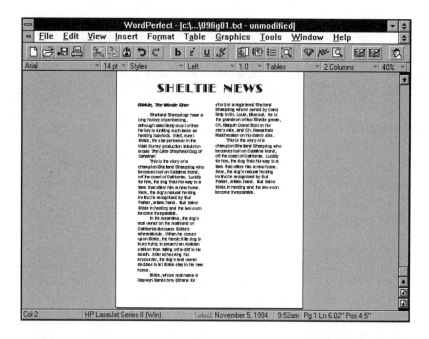

Figure 9.2
A document using two balanced newspaper columns.

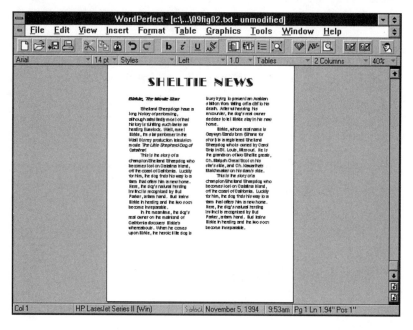

Parallel columns
Text flows across the page in rows.

- *Parallel columns.* Text flows across the page in rows. Parallel columns are useful for inventory lists, resumes, schedules, and itineraries (see figure 9.3).

- *Parallel columns with block protect.* WordPerfect makes sure that all text within each parallel column always stays together on the page without being split by a page break. This effect is accomplished much more easily in tables.

Figure 9.3
Text set in three parallel columns.

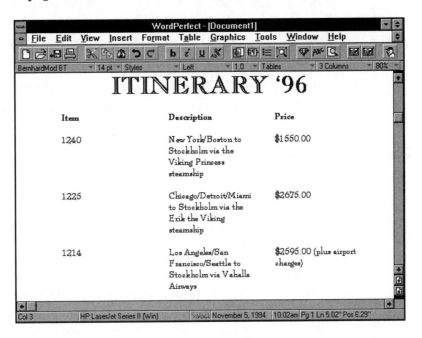

Text columns
Newspaper or parallel Columns created with the Columns command on the Format menu or the Columns button on the Power Bar.

Newspaper and parallel columns are known as *text columns* in order to differentiate them from *tabular columns* (columns created with tabs). When using the WordPerfect Columns feature, the Tab key is used as with any text entry. You do not have to determine tab settings before starting the document. When you want to create newspaper columns, it is easiest to enter the text first and then define the column characteristics.

In order to work through the following tutorials, you must create the document shown in figure 9.4. Save the document as COLUMNS.DOC and keep it displayed on-screen. Type the document exactly as shown, including the centered title.

9

Figure 9.4
The sample
document.

The Depth Gauge

Dive Trip to Cozumel

That's right, folks, this year No Sierra Divers is taking its Fall dive trip to the island of Cozumel. If you've never been there before, Cozumel is an island off the coast of Mexico's Yucatan Peninsula, about 30 miles south of Cancun. It has one small city, a dozen or so hotels, twice as many dive shops, and miles and miles of coral reefs.

The water is 80 down to 100 feet, so you won't need a wetsuit! This means less weight, too. You may want to wear a T-shirt to keep your straps from chafing, but otherwise all you'll need are mask, fins, snorkel, regulator, and BC (and a swim suit, of course). You can rent tanks anywhere.

By law you can't wear gloves or a dive knife into the water. The entire island is a national park, and everything underwater is protected: fish, plants, and especially coral. Believe me, it's a lot harder to grab a piece of coral for a souvenir without gloves. So, while they can't watch every driver underwater every minute, they can stop you from going under equipped to do damage.

There's a good reason for it, too. Did you know that coral only grows a fraction of an inch per year? At Palancar Gardens, you will see blocks of coral the size of apartment buildings. The reefs are thousands of years old. Yet it only takes one careless move to break off a piece of fan coral that took hundreds of years to grow. (We're assuming that no one's going souvenir hunting on purpose, right?)

For those of you who can bear to spend a day out of water, there is an optional day trip to Tulum, a Mayan archeological site on the mainland. The day won't be a complete waste, however, since the trip includes a stop at Xelha, a protected lagoon that has to be seen in order to appreciate it.

You can use the Columns button on the Power Bar to set as many as five standard newspaper columns. You learn how to do this in the following tutorial.

Defining Newspaper Columns with the Columns Button

To use the Columns button to define newspaper columns, follow these steps:

Note: *If you did not create the document shown in figure 9.4, you must do so before proceeding.*

❶ Position the insertion point at the place in the document where you want the columns to begin.

❷ Click the Columns button on the Power Bar.

The Columns pop-up menu is displayed (see figure 9.5).

Figure 9.5
The Columns
pop-up menu.

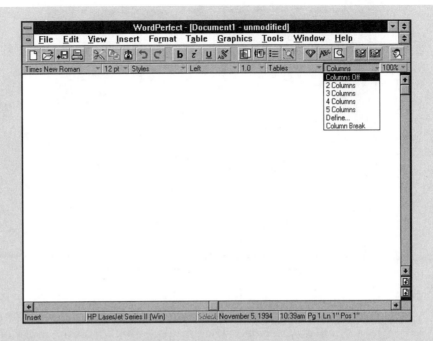

❸ Drag to the Columns command that you want in the pop-up menu. Release the mouse button to choose the command.

You can turn off the Columns feature anywhere in the document to return to normal text.

Turning Off the Columns Feature

To turn off the Columns feature, choose one of the following methods:

❶ Click the Columns button on the Power Bar and select the Columns Off command.

❷ Open the Format menu, choose Columns, and then choose Off from the cascading menu.

Defining Columns Using the Columns Dialog Box

If you need to create more than five columns or you want to choose a column type other than the standard newspaper type, you must use the options available in the Columns dialog box. In this dialog box, you designate the number and type of columns, the spacing between columns, and the column width (see figure 9.6).

9

Figure 9.6

The Columns dialog box.

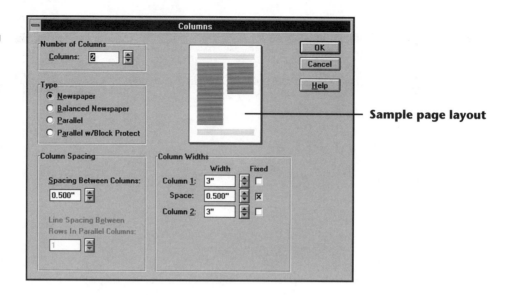

Sample page layout

The following options appear in the Columns dialog box:

- *Number of Columns.* The default setting for Number of Columns is 2. You can create as many as 24 columns.

- *Type.* You can choose from four types of columns: **N**ewspaper (the default), **B**alanced Newspaper, **P**arallel, and P**a**rallel w/Block Protect.

- *Column Spacing.* By default, WordPerfect divides the line length into columns of equal size with a distance of one-half inch between columns. To change the amount of space between each column (this space is known as the *gutter*), enter a new value in the **S**pacing Between Columns text box or click the up- or down-arrow button to increase or decrease the value in the text box.

- *Line Spacing Between Rows in Parallel Columns.* This option appears when choosing either type of parallel column. When you want to use spacing other than single spacing in the lines of text in each column, choose this option and enter the new line spacing in its text box.

You can use the options in the Column Widths area of the Columns dialog box to make adjustments to the widths of the columns or to the amount of space between each pair of columns. These options follow:

- *Width.* To vary the width of the columns, enter a new column width measurement in the text box of the appropriate column. As with other measurements in WordPerfect, enter column width measurements as whole numbers or decimal expressions.

- *Space.* To vary the gutter space for a particular pair of columns, enter the new settings in the **S**pacing Between Columns text box.

- *Fixed.* Choose this check box to ensure that the chosen column or spacing dimension remains fixed as you defined it. If the Fixed check box does not contain an x, WordPerfect may vary the dimensions you enter for column width or spacing in order to fit all columns within the specified margins.

Creating Newspaper Columns

To create newspaper columns for COLUMNS.DOC using the Columns dialog box, perform these steps:

1 Position the cursor at the location in the document where you want the columns to begin. For this tutorial, place the cursor at the beginning of the first sentence of the first paragraph (before the word *That's*).

2 Open the Format menu, choose Columns, and then choose Define.

The Columns dialog box appears (refer to figure 9.6).

3 In the Number of Columns text box, enter the number of columns you want (you can create up to 24). For this tutorial, use the default setting of 2 Columns.

4 Choose the Newspaper command button (the default) in the Type area as the type of column to use.

5 To change the amount of space between columns (the gutter), enter a value in the Spacing Between Columns text box. For this tutorial, keep the spacing set to a distance of one-half inch (0.500"), which is the default.

6 To see how the columns will appear, refer to the layout of the sample page in the upper right of the Columns dialog box.

7 Click OK to turn on the columns in your document (see figure 9.7).

Make any needed adjustments to improve the document's appearance.

Figure 9.7
COLUMNS.DOC has been split into two columns.

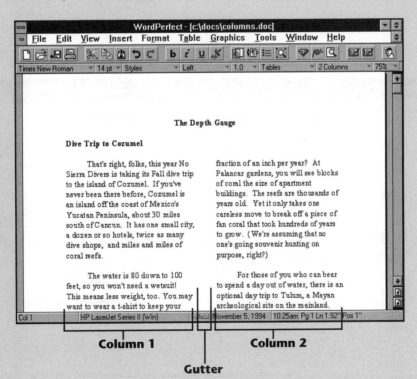

9

Objective 2: Edit in Columns

In the preceding tutorial, you learned to add newspaper-style columns to text you already created. Defining newspaper columns first and then creating the text can be painfully slow because WordPerfect constantly must adjust everything you type to fit within the columns.

Note: *Defining parallel columns first and then adding text is the only recommended way to use parallel columns. Information you normally format in parallel columns, however, is much more easily accomplished in WordPerfect tables. Because you learn about tables later in this chapter, parallel columns are not discussed here. (For more information on parallel columns, see your WordPerfect reference manual, or use the online help.)*

After you format your text in newspaper columns, you still can add or edit text and adjust column widths.

Moving the Insertion Point through Columns

You often need to edit text in columns—for content or to change the length of sentences so that paragraphs fit more neatly. Moving the insertion point with the cursor keys can be quite slow. Instead, consider these shortcuts for moving the insertion point:

- Move the insertion point to a new location by clicking in the text you want to edit.

- Press Alt+≤ to move the insertion point to the next column to the left.

- Press Alt+≥ to move the insertion point to the next column to the right.

- Choose **G**o To from the **E**dit menu and use the Go To dialog box to place the insertion point in different columns.

Using the Ruler to Adjust the Widths of Newspaper Columns

To change the width of a column by using the Ruler, perform the following steps:

1 Display the Ruler Bar by choosing **R**uler Bar from the **V**iew menu.

2 Position the insertion point at the place in the text where you want to adjust the column's width.

3 Drag the appropriate Column-Margin icon to the desired position on the Ruler (see figure 9.8). Notice the dotted line that appears as you drag the margin icon to the new position. When you release the mouse button, WordPerfect reflows the text according to the new column widths.

Figure 9.8
The Column-
Margin icon
dragged to
adjust the
column margin
setting.

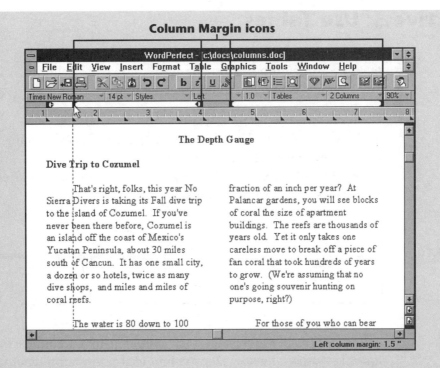

④ To adjust the size of two adjacent columns without changing the size of the gutter, position the cursor where the columns begin. Click the gutter area (the gray area between the Column Margin icons) to drag it to a new position on the Ruler. Notice a double set of dotted lines as you drag the gutter (see figure 9.9).

Figure 9.9
Adjusting two
adjacent
columns by
moving the
gutter area.

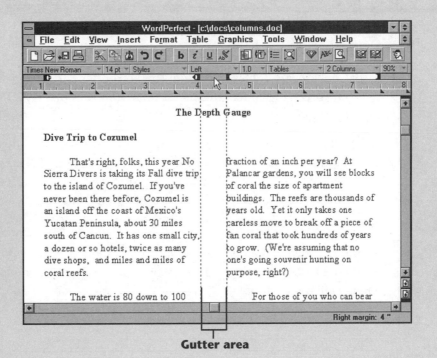

9

Objective 3: Use Tables

The Tables feature is one of the most useful features found in WordPerfect. A *table* is a grid of information arranged in rows and columns. The format is similar to parallel columns, but much easier to work with.

Understanding Table Layout

Tables are very much like spreadsheets. Data in tables is arranged in columns (column A, column B, and so on) and in rows (row 1, row 2, and so on). The intersection of rows and columns is called a *cell* (for example, cell A1). Figure 9.10 shows a table with columns, rows, and cells.

Figure 9.10
A table of Columns and rows, with data in cell A1.

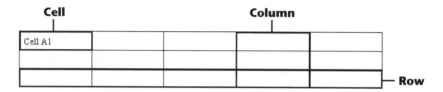

Before you create a table, take a few moments to determine what your table must look like—especially how many columns of information your table will need. If you want to create a simple phone roster that includes employee names, office numbers, and phone numbers, for example, you create a table with three Columns. You may not know the exact number of rows you need, but you can add rows as you enter data in the table.

Creating a Table

There are two methods for creating a table. To use the easier method first, follow these steps:

❶ Click on the Tables button on the Power Bar and hold down the mouse button. WordPerfect displays a small grid that displays the words No Table at the top.

❷ Drag the mouse down and to the right until you have highlighted the number of columns and rows you need (see figure 9.11). WordPerfect also displays the number of columns and rows you have selected in the Title Bar of the dialog box. Highlight three columns and three rows, for example, and note that the Title Bar indicates 3x3. Release the mouse button.

WordPerfect creates a perfectly proportional table of three columns. Note that when the insertion point is in the table, the Toolbar changes by adding several table-related functions.

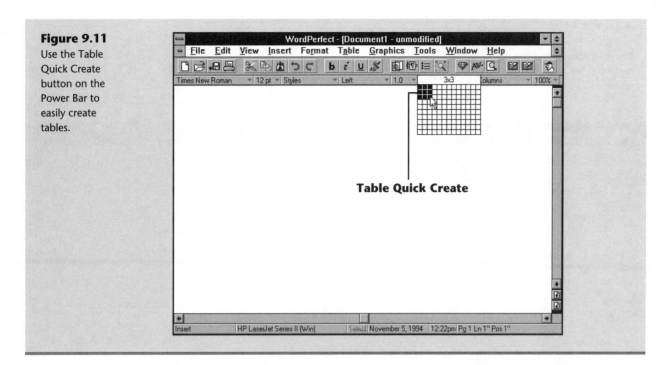

Figure 9.11
Use the Table Quick Create button on the Power Bar to easily create tables.

The second method for creating a table is to open the T**a**ble menu and choose **C**reate; or press F12. In the Table Create dialog box that appears, specify the number of **C**olumns and **R**ows you want and click OK.

Entering Data in a Table

To enter data in a table, position the cursor in the cell where you want data and begin typing. As you reach the right margin of the cell, your data wraps to a second line and the table row expands to accommodate the additional line (see figure 9.12 and enter the text you see there).

Figure 9.12
Entering more than one line of text in a cell expands the table row.

Employee Name (Last Name First) I		

To continue entering text in the next adjacent cell, press Tab. The cursor advances to the next cell to the right. To move the cursor to the preceding cell, press ⬆Shift+Tab. If the cursor is in the last cell of a row, pressing Tab moves the cursor to the far left cell of the next row.

Enter the information you see in figure 9.13 before proceeding to the next section.

As you continue to add data, you need to add rows to your table. To do so, simply position the cursor in the last cell of the table (cell C3, for example) and press Tab. WordPerfect expands the table by adding a row.

9

Figure 9.13
A table with one row for headings and two rows of data

Employee Name (Last Name First)	Office Number	Phone Number
Jones, Regina M.	B-3444	2-1408
Swenson, Marla S.	B-3466	2-1498

Adding and Deleting Table Rows

Suppose that you need to add a row in the middle of the table for Robin Adams, so that her name will appear in alphabetical order. Follow these steps:

1 Position the cursor at the location in which you need the new row (for example, in the Jones row).

2 Open the **T**able menu and choose **I**nsert. WordPerfect displays the Columns/Rows dialog box.

3 Choose the **R**ows (1 row), and **B**efore option buttons, and click OK.

WordPerfect inserts a row between your header row and the Jones row.

> **Tip**
>
> A shortcut method for adding a row in the middle of the table is to position the cursor where you want the new row to appear and press (Alt)+(Insert). You also can choose **I**nsert from the Tables QuickMenu.

4 If you need to delete a row, position the cursor in the row you want to delete, open the **T**able menu, and choose **D**elete. Then, from the Delete dialog box, choose **R**ows (1 row) and click OK.

> **Tip**
>
> Any time you make a change to your table, you can reverse the change by clicking the Undo button on the Toolbar or choosing **U**ndo from the **E**dit menu. Using Undo makes working with tables much easier.

5 Finish adding data to your table until it matches the table in figure 9.14.

Figure 9.14
A table complete with a header row and four rows of data.

Employee Name (Last Name First)	Office Number	Phone Number
Adams, Robin	C-4333	2-1467
Jones, Regina M.	B-3444	2-1408
Swenson, Marla S.	B-3466	2-1498
Ziegler, Jonathan	D-3244	2-1356

By default, WordPerfect creates evenly spaced columns. If your data varies in length, you may want to adjust the column widths to make your data more readable. The first column could be slightly wider so that the header fits on one line, for example.

Adjusting Table Column Widths

To adjust the width of a column, follow these steps:

❶ Position the mouse pointer on the line separating columns A and B. The pointer turns to a double arrow.

❷ Click-and-drag the column separator line to the right. WordPerfect displays a dashed line to show the new location of the line you are dragging (see figure 9.15).

Figure 9.15
Drag the table column separator line to adjust table column widths

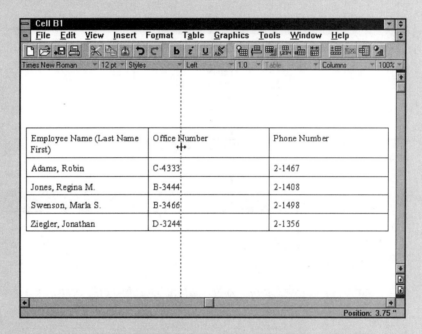

❸ When the column width is the way you want it, release the mouse button; WordPerfect adjusts the column accordingly.

Note: *You cannot drag a column line past another column line.*

Another quick and useful method for adjusting table columns is to use the Size Column to Fit feature, which adjusts the width of the column to fit the longest line of text.

Using the Size Column to Fit Feature

To use the Size Column to Fit feature, follow these steps:

❶ Position the cursor in the column you want to adjust (for example, column A).

9

(continues)

Using the Size Column to Fit Feature (continued)

2 Position the mouse pointer anywhere on the table and open the QuickMenu by clicking the right mouse button.

3 From the QuickMenu, choose Size Column to Fit (see figure 9.16).

Figure 9.16
Use the QuickMenu to size the column width.

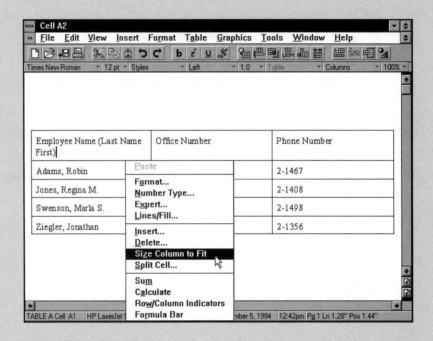

Use the Size Column to Fit feature to adjust each of the columns in your phone roster table.

Note: *The Size Column to Fit feature usually works best if you start with the far left column and then continue to adjust each column to the right.*

Joining Table Cells

Suppose that you want a single cell across the top of the table as a title for your roster. Follow these steps:

1 Use the method described in "Adding and Deleting Table Rows" to add a row to the beginning of your table.

2 Click the mouse in cell A1 (a blank cell) and drag to cell C1 (the last cell in the first row). WordPerfect selects each cell in the row.

3 Open the Table menu, choose Join, and then choose Cell. Or choose Join Cells from the QuickMenu.

Your table now has one single cell across the top (cell A1), as shown in figure 9.17.

Figure 9.17
You can join two
or more cells
into one cell.

Employee Name (Last Name First)	Office Number	Phone Number
Adams, Robin	C-4333	2-1467
Jones, Regina M.	B-3444	2-1408
Swenson, Marla S.	B-3466	2-1498
Ziegler, Jonathan	D-3244	2-1356

Note: *You also can split cells into columns or rows by choosing **S**plit Cells from the QuickMenu.*

You can select and format table text as you do any other text in your document. However, you also can format entire cells, rows, or columns so that whenever you enter data into a formatted cell, the data takes on the format attributes of the cell.

Formatting Table Cells

Suppose that you want the text you enter in cell A1 to be centered and in bold-face. Follow these steps to format a cell:

1 Position the cursor in the cell you want to format (for example, cell A1).

2 From the Tables menu or from the QuickMenu, choose Format. WordPerfect displays the Format dialog box (see figure 9.18). The various options apply to cells (the current cell or selected cells).

Figure 9.18
The table
Format dialog
box, used here
for formatting
cells.

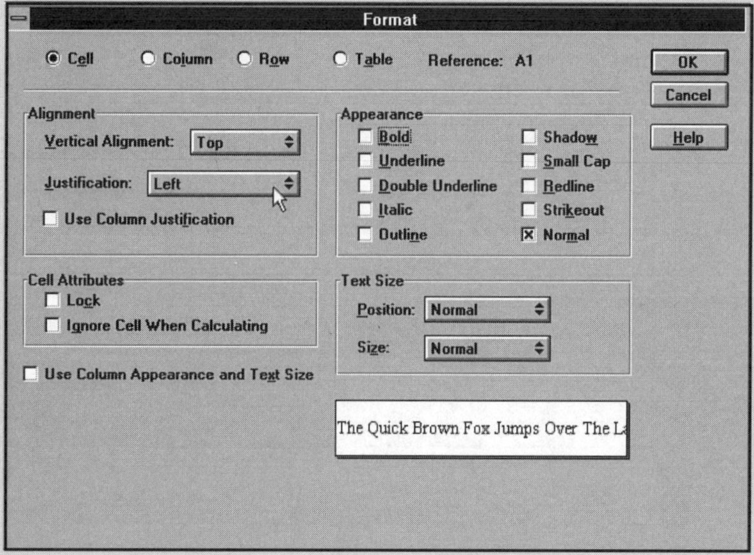

3 Choose Center from the Justification drop-down list.

(continues)

Formatting Table Cells (continued)

❹ From the Appearance area, choose **B**old. Note the text in the preview box at the lower right of the dialog box.

❺ Click OK to apply the attributes to your selected cell.

Now, with the cursor in cell A1, type **Megabucks Corporation Employee Roster**. Note that the text is formatted automatically as centered and in bold-face.

Formatting Table Columns

You also can format entire columns of cells at once. To center the phone numbers column, for example, follow these steps:

❶ Position the cursor in any cell in column C.

❷ From the **T**ables menu or from the QuickMenu, choose **F**ormat. WordPerfect displays the Format dialog box.

❸ Choose the Co**l**umn radio button. Note that the bottom part of the Format dialog box changes to display options that apply to entire columns (see figure 9.19). When formatting columns, for example, you can specify an exact column width.

Figure 9.19
Use the table Format dialog box to format entire columns.

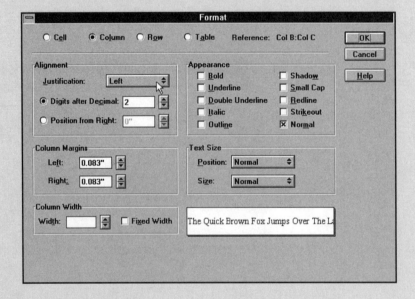

❹ Choose **C**enter from the **J**ustification drop-down list.

❺ Click OK to apply your chosen attributes to the entire column.

You can enhance the readability of your table by adding shading to certain cells. A light gray fill pattern in the headings row would help set it off from the rest of the table data, for example.

Adding Fill Attributes to Table Cells

To add a fill to selected cells, follow these steps:

❶ Click in cell A2 and drag to cell C2 to select all the cells in the headings row.

❷ From the Tables menu or from the QuickMenu, choose Lines/Fill. WordPerfect displays the Table Lines/Fill dialog box (see figure 9.20). The changes you make in this dialog box apply to the current selection of cells.

Figure 9.20

The Table Lines/ Fill dialog box, used for adding shading and lines to table cells.

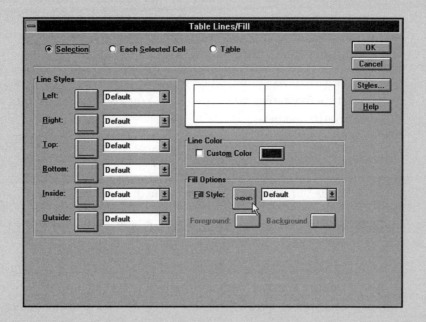

❸ Click on the Fill Style palette button and choose a style from the palette. Alternatively, you can choose a style from the Fill Style drop-down list. Choose a light gray pattern (for example, 5%, the first button on the palette). Note that choosing a dark gray (30% or more) makes it difficult to read the text in the cell.

❹ Click OK to apply the fill style to your selected cells.

❺ Click anywhere else in the table to deselect the table cells and to see the effect of the fill on your table (see the completed phone roster table in figure 9.21).

(continues)

Adding Fill Attributes to Table Cells (continued)

Figure 9.21

A completed phone roster table.

MEGABUCKS CORPORATION EMPLOYEE ROSTER		
Employee Name (Last Name First)	Office Number	Phone Number
Adams, Robin	C-4333	2-1467
Jones, Regina M.	B-3444	2-1408
Swenson, Marla S.	B-3466	2-1498
Ziegler, Jonathan	D-3244	2-1356

Exploring Other Table Features

In this chapter, you learned some of the very basic Tables features. You should have noted that tables format data very much like parallel columns do, but with much greater ease and with more style. You should take the time to study the WordPerfect reference, or to consult WordPerfect on-line help to learn more about other Tables features such as the following:

- *Table Experts.* Table expert styles offer predefined formats that make creating attractive tables quick and easy. You also can save your own formats as customized experts.

- *Change Lines, Borders, and Fills.* Create custom line and fill styles to create just the type of table you need.

- *Table Sort.* You easily can sort the data in your tables.

- *Join or Split Tables.* You can split a table into two tables, or join two tables into one.

- *Table Formulas.* WordPerfect tables feature full spreadsheet functionality, including nearly 100 mathematical, financial, and scientific functions. You also can import spreadsheets directly into WordPerfect tables.

- *Floating Cells.* You can create table cells that appear to be part of your document text, but that function just like table or spreadsheet cells.

As you explore the various Tables features, you will begin to find more and more uses for tables, such as fill-in forms, calendars, rosters, spreadsheets, and more.

Chapter Summary

In this chapter, you learned how to create and edit the four types of WordPerfect columns. You learned how to use the Columns dialog box and the Ruler Bar to adjust column widths; and you also learned how to turn off the Columns feature. Finally, you learned how to create tables and how to change shape, format, and fill patterns of table cells.

Checking Your Skills

True/False Questions

For each of the following statements, circle *T* or *F* to indicate whether the statement is true or false.

T F **1.** WordPerfect for Windows provides four types of columns that can be inserted into a document.

T F **2.** You can define up to 24 columns by using the Columns button.

T F **3.** The *gutter* is the space between the top and bottom margin in a column.

T F **4.** Parallel columns are known as *tabular columns*.

T F **5.** Text columns are set up by pressing ⭾Tab⭾ or using the Indent option.

T F **6.** In newspaper columns, text flows across the page in rows.

T F **7.** Balanced newspaper columns wrap when necessary so that they always line up with each other at the top and bottom of the page.

T F **8.** Parallel columns are easier to use than tables for arranging columns and parallel rows of data.

T F **9.** You can change the width of a table column by dragging the column margin with the mouse.

T F **10.** You can perform math calculations by joining table cells together.

Multiple-Choice Questions

In the blank provided, write the letter of the correct answer for each of the following questions.

___**1.** The default number of columns WordPerfect uses is _____.

   a. 3

   b. 2

   c. none; you must specify the number

   d. none of these answers

___**2.** Newspaper columns commonly are used in all of the following except _____.

   a. magazine articles

   b. inventory lists

   c. newsletters

   d. brochures

9

___**3.** In balanced newspaper columns, _____.

    a. text in each column always stays together on the page

    b. text flows down the first column and then wraps at the bottom of the page and starts the next column

    c. WordPerfect wraps the columns when necessary to make sure that they always align with each other at the top and bottom

    d. text flows across the page

___**4.** WordPerfect supports a maximum of _____ columns.

    a. 24

    b. 5

    c. 42

    d. 3

___**5.** To terminate a column entry and move to the next column when entering text in parallel columns, press _____.

    a. Ctrl+End

    b. Ctrl+↵Enter

    c. Alt+→

    d. none of these answers

___**6.** The *gutter area* is the _____.

    a. gray area on the far right side of the Ruler Bar

    b. gray area between the Column Margin icons

    c. gray area on the far left of the Ruler Bar

    d. white space area in the Ruler Bar for each column

___**7.** To select a number of columns from the pop-up menu on the Power Bar, _____.

    a. type the number of columns needed

    b. scroll through the numbers until the number of your choice appears, and then select it

    c. click on the number you want to use

    d. none of these answers

___**8.** _____ is not possible in a table cell.

   a. Center justification of text and numbers

   b. Use of fill patterns for highlighting effects

   c. Formatting the cell's text into columns

   d. Splitting the cell into two or more rows

___**9.** To change the width of a table column, _____.

   a. change the column line style

   b. use the Make It Fit feature

   c. use Column Width in the Format dialog box

   d. none of these answers

___**10.** To move from one cell to the next in a table, _____.

   a. press ⏎Enter

   b. press Tab↹

   c. press Alt+Tab↹

   d. none of these answers

Fill-in-the-Blank Questions

In the blank provided, write the correct answer for each of the following questions.

1. Use the _____ command to create columns in a document.

2. To change the amount of space between columns, enter a new value in the _____ _____ _____ text box.

3. To adjust the size of two adjacent columns without changing the size of the space between columns, click the _____ area in the Ruler Bar.

4. When editing text in columns, use the _____ key combination to move to a column to the right.

5. You also can use the _____ dialog box to reposition the insertion point in a column.

6. When creating newspaper columns, it is easier to type the text first, then _____ and _____ on columns.

7. When you reach the bottom of a column, WordPerfect moves the insertion point to the _____ of the next _____.

8. When you reach the last cell in a table and press Tab↹, WordPerfect adds a _____ to the table.

9. The intersection of a table column and row is called a _____.

10. The Size Column to Fit feature is found on the _____ menu.

9

Applying Your Skills

Review Exercises

Exercise 1: Editing Columns

Practice editing columns by following these steps:

1. Open the COLUMNS.DOC file.

2. Edit the document by changing the title to a larger font size and making it boldface.

3. Change the subtitle heading by changing the font size and making it boldface.

Notice what happens to the columns in the document due to your editing changes.

Exercise 2: Removing Columns

Practice removing columns by following these steps:

1. Turn off the Columns option for COLUMNS.DOC.

2. Print a copy of the document, displaying the new edited changes that you made in exercise 1.

Exercise 3: Adjusting Column Widths with the Ruler Bar

Practice using the Ruler Bar to adjust column widths by following these steps:

1. Turn Columns back on.

2. Using the Ruler Bar, adjust the width of the columns to a two-inch left margin and a half-inch right margin.

3. Print a copy of the document.

4. Close the document and do not save your changes.

Exercise 4: Creating a Newsletter with Columns

Create a newsletter on a topic of your choice. The newsletter should use the following formats:

1. The title of the newsletter should be in 18-point type and in boldface.

2. Subtitles should be in bold and in a 14-point type size.

3. The body of the text should be in a 12-point type size.

4. The information in the first half of the page should be in two standard newspaper columns. The second half of the document should be in four columns using parallel columns.

5. Save the document as **MYCOLUMN.DOC**.

6. Print the document.

Exercise 5: Editing a Newsletter with Columns

In this exercise, you modify the column structure of the newsletter you created in the preceding exercise.

Open MYCOLUMN.DOC and make the following changes:

1. Change the first half of the document to two balanced newspaper columns.

2. Change the margin setting for the balanced newspaper columns to .5" for the left margin, with a gutter area of 1" beginning at 3.5" and ending at 4.5". Set the right margin at 7.5".

3. In the Parallel Columns with Block Protect section, reset the column margins to the following:

   Col 1: Starts at .5" and ends at 1.5"

   Col 2: Starts at 2" and ends at 3"

   Col 3: Starts at 3.5" and ends at 4.5"

   Col 4: Starts at 5" and ends at 6"

4. Print the document.

5. Save the document as **MYCOLEDT.DOC**.

Continuing Projects

Project 1: Creating and Editing Newspaper Columns

Open the file NEWS.DOC. Create standard newspaper columns for the document. Make the following changes to the document:

1. Insert a subheading above the first paragraph of the document: **New Employees**. Make the font two point sizes larger than the regular text. Underline the text and make it boldface.

2. Insert a second subheading above the paragraph about Mary Foist's promotion: **Employee Promotion**. Follow the same format that you used on the first subtitle.

3. Insert a subheading above the paragraph about the golf outing: **Golf Outing**. Again, use the same format you used for the previous headings.

4. Double space between each subheading and the text that follows it. Single space the remainder of the text. Make any needed adjustments in spacing required to create an attractive document.

5. Save the document as **NEWS.DOC**.

Project 2: Creating Balanced Newspaper Columns

In this project, you balance the columns in the NEWS.DOC file and make other changes to improve its appearance. Follow these steps:

1. Open the NEWS.DOC file.

9

2. Change the columns to balanced newspaper columns.

3. Make changes you think are necessary to make the page look attractive.

4. Print a copy of the document.

5. Close the document, but do not save the changes.

Project 3: Adding a Table to an Existing Document

In this project, you add a table to your training document. You then format the table and print the document. Follow these steps:

1. Open TRAIN5.DOC.

2. Add the following paragraph, beginning on a new page:

> **Once again this year Compuvise will sponsor the Annual Office Automation Seminar that will take place on July 5, 1995. Please check the enclosed schedule to check the specific times of presentations that will be given.**

3. Create a table for the following schedule:

Schedule of Events for Office Automation Seminar		
Time	**Room**	**Session**
9:00 a.m.	Lobby	Registration/Coffee
10:00 a.m.	Pines	"Beyond Mail Merge"
10:45 a.m.	Dells	"Spice up Documents with Graphics"
11:30 a.m.	Flambeau	Lunch
12:30 p.m.	Oshkosh	"Don't Print It. E-mail It."
1:30 p.m.	Oshkosh	"Find What You Need on the Internet"
2:30 p.m.	Pines	Open Discussion of Topics
3:30 p.m.	Pines	Summary

4. Join the top row of cells and boldface and center the title.

5. Right justify the Time column and size it to fit.

6. Center the Room column and size it to fit.

7. Add a gray fill pattern to the heading row.

8. Type the remainder of the text after the table:

> **Please make your reservations early so you will be ensured a seat. We accept all types of major credit cards or cash. No checks, please.**

9. Save the document as **TRAIN6.DOC**.

10. Print the document.

CHAPTER 10

Adding Graphics to Documents

In Chapter 5, "Formatting Paragraphs and Characters," you learned how to enhance text by selecting fonts and adding text attributes. Adding graphics is another way to enhance your documents. WordPerfect makes adding graphics to your documents easy. In this chapter, you learn how to combine graphics with text, and how to resize and reposition them. You also learn how to insert borders and lines into a document.

Objectives

By the time you finish this chapter, you will have learned to

1. Work with Graphics

2. Edit Graphics Using the Image Tools Palette

3. Use Borders and Lines

Objective 1: Work with Graphics

Graphics box
A box defined to hold a figure, a table, text, user-defined elements, or an equation.

In a WordPerfect for Windows document, you can place images in one of four types of graphics boxes: image, equation, text, and custom. Each box also can hold certain characteristics such as border style and caption style. You can use a WordPerfect graphics box to insert text, graphics, charts, or graphs created with other software programs such as Microsoft Excel or Lotus 1-2-3. You can place graphics boxes in the body of a document and in headers and footers.

To complete the following tutorials, open the document named COLUMNS.DOC.

Inserting a Graphics Image into a Document

To place a graphics image into COLUMNS.DOC, perform the following steps:

1 Position the insertion point at the place in the document where you want the graphics image to appear. For this tutorial, place the cursor two lines below the last paragraph in the second column.

2 Open the **G**raphics menu and choose **I**mage.

WordPerfect displays the Insert Image dialog box and the contents of the GRAPHICS directory (see figure 10.1).

Figure 10.1

The Insert Image dialog box.

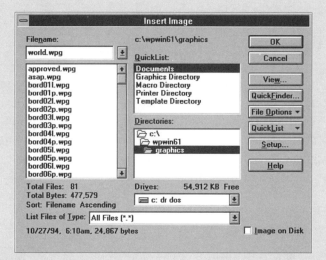

3 Select the directory in which the graphics files reside; then enter the file name in the File**n**ame text box. For this tutorial, use WordPerfect's GRAPHICS directory. WordPerfect supplies a number of graphics files that come with the program. By default, WordPerfect displays only WordPerfect graphics files (with the extension WPG) in the File**n**ame list box.

4 Choose WORLD.WPG from the File**n**ame list box.

5 To preview the image before retrieving it and placing it in the document, click the Vie**w** button.

The graphic is displayed in the Viewer window.

Note: *If you are using a graphics image that was created in a different software package, the program must be compatible with WordPerfect in order for you to view the graphics image in the Viewer window.*

6 Click OK in the Open File dialog box.

WordPerfect returns you to the document window and inserts the graphics image into a figure box at the location of the insertion point. The Graphics Feature Bar also is displayed (see figure 10.2).

Figure 10.2

The document with the inserted graphics image and Graphics Feature Bar.

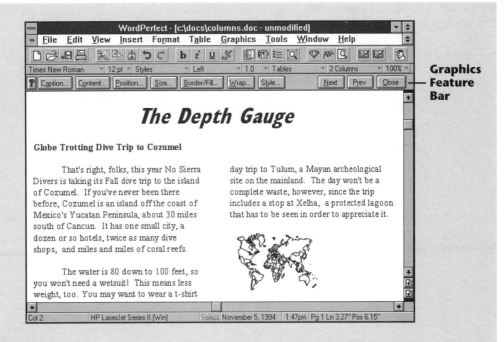

Graphics Feature Bar

10

❼ Click the left mouse button outside the graphics box to deselect it. (You cannot move the cursor down the page until you deselect the box.)

Repositioning a Graphics Image

Any time you retrieve a graphics image into a document, you can use the mouse to move the graphic to a new position on the page.

If you position a graphics image in the middle of the page in a single-column layout, WordPerfect does not split the text around the left and right sides of its graphics box, but instead wraps all the text on the left side.

To wrap text around the left and right sides, as well as on the top and bottom, of a graphic that is centered on the page, you must change the way the text wraps around the graphics box or set the text on the page in two newspaper columns before you position the image between them.

Repositioning a Graphics Image

To reposition the graphics image placed in the preceding tutorial, perform the following steps:

❶ Position the pointer anywhere in the graphics box and click the left mouse button.

The pointer changes to a four-headed arrow, and sizing handles appear around the graphics box (see figure 10.3).

(continues)

Repositioning a Graphics Image (continued)

Figure 10.3
The pointer changed to a four-headed arrow, with sizing handles.

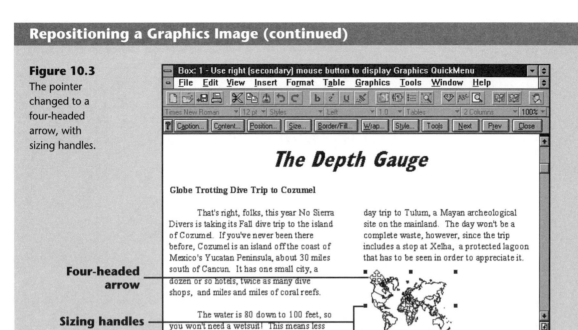

Four-headed arrow

Sizing handles

➋ Use the four-headed arrow pointer to drag the graphics box to the desired location on the page. (You actually drag a dotted outline of the graphics box and the mouse pointer changes to a drag-and-drop icon; WordPerfect does not redraw the picture until you release the mouse button.)

For this tutorial, drag the graphics box to directly below the first heading, "Globe Trotting Dive Trip to Cozumel" (see figure 10.4).

Figure 10.4
Drag the dotted outline to below the first heading in the document.

Drag-and-drop icon

New graphics box position

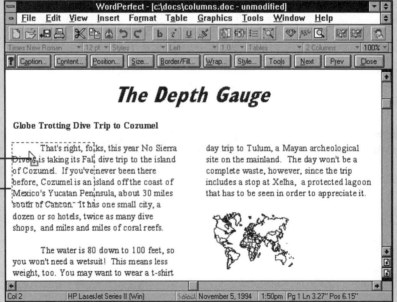

3 Release the mouse button when the graphics box is in the position you want on the page (see figure 10.5). Note that your text wraps around the graphics box.

Figure 10.5
The repositioned graphics box.

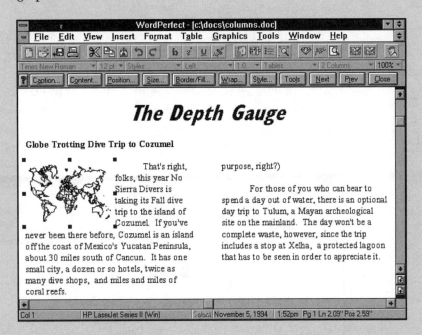

4 Click the pointer somewhere on the page outside the graphics image to deselect the graphics box.

You can change the text flow around your graphics box by choosing the **W**rap command in the Graphics Feature Bar.

Tip

You can select many features related to graphics boxes by clicking the right mouse button on the graphics box to display the Graphics QuickMenu.

Resizing a Graphics Image

To change the size of a graphics image, follow these steps:

1 Position the pointer within the graphics box and click the left mouse button.

The mouse pointer changes to the four-headed arrow and sizing handles appear around the sides of the graphics box.

(continues)

Resizing a Graphics Image (continued)

2 Position the mouse pointer on the appropriate sizing handle until the pointer changes to a double-headed arrow. Then drag the handle until the graphics box is the size you want it.

To make the image wider or narrower, drag the sizing handle on either side of the graphics box. To make the image shorter or taller, drag the sizing handle on the bottom or top side upward or downward. To change both the width and length of the graphics image at the same time, drag the sizing handle in any corner diagonally upward or downward. WordPerfect redraws the graphics box along with the image, and existing text reflows around the new size (see figure 10.6).

Figure 10.6
The resized graphics image.

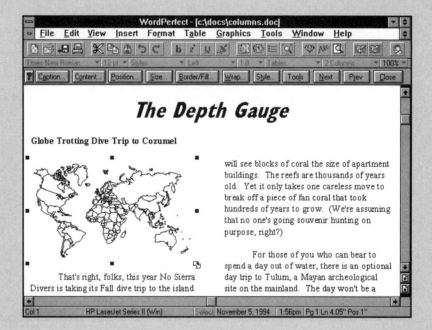

3 When the image is the size you want, release the mouse button and click the pointer outside the graphic to deselect the graphics box.

WordPerfect 6.1 for Windows makes it easy to add captions to graphics boxes. Captions are used to explain the contents of the graphics box. The program sequentially numbers each type of graphics box. You can use the figure number that WordPerfect provides for you, or you can enter a caption of your own.

Adding a Caption to a Graphics Image

To add a caption of your own to the graphics image, perform the following steps:

1 Click the graphics box containing the graphics image for which you want to add a caption. This action selects the graphics box.

2 Choose the Caption command from the Graphics Feature Bar.

The Box Caption dialog box appears (see figure 10.7).

Figure 10.7
The Box Caption
dialog box.

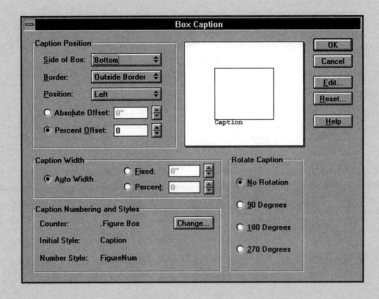

The Box Caption dialog box includes a variety of options you can use to customize the way a caption appears. Some of these follow:

- *Side of Box*. Places the caption on the desired side of the graphics box.

- *Border*. Displays the caption inside the box border or outside the box border.

- *Position*. Specifies how the caption is aligned relative to the side of the box where it is placed.

- *Caption Width*. Enables you to avoid excessive white space above or below the caption.

- *Caption Numbering and Styles*. Enables you to choose numbering styles other than the default, which is Figure 1, Figure 2, and so on.

3 Change any of the Caption options you want to modify, including the position of the caption in relation to the graphics box and the rotation of the caption text (for example, vertical or horizontal text captions).

4 Change any other caption Position to Center.

5 Click the Edit button from the Box Caption dialog box. You are returned to the actual figure box to make changes to the caption (see figure 10.8).

(continues)

Adding a Caption to a Graphics Image (continued)

Figure 10.8

Editing your caption directly on the graphics box.

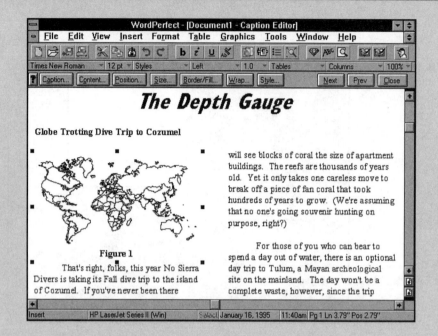

Note: *If you are in Draft mode, WordPerfect displays the Caption Editor screen.*

For this tutorial, you are going to change the figure number to a caption with words.

6 Press Del to delete the Figure #.

7 Type **Come to Cancun!**

8 Click outside the graphics box or, if you are in Draft mode, click **C**lose to return to the document from the Caption Editing screen.

The caption is placed directly below the graphics figure box (see figure 10.9).

Figure 10.9
The caption is inserted under the graphics image box.

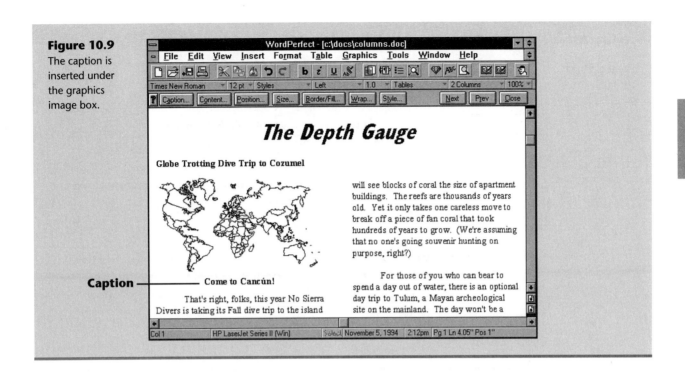

Caption ————

Objective 2: Edit Graphics Using the Image Tools Palette

With WordPerfect for Windows, you can edit graphics images directly in the document with the Image Tools palette. You can use the tools to crop an image in its graphics box; rotate, invert (flip), or scale an image; and reset the brightness and contrast for an image.

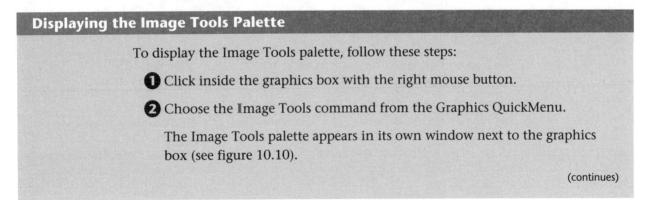

Displaying the Image Tools Palette

To display the Image Tools palette, follow these steps:

1 Click inside the graphics box with the right mouse button.

2 Choose the Image Tools command from the Graphics QuickMenu.

The Image Tools palette appears in its own window next to the graphics box (see figure 10.10).

(continues)

Displaying the Image Tools Palette (continued)

Figure 10.10
The Image Tools palette.

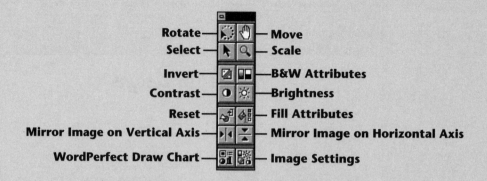

Rotate — Move
Select — Scale
Invert — B&W Attributes
Contrast — Brightness
Reset — Fill Attributes
Mirror Image on Vertical Axis — Mirror Image on Horizontal Axis
WordPerfect Draw Chart — Image Settings

❸ To find out the function of a particular button in the Image Tools palette, position the mouse pointer on any tool. A brief description of that tool's function appears in the Title Bar of the WordPerfect program window.

❹ To close the Image Tools palette, click the Control menu box and choose Close.

Because the Image Tools palette is displayed in its own window, you can move it around the document editing window by dragging it by its Title Bar. You cannot resize the Image Tools palette, however.

After you have displayed the Image Tools palette, you can enlarge the figure in its graphics box by scaling it; you also can crop the figure by moving it within its graphics box so that only part of the total image is seen.

Scaling a Graphics Image

To scale a graphics image, perform these steps:

❶ Click the Scale Image button (the one with the magnifying glass) to display the three additional buttons to the right (see figure 10.11).

Figure 10.11
Choosing the
Scale Image
button produces
three additional
tool buttons.

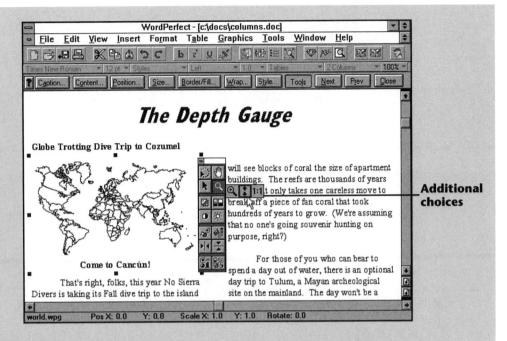

Additional
choices

2 To enlarge just a part of the image, click the Magnifying Glass icon to change the pointer to a magnifying glass with crosshairs.

3 Use this pointer to drag a bounding box around the part of the graphics image you want to enlarge.

4 Release the mouse button.

The part of the image you selected is enlarged to the size of the entire graphics box.

Enlarging or Decreasing the Size of an Image

To enlarge or decrease the size of an image in its graphics box using the Image Tools palette, follow these steps:

1 Choose the second button that appears to the right when you click the Scale Image button (the one with the up and down arrows).

WordPerfect adds a vertical scroll bar to the graphics box. You use this scroll bar to make the image larger or smaller.

(continues)

Enlarging or Decreasing the Size of an Image (continued)

② Click the down arrow to decrease the image size or the up arrow to increase the image size.

You also can quickly change the image size by dragging the scroll box in the scroll bar.

Cropping a Graphics Image

To crop an image so that only a part of it is displayed, perform the following steps:

❶ Click the Move button on the Tools palette (refer to figure 10.10).

When you position the pointer within the graphics box, the pointer changes to a hand.

❷ Use the hand pointer to drag the image within the graphics box, and then release the mouse button when the image is cropped to your satisfaction.

Tip

To correct any mistakes you make when editing a graphics image, you can restore the image to its original appearance by clicking the Reset button on the Image Tools palette.

You can use the Rotate button from the Image Tools palette to rotate a graphics image so that the image appears in the graphics box at a different angle; the following tutorial tells you how to do this.

Rotating a Graphics Image

To rotate a graphics image, follow these steps:

❶ Click the Rotate button on the Image Tools palette.

WordPerfect displays rotation handles at each of the inside corners of the graphics box (see figure 10.12).

Figure 10.12
Rotating an
image.

Rotation
handle

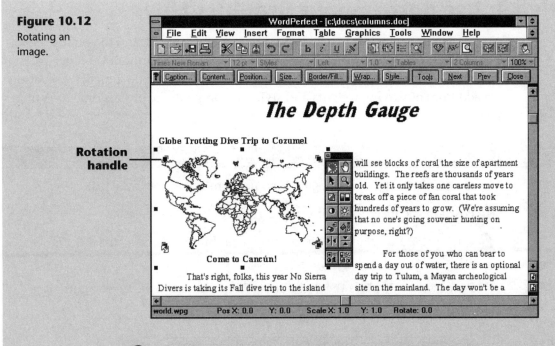

2 Click on one of the rotation handles, and drag in the direction you want to rotate the graphics image (clockwise or counter-clockwise). As you drag, the program indicates the degree of rotation on the Status Bar.

3 Release the mouse button.

WordPerfect redraws the image rotated to the desired angle.

You may want to flip a graphics image so that a mirrored image appears in the graphics box; the following tutorial explains how to do this.

Flipping a Graphics Image

To flip an image, perform the following steps:

1 Select the graphic you want to flip.

2 Open the Image Tools palette.

3 Choose the Mirror Image on Vertical Axis button or the Mirror Image on Horizontal Axis button (refer to figure 10.10) to flip the image.

Before beginning the next set of tutorials, reset your graphics figure to its original form (the way it appeared prior to scaling a graphics image). Click on the Reset button on the Image Tools palette (the fifth button on the left side of the palette).

Objective 3: Use Borders and Graphics Lines

Borders
Graphics lines around a paragraph or page, or between or around newspaper columns in a document.

WordPerfect contains many decorative borders that you can add to your documents. These ready-made designs are perfect additions for announcements or invitations, or you can use them to set off text within other documents. You also can add lines of varying weights and styles to complete the professional look of a document.

Adding Borders to a Graphics Box

To add a border to a graphics figure box, perform the following steps:

1 Position the insertion point in the graphics box and select it.

2 Click the Border/Fill button from the Graphics Feature Bar (refer to figure 10.12).

WordPerfect displays the Box Border/Fill Styles dialog box (see figure 10.13).

Figure 10.13
The Box Border/ Fill Styles dialog box.

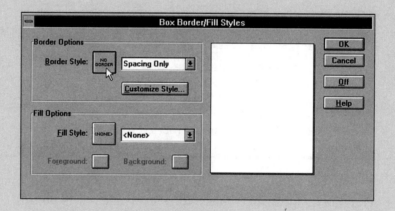

3 To choose a border style to apply to the graphics figure box, click the down arrow of the text box for the Border Style option to activate the drop-down list.

4 Choose Shadow from the drop-down list.

5 To add a fill style to the graphics figure box, click the down arrow of the text box for the Fill Style option to activate the drop-down list.

6 Choose 40% from the drop-down list.

7 When the border appears in the example box, click OK to return to your document.

WordPerfect redraws the border to suit the graphics figure (see figure 10.14).

Figure 10.14
The document displays the graphics figure with a shadow style and a 40 percent border fill.

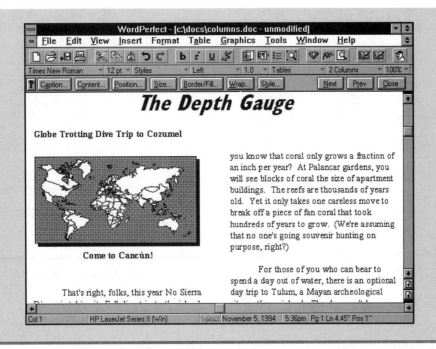

Removing a Border

To remove a border from around a figure box, follow these steps:

1 Position the insertion point somewhere in the figure box, and click the **B**order/Fill button on the Graphics Feature Bar.

2 In the **B**order Style text box, click on the down arrow to activate the drop-down list.

3 Choose None for the border style.

If you want to emphasize or set off text, you can create a graphics text box. An easier method, however, is simply to place a border around existing text.

Adding Borders to Paragraphs

To place a drop shadow border around a paragraph of text, follow these steps:

1 Position the cursor in the paragraph around which you want to place the border.

2 Open the Fo**r**mat menu, choose **P**aragraph, and then choose **B**order/Fill. WordPerfect displays the Paragraph Border dialog box (see figure 10.15).

(continues)

Adding Borders to Paragraphs (continued)

Figure 10.15
Use the Paragraph Border dialog box to add borders and fills to paragraphs.

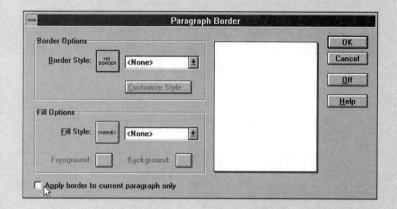

❸ Click on the **B**order style palette button or the drop-down list and choose a border style (for example, the Shadow style).

❹ If you want the style to apply only to the current paragraph, make sure the A**p**ply Border to Current Paragraph Only box is checked.

❺ Make any other changes you want. Choose a 5 percent fill pattern, for example, from the **F**ill Style palette or drop-down menu.

❻ Click OK to apply the border to your paragraph (see figure 10.16).

Figure 10.16
An easy way to highlight a paragraph is to use the Paragraph Border/Fill feature.

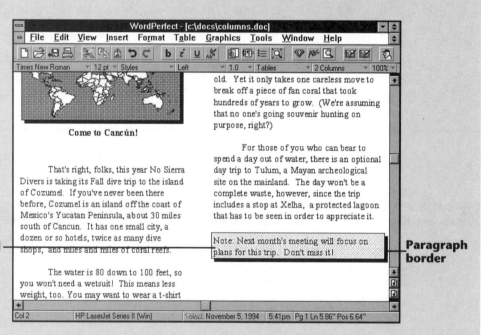

You also can quickly and easily add borders to entire pages; you can use the Page Borders feature or the special page border graphics that come with WordPerfect.

Adding Borders to Pages

To use the Page Border feature, follow these steps:

1 Position the cursor on the page on which you want to place the border.

2 Open the Format menu, choose Page, and then choose Border/Fill. (The Page Border dialog box is functionally identical to the Paragraph Border dialog box shown in figure 10.15.)

3 From the Border Style palette or drop-down list, choose the border style you want to use.

4 If you want the style to apply only to the current page, make sure that the Apply Border to Current Page Only box is checked.

5 Make any other changes you want, such as the fill pattern.

6 Click OK to apply the border to your page.

To use WordPerfect special page border graphics, you can use the PGBORDER macro:

1 Position the cursor on the page on which you want to place the border.

2 Open the Tools menu, choose Macro, and choose Play. Or press Alt+F10.

3 In the Play Macro dialog box, type **pgborder** and click OK. WordPerfect then displays a list of special borders, such as Confetti, Pencil, and so on (see figure 10.17).

Figure 10.17
The PGBORDER macro enables you to choose a fancy page border.

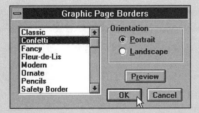

4 Choose the pattern you want. You can preview the pattern.

5 Click OK to apply the border to your document page (see figure 10.18).

(continues)

Adding Borders to Pages (continued)

Figure 10.18

The document with page, paragraph, and graphics box borders.

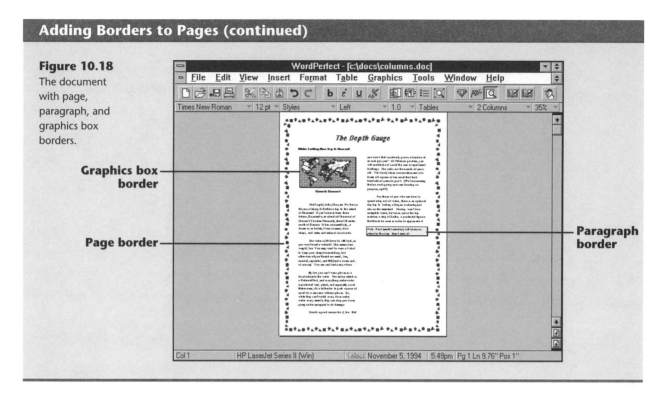

Graphics box border

Page border

Paragraph border

Graphics lines

Horizontal or vertical rules of various weights and lengths that you can move and size with the mouse.

Creating Horizontal and Vertical Graphics Lines

With WordPerfect, you can create vertical and horizontal *graphics lines* and place them anywhere on the page. A graphics line can be various colors, lengths, or weights. After you draw a graphics line, you can move or size it directly in the document.

Adding a Horizontal or Vertical Graphics Line to a Document

To add a horizontal or vertical line to a document, perform the following steps:

1 Position the insertion point in the document where you want the graphics line to appear. For this tutorial, place the cursor one line under the title of the document.

2 Open the **G**raphics menu and choose **H**orizontal Line option.

WordPerfect draws a single horizontal line the width of the current left and right margin settings under the title of the document.

If you choose **V**ertical Line, the program draws a single vertical line the length of the current top and bottom margins.

3 To edit the horizontal line setting in order to make it thicker, open the **G**raphics menu and choose the **E**dit Line command.

4 Choose **L**ine Style; then choose the Thick Double option (see figure 10.19).

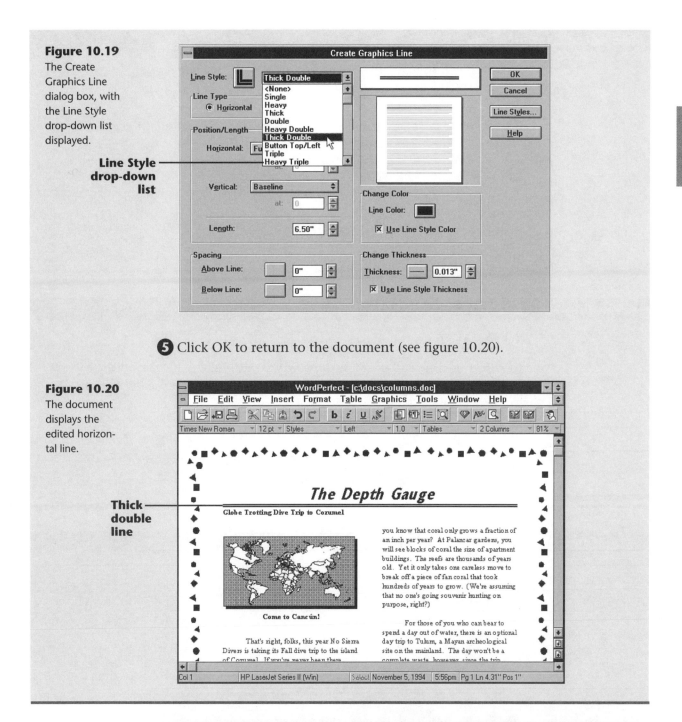

Figure 10.19
The Create Graphics Line dialog box, with the Line Style drop-down list displayed.

Line Style drop-down list

5 Click OK to return to the document (see figure 10.20).

Figure 10.20
The document displays the edited horizontal line.

Thick double line

° Tip

It's a good idea to limit your graphics line styles and thickness amounts to one or two types. When you add too many styles of lines to a document, it can cause the reader to become distracted and produce a very unprofessional look.

Moving a Graphics Line

To move a graphics line, follow these steps:

1 Position the I-beam pointer on the line.

2 When the pointer changes to an arrowhead, click the line to select it. Sizing handles appear around the line.

3 Position the pointer on the line until the pointer changes to a four-headed arrow. Then drag the line to its new position on the page.

Text does not wrap around graphics lines. If you place a graphics line in the middle of text, the line prints over the text.

Changing the Thickness of a Graphics Line

To change the thickness of a graphics line, follow these steps:

1 Select the line and position the pointer on the sizing handle on the top or bottom of a horizontal line, or on the sizing handle on the left or right of a vertical line.

The pointer becomes a double-headed arrow.

2 Drag the pointer away from the line to make the line thicker; drag the pointer toward the line to make it thinner.

Modifying the Length of a Graphics Line

To modify the length of a graphics line, follow these steps:

1 Select the line and position the pointer on the sizing handle on the left or right of a horizontal line, or the top or bottom of a vertical line.

The pointer becomes a double-headed arrow.

2 Drag the pointer away from the line to make the line longer, or drag the pointer toward the line to make the line shorter.

3 When you have finished editing the graphics line, click outside the line to deselect it.

Chapter Summary

In this chapter, you learned how to place graphics images in a document and to move, resize, and add captions to graphics. You also learned how to add borders to a graphics figure and add graphics lines to a document.

Checking Your Skills

True/False Questions

For each of the following statements, circle *T* or *F* to indicate whether the statement is true or false.

T F **1.** Four kinds of graphics boxes can be inserted into a document.

T F **2.** When dragging a graphics box to a new location, you actually drag the border of the graphic.

T F **3.** To make an image taller or shorter, you must drag the sizing handle on the bottom of the figure box upward or downward.

T F **4.** In order for you to see in the Viewer window a graphic created in some other software package, the software must be compatible with WordPerfect.

T F **5.** When repositioning a graphics image in the middle of a page in a single-column layout, WordPerfect splits the text around the left and right sides of the graphics box.

T F **6.** After you bring a graphics image into a document, you cannot move the cursor down the page until you deselect the graphics box.

T F **7.** You can reposition a graphics image with the keyboard or the mouse.

T F **8.** When you enter a caption for a graphics figure, WordPerfect centers it under the graphics box for you.

T F **9.** The Image Tools command is located on the graphics QuickMenu.

T F **10.** The Fill Attributes button has three additional icons that appear to the right when chosen.

Multiple-Choice Questions

In the blank provided, write the letter of the correct answer for each of the following questions.

___ 1. Graphics images provided by WordPerfect have a file name extension of _____.

    a. WGG

    b. WPG

    c. WGR

    d. WGP

___ **2.** To reposition a graphics image, the pointer must change to a _____.

     a. two-headed arrow

     b. cupped hand

     c. four-headed arrow

     d. pointing finger

___ **3.** To make an image wider or narrower, drag the _____.

     a. border around the box

     b. sizing handles

     c. dotted line

     d. none of these answers

___ **4.** The Image Tools palette is found directly under the _____.

     a. **T**ools menu option

     b. **G**raphics menu option

     c. Graphics QuickMenu

     d. **L**ayout menu option

___ **5.** The Magnifying Glass icon enables you to _____.

     a. enlarge an object

     b. enlarge only a part of an object

     c. zoom in on an object

     d. change the pattern of an object

___ **6.** You can do all of the following with the Image Tools palette except _____.

     a. display it

     b. drag it to another location

     c. select from it

     d. resize it

___ **7.** When you drag the mouse in a clockwise or counter-clockwise direction, you are _____.

     a. cropping an image

     b. scaling an image

     c. flipping an image

     d. rotating an image

___**8.** The Mirror Image on Vertical Axis and Mirror Image on Horizontal Axis buttons enable you to _____.

    a. flip an image

    b. rotate an image

    c. crop an image

    d. scale an image

___**9.** You use the _____ option to remove a border from a figure box.

    a. Remove

    b. Delete

    c. Cancel

    d. none of these answers

___**10.** To put a border around a paragraph of text, you use _____.

    a. the Graphics text box

    b. Paragraph Border/Fill

    c. both a. and b.

    d. neither a. nor b.

Fill-in-the-Blank Questions

In the blank provided, write the correct answer for each of the following questions.

1. To make a graphics line thicker, drag the pointer _____ from the line.

2. To turn off borders, select _____ from the Borders Style option box.

3. To create a border for a graphics box, choose the **B**order/Fill button from the _____ _____ _____.

4. To deselect a figure, click the _____ of it.

5. To add a caption to a figure box, click the **C**aption button from the _____ _____ _____.

6. To preview an image before retrieving it and placing it into a document, click the _____ button.

7. When entering a graphics image from another software package into a WordPerfect document, it must be _____ with WordPerfect in order for you to view it.

8. When repositioning a graphics image, you actually drag the _____ _____ of the graphics box.

9. You can change the text flow around a graphics box by choosing the
_____ command in the graphics _____.

10. Use the_____ _____ _____ option to place a
caption on the desired side of a graphics box.

Applying Your Skills

Review Exercises

Exercise 1: Editing a Caption

Practice editing a caption by following these steps:

1. Change the caption in the COLUMNS.DOC file to something of your own
choice.

2. Print the document with the change included.

Exercise 2: Placing a Border

Practice placing a border by following these steps:

1. Place an attractive border around a graphics box in the COLUMNS.DOC
file, using the various Border Style and Border Fill options.

2. Print the document with the changes included.

Exercise 3: Adding a Vertical and Horizontal Line

Practice adding a vertical and horizontal line by following these steps:

1. Add vertical and horizontal lines to the COLUMNS.DOC file. Be creative!
Change the appearance by using the Edit Line option.

2. Record the steps you use to do this project.

3. Print the document when finished.

Exercise 4: Using Page Breaks

In this exercise, you create several descriptions of jobs you have held—each on a
separate page. Follow these steps:

1. Create a document that includes one or two short paragraphs describing
each of the previous jobs you had, as referred to in the JOB3.DOC file. Each
job description should be on its own page.

2. Save the document as **PRTFOLIO.DOC**.

Exercise 5: Adding Graphics to a Document

In this exercise, you add graphic images to your portfolio and print the document. Follow these steps:

1. Open the PRTFOLIO.DOC file.

2. In addition to the one or two paragraphs describing your role at each company, place a graphic on each page that could relate to the company, demonstrating your advertising talent.

3. Print the document.

Continuing Projects

Project 1: Adding Graphics and Lines to Newsletters

In this project, you add a graphics image and a caption. Then, you place lines in a newsletter document. Follow these steps:

1. Place an appropriate WordPerfect graphics image in the NEWS.DOC document.

2. Size and reposition the image.

3. Add a caption to the graphics image box.

4. Add a horizontal line under the title of the document.

5. Save the document and print a copy of it.

Project 2: Using the Image Tools Palette

Practice using the Image Tools palette by following these steps:

1. Use the Image Tools palette to flip, rotate, scale, enlarge, and minimize the graphic you placed in the NEWS.DOC file.

2. Record your steps for each action.

Project 3: Creating a Flyer

In this project, you use your graphics skills to create a flyer promoting your training classes. Follow these steps:

1. Create a flyer to go with the TRAIN5.DOC letter. The flyer should include information on classes being offered at Compuvise. The classes should include "Introduction to Word Processing," "Introduction to Spreadsheets," and "Introduction to Graphics." Provide a time and date for each class offered, as well as any graphical depictions you may think of as conducive to the marketing of the classes.

2. Save the document as **FLYER.DOC**.

3. Print the document.

Appendix A

Working with Windows

Graphical user interface
An easy-to-use method of combining graphics, menus, and plain English commands so that the user communicates with the computer.

Microsoft Windows is a powerful operating environment that enables you to access the power of DOS without memorizing DOS commands and syntax. Windows uses a *graphical user interface* (GUI) so that you can easily see on-screen the tools you need to complete specific file and program management tasks.

This appendix, an overview of the Windows environment, is designed to help you learn the basics of Windows.

Objectives

By the time you finish this appendix, you will have learned to

1. Start Windows

2. Use a Mouse in Windows

3. Understand the Windows Desktop

4. Understand the Program Manager

5. Get Help

6. Get Comfortable with Windows

7. Exit Windows

Objective 1: Start Windows

Many computers are set to open in Windows. If your computer does not automatically open in Windows, however, you can easily access the program.

Starting Windows
To start Windows from the DOS command prompt, follow these steps:

1. Type **win**.

2. Press ⏎Enter. Windows begins loading. When it is loaded, you see the Program Manager window open on-screen.

Window
A rectangular area on-screen in which you view program icons, applications, or documents.

The Program Manager *window* includes many different elements, such as the Menu Bar, Title Bar, and icons. (You open windows, start applications, and select items by selecting the appropriate icon.) Your Program Manager window may look different from the window used in this book's illustrations. For example, you may have different program group icons across the bottom of the Program Manager window (see figure A.1).

Figure A.1
The first time you start Windows, a group window may be open on the desktop.

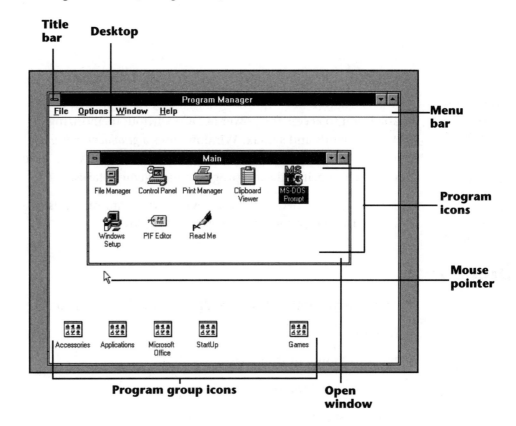

Objective 2: Use a Mouse in Windows

Mouse
A pointing device used in many programs to make choices, select data, and otherwise communicate with the computer.

Windows is designed for use with a *mouse*. Although you can get by with just a keyboard, using a mouse is much easier. This book assumes that you are using a mouse.

In the Windows desktop, you can use a mouse to

- Open windows

- Close windows

- Open menus

- Choose menu commands

- Rearrange on-screen items, such as icons and windows

Mouse pointer

An on-screen symbol that indicates the current location of the mouse.

Mouse pad

A pad that provides a uniform surface for a mouse to slide on.

The position of the mouse is indicated on-screen by a *mouse pointer*. Usually, the mouse pointer is an arrow, but it sometimes changes shape depending on the current action.

On-screen the mouse pointer moves according to the movements of the mouse on your desk or on a *mouse pad*. To move the mouse pointer, simply move the mouse.

There are three basic mouse actions:

- *Click.* To point to an item and press and release quickly the left mouse button. You click to select an item, such as an option on a menu. To cancel a selection, click an empty area of the desktop.

- *Double-click.* To point to an item and then press and release the left mouse button twice, as quickly as possible. You double-click to open or close windows and to start applications from icons.

- *Drag.* To point to an item, press and hold down the left mouse button as you move the pointer to another location, and then release the mouse button. You drag to resize windows, move icons, and scroll.

  Note: *Unless otherwise specified, you use the left mouse button for all mouse actions.*

If you have problems...   If you try to double-click but nothing happens, you may not be clicking fast enough. Try again.

Objective 3: Understand the Windows Desktop

Desktop

The background of the Windows screen, on which windows, icons, and dialog boxes appear.

Your screen provides a *desktop*, the background for Windows. On the desktop, each application is displayed in its own window (hence the name *Windows*). All windows have the same set of elements that enable you to move, resize, and manipulate the window.

If you have multiple windows open, they may overlap on the desktop, just as papers on your desk can be stacked one on top of the other. You may have one or more windows open when you start Windows.

The Title Bar

Icon

A picture that represents a group window, an application, a document, or other element in a GUI-based program.

Across the top of each window is its Title Bar. At the right side of the Title Bar are the Minimize button for reducing windows to icons and the Maximize button for expanding windows to fill the desktop. At the left side of the Title Bar is the Control menu *icon*, a box with a small hyphen in it. The Control icon activates a window's Control menu (see figure A.2).

Figure A.2
Every open window
has a Title Bar, used
to identify the
contents of the
window.

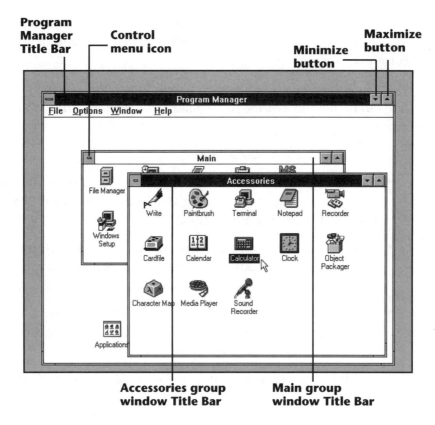

Menus

Menus enable you to select options to perform functions or carry out commands
(see figure A.3). The Control menu, for example, enables you to control the size
and position of its window.

Figure A.3
Menus, like the
Control menu
shown here, enable
you to choose
commands without
remembering DOS
syntax, switches, or
parameters.

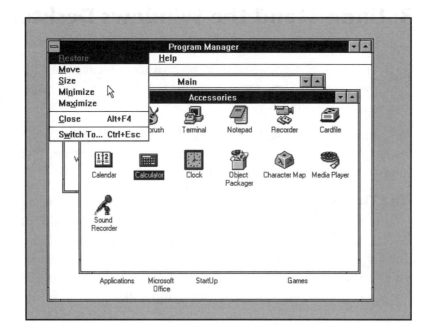

Dialog box
A window that opens on-screen to provide information or to ask for the additional information.

Dialog Boxes

Some menu options require you to enter additional information. When you select one of these options, a *dialog box* opens (see figure A.4). You either type the additional information into a text box, select from a list of options, or select a button.

Figure A.4
In a dialog box, you provide additional information that Windows needs to complete the command.

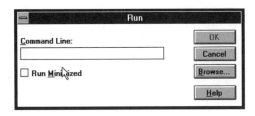

Buttons

Buttons are on-screen areas with which you select actions or commands. Most dialog boxes have at least a Cancel button, which stops the current activity and returns to the preceding screen; an OK button, which accepts the current activity; and a Help button, which opens a Help window (see figure A.5).

Figure A.5
The Search dialog box of the Help features, with buttons you click to select topics and perform actions.

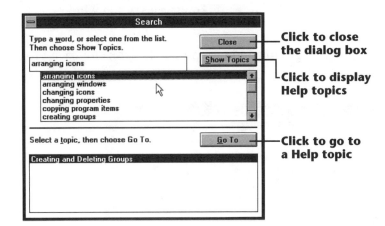

Objective 4: Understand the Program Manager

The Program Manager is the central Microsoft Windows program. When you start Microsoft Windows, the Program Manager starts automatically. When you exit Microsoft Windows, you exit the Program Manager. You cannot run Microsoft Windows if you are not running the Program Manager.

Program group
Application programs organized into a set that can be accessed through a program group window.

The Program Manager does what its name implies—it manages programs. You use the Program Manager to organize programs into groups called *program groups*. Usually, programs in a group are related, either by function (such as a group of accessories) or by usage (such as a group of programs used to compile a monthly newsletter).

Each program group is represented by a program group icon (see figure A.6).

Figure A.6
When you double-click a program group icon, a group window opens on-screen.

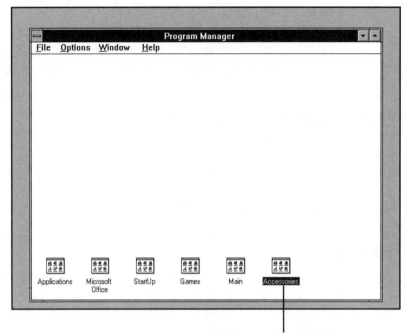

**Double-click to open the
Accessories group window**

In each program group window, you see the icons for each program item in the group (see figure A.7).

Figure A.7
When you double-click a program icon, the program starts.

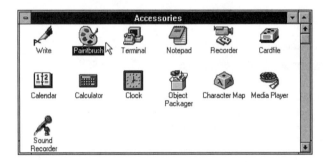

Objective 5: Get Help

Almost every Windows application has a Help menu. From the Help menu, you can start a Help program to display information about many aspects of the program.

To display Help information, take one of the following actions:

Context-sensitive

Pertaining to the current action.

- Press F1. The Help program starts, and a *context-sensitive* Help window opens on-screen.

- Choose **H**elp from the menu bar, and choose one of the Help menu commands.

Note: *To choose a menu item, point to it with the mouse pointer; then click the left mouse button.*

Displaying Help for a Topic

To display Help for a particular topic, follow these steps:

1. Choose **H**elp from the menu bar.

2. Choose **C**ontents from the Help menu. A Help Window opens; it displays the main topics for which Help is available (see figure A.8).

Figure A.8
The Help window groups topics into How To and Commands categories.

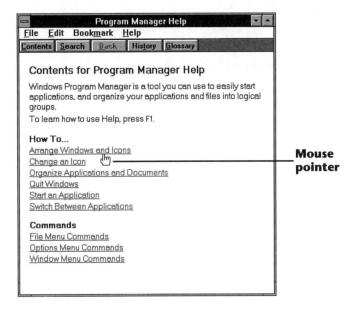

3. Choose the topic for which you want additional information. Windows displays the Help information.

Closing the Help Window

To close the Help window, take one of the following actions:

- Choose **C**lose from the Help window's Control menu.

- Choose E**x**it from the Help window's File menu.

- Double-click the Control menu button.

If you have problems... To open the Control menu, click the Control menu button at the far left end of the window's Title Bar.

Objective 6: Get Comfortable with Windows

To be comfortable using Windows, you need to know how to control your Windows desktop, which in large part means controlling the windows themselves.

You can open, close, move, and resize all the windows that appear in Windows, including the Program Manager.

Opening a Window

To open a window, double-click the appropriate icon (see figure A.9). When you double-click a program group icon, you open a group window. When you double-click a program icon, you start that program.

Figure A.9
You can continue opening windows until the desktop is full or until you run out of memory.

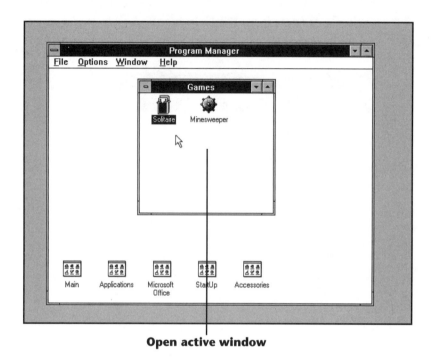

Open active window

If you have problems... If a Control menu opens instead of a window, you are not double-clicking fast enough. Try again, or choose **R**estore from the Control menu.

Don't worry if your screen looks different from the screens used to illustrate this book. Your desktop may be organized differently. You still can perform all the same tasks.

Note: *You can also use the Control menu to open a window. Click the icon once to display the Control menu. Then click **R**estore.*

Changing the Active Window

No matter how many windows are open on the desktop, you can work only in the *active window*.

Active window
The window in which you are currently working.

You can tell which window is active in two ways:

- The active window is on the top of other open windows on the desktop.

- The Title Bar of the active window is highlighted (see figure A.10).

Figure A.10
Four windows are
open. The Games
group window is
the active window.

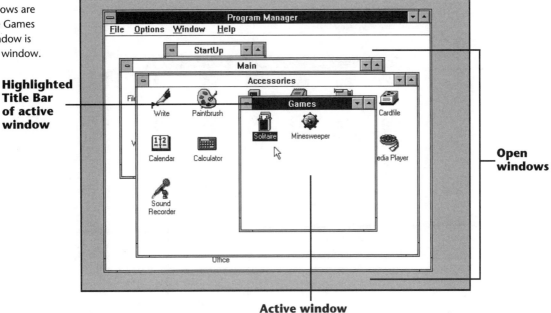

**Highlighted
Title Bar
of active
window**

**Open
windows**

Active window

To make a window active, click anywhere in it. The window moves to the top of
the desktop, and its Title Bar appears in a different color or shade.

**If you have
problems...**   If the window you want to make active is hidden behind another window, click
Window on the menu bar to open the Window menu. From the list of available
windows, choose the one you want to make active.

Resizing a Window

You can change the size of any open window by dragging its borders with the
mouse.

To resize a window, follow these steps:

1. Point to the border you want to move.

    Note: *When you are pointing to the border, the mouse pointer changes to a
    double-headed arrow.*

2. Press and hold down the left mouse button, and drag the border to its new
    location. As you drag, you see the border move along with the mouse
    pointer.

3. Release the mouse button. The window adjusts to the new size (see
    figure A.11).

    Note: *To change the height and width of the window simultaneously, drag one of
    the window's corners.*

Figure A.11

To resize a window, drag one of its borders.

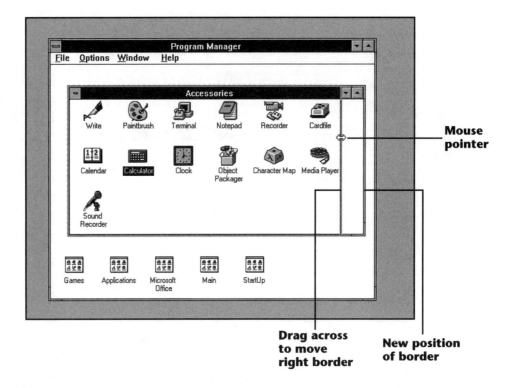

If you have problems... If nothing happens when you try to change a window size, you probably are not pointing at a border. Make sure that the mouse pointer changes shape to a double-headed arrow before you drag the border.

Moving a Window

You can move a window to a different location on the screen by dragging it with the mouse.

To move a window, follow these steps:

1. Point to the window's Title Bar.

2. Press and hold down the left mouse button, and drag the window to the new location. You see the borders of the window move with the mouse pointer (see figure A.12).

3. Release the mouse button.

If you have problems... If nothing happens when you try to move a window, you are probably not pointing to the window's Title Bar. Make sure that the mouse pointer is within the Title Bar before you drag the window.

Maximizing a Window

You can maximize a window to fill the entire desktop. Maximizing a window gives you more space in which to work.

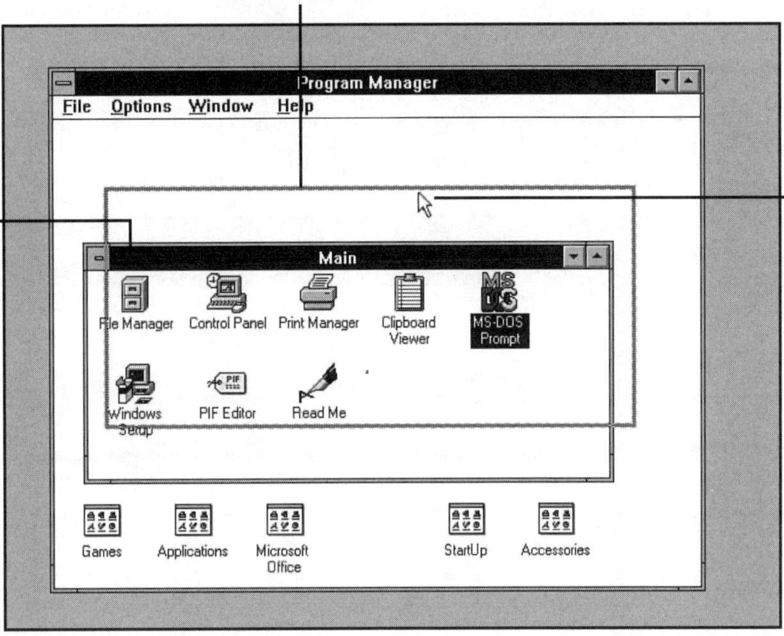

New window position

Figure A.12
You can move a window to any location on the desktop.

Drag Title Bar to move window

Mouse pointer

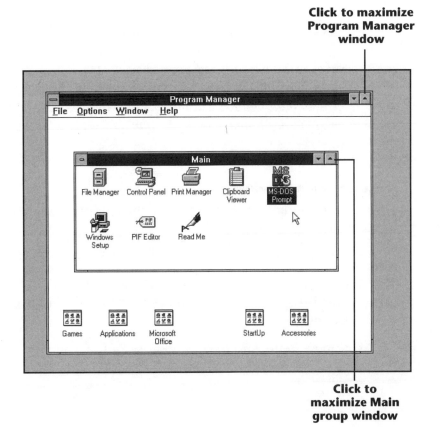

Maximize
To increase the size of a window until it covers the desktop.

To *maximize* a window, do one of the following:

- Click the Maximize button at the far right of the window's Title Bar. This button has an arrowhead pointing up (see figure A.13).

- Choose **M**aximize from the window's Control menu.

Click to maximize Program Manager window

Figure A.13
Each window has a Maximize button at the right end of its Title Bar.

Click to maximize Main group window

Minimize
To reduce a window to an icon.

Minimizing a Window

You can *minimize* a window that you are not currently using.

To minimize a window, take one of the following actions:

- Click the Minimize button on the Title Bar. This button has an arrowhead pointing down (see figure A.14).

Figure A.14
Each window has a Minimize button, which you can use to minimize the window to an icon.

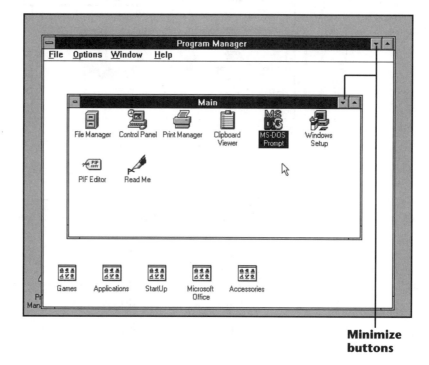

Minimize buttons

- Choose Minimize from the window's Control menu.

    Note: *Program group windows, such as the Main group, are reduced to program group icons at the bottom of the Program Manager. Application, utility, or document icons are positioned at the bottom of the desktop, behind any active windows. The application that has been minimized is still active; it is just out of the way.*

Restoring a Window

Restore
To return a window to its most recent size and position on the desktop.

You can *restore* a window that has been maximized or minimized to its most recent size and location.

To restore a window to its most recent size, take one of the following actions:

- Click the Restore button, which replaces the Maximize button on the Title Bar. The Restore button has arrowheads pointing up and down (see figure A.15).

- Choose **R**estore from the window's Control menu.

Figure A.15
When you maximize a window, the Restore button appears at the left end of the Title Bar in place of the Maximize button.

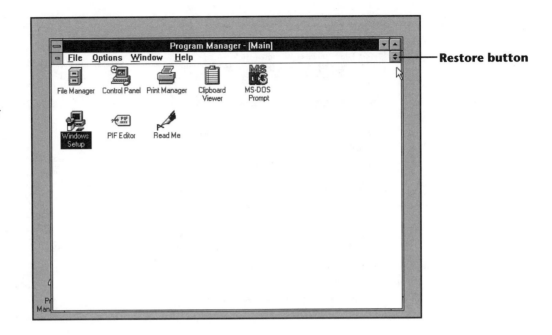

──

If you have problems... If you try to restore the window but nothing happens, the window has not been maximized or minimized. You cannot restore a window unless it has been maximized or minimized first.

Arranging the Windows on Your Desktop

Sometimes a desktop becomes so cluttered with open windows that you cannot tell what you are using. When that happens, you can choose either to *tile* or to *cascade* the open windows on-screen so that you can see them all.

To arrange the windows on the desktop, follow these steps:

1. Choose **W**indow from the menu bar to display the Window menu.

2. Choose one of the following:

- **T**ile, to arrange the windows on-screen so that none is overlapping (see figure A.16).

- **C**ascade, to arrange the windows on-screen so that they overlap (see figure A.17).

Tile
To arrange open windows on the desktop so that they do not overlap.

Cascade
To arrange open windows on the desktop so that they overlap, but at least a portion of each window is displayed.

Figure A.16
The windows are tiled on the desktop.

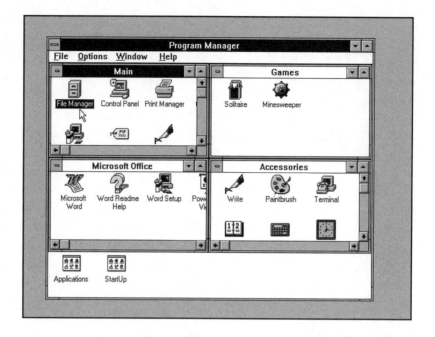

Figure A.17
The windows are cascaded on the desktop.

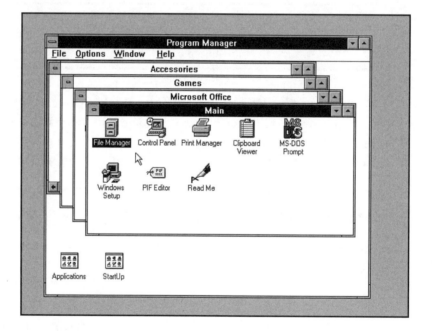

Closing a Window

To close a window, take one of the following actions:

- Choose **C**lose from the window's Control menu.

- Choose **C**lose from the window's **F**ile menu.

- Double-click the Control menu button. (To open the Control menu, click the Control menu button at the far left end of the window's Title Bar.)

If you have problems... If the Exit Windows dialog box appears, you clicked the Control menu box for the Program Manager rather than the Control menu box for the window you want to close. Click Cancel.

Objective 7: Exit Windows

You should always exit Windows before turning off your computer. To exit Windows and return to the DOS command prompt, follow these steps:

1. Close all open windows and applications.

2. Point to File in the Menu Bar, and click the left mouse button.

3. Point to Exit Windows, and click the left mouse button. Windows prompts you to confirm that you want to exit.

4. Point to OK, and click the left mouse button. Windows closes, and the DOS command prompt is displayed.

   Note: *As a shortcut, simply double-click the Control menu button at the far left of the Program Manager Title Bar. Windows asks you to confirm that you want to exit. Click OK.*

Index

F

File command (Insert menu), 58

File menu commands
Close, 30, 57
Document Summary, 166
New, 28
Open, 29, 51
Paste, 64
Print, 41, 164
Save, 40

files
copying, 173
deleting, 173
directories
creating, 175
deleting, 175-176
displaying file types, 180
inserting into documents, 57-58
naming, 168-172
opening, 179-180
printing
document summaries, 167
lists, 174
QuickLists
creating, 168-169
deleting, 170-171
displaying files, 171-172
editing, 169
sort order, 180
see also documents

filling table cells, 233-234

Find and Replace command (Edit menu), 79

Find and Replace operations
backward searches, 81
codes, 81
customizing, 81-82
fonts, 81
replacing text, 61-62, 84-85
scope, 79
wildcards, 82-83
Wrap at Beg/End of Document option, 79

Find and Replace Text dialog box, 79

Find Text dialog box, 198

fitting columns, 229-230

fixed columns, 222

flipping graphics, 253

floating cells (tables), 234

flush right text, 112-113

Font command (Format menu), 114-116

Font dialog box, 114-118

fonts, 114
addressing envelopes, 206
attributes, 115
envelopes, 141
points, 114
rotating, 140
Search and Replace operations, 81
selecting, 114-115
sizing, 115
Status Bar, 177

FOOTEND macro, 184

footers, 144-145
creating, 146-147
discontinuing, 148
editing, 147-148
options, 146

Footnote command (Insert menu), 120

footnotes
creating, 120-121
viewing, 122

foreign language characters, 123

form files, 193-194
letter-type, 199-201
spacing, 201

Format menu commands
Envelope, 140
Font, 114-116
Header/Footer, 146
Line, 17, 126
Margins, 143
Page, 139
Paragraph, 108

formatting
pages
binding options, 142
centering text, 144
margins, 143
numbering pages, 148-152
page breaks, 152-155
paper definitions, 137-142
table cells, 231-234
text
Font dialog box, 116-118
Toolbar, 116
see also codes

formulas (tables), 234

full justification, 110

function keys, 18-20

G

Go To command (Edit menu), 36

Go To dialog box, 36

Grammatik
document statistics, 91
options, 92-93

Grammatik command (Tools menu), 91

graphics, 241-249
borders
appending, 254
deleting, 255
captions, 246-247
cropping, 252
editing, 249-253
flipping, 253
Image Tools palette, 249-250
inserting, 242-243
lines
appending, 258-259
length, 260
moving, 260
thickness, 260
positioning, 243-245
restoring to original, 252
rotating, 252-253